Liberalism after Communism

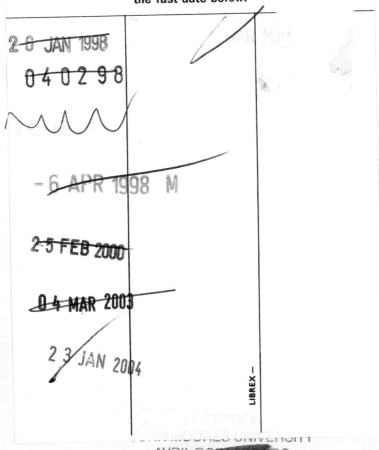

Liberalism after Communism

JERZY SZACKI

Translated by Chester A. Kisiel

CENTRAL EUROPEAN UNIVERSITY PRESS

Budapest · London · New York

This edition first published in 1995 by
Central European University Press
1051 Budapest,
Nádor utca 9,
Hungary

First published in Polish as *Liberalizm po komunizmie* in 1994

Distributed by
Oxford University Press, Walton Street, Oxford OX2 6DP
Oxford New York Athens Auckland Bangkok Bombay Toronto
Calcutta Cape Town Dar es Salaam Delhi Florence Hong Kong
Istanbul Karachi Kuala Lumpur Madras Madrid Melbourne
Mexico City Nairobi Paris Singapore Taipei Tokyo Toronto
and associated companies in Berlin Ibadan
Distributed in the United States
by Oxford University Press Inc., New York

British Library Cataloguing in Publication Data
A CIP catalogue record for this book is available from the British Library

ISBN 1-85866-015-7 Hardback
ISBN 1-85866-016-5 Paperback

Library of Congress Cataloging in Publication Data
A CIP catalog record for this book is available from the Library of Congress

Designed, typeset and produced by John Saunders Design & Production, Reading, UK
Printed and bound in Great Britain by Biddles of Guildford, UK

Contents

Acknowledgments

In writing this book I was helped by many people, who supplied me with materials not available in any library. I am very grateful to them for this. However, special thanks are due to the institutions which enabled me to concentrate on writing this book and created ideal working conditions for me. These institutions are the Woodrow Wilson International Center for Scholars in Washington DC, and the National Humanities Center in North Carolina.

Jerzy Szacki

The publisher wishes to acknowledge the generosity of the Central and East European Publishing Project in supporting the translation costs of this book.

I   Introduction

1. *The discovery of liberalism in Eastern Europe*

This book can be started with a paraphrase of the first sentence of the now so unpopular *Communist Manifesto* of Marx and Engels, a paraphrase which at the same time is a restatement of other paraphrases, proliferating for some time past, in which 'Eastern' was added to the word 'Europe', and the word 'communism' was replaced by the words 'dissidentism', 'democratic opposition', 'democracy', 'civil society', etc., as well as – ever more often – by 'nationalism' and 'populism'. My paraphrase reads as follows: A spectre is haunting Eastern Europe – the spectre of *liberalism*.

In countries which have almost no liberal tradition (see Chapter III) and which barely a few years after the revolution of 1989 (or what Timothy Garton Ash facetiously called a 'refolution') and after the political fall of real socialism[1] cannot be called liberal in any of the innumerable meanings of this word, 'liberal values . . . codified in the writings of John Stuart Mill

---

[1] In my opinion, the terminology used in expounding on Eastern Europe leaves a lot to be desired. *Communism*, the most frequently used term, does not seem appropriate to me, because in the strict sense it denotes an ideology which, firstly, was never carried into effect anywhere and, secondly, was already dead long before 1989. The term *state socialism* in turn has the flaw that it immediately is associated with a well-defined conception of the political system to which it is applied. For this reason I use the term *real socialism*, even though it is odd and comes from communist new-speak, to which it was introduced in the times of Brezhnev in order to convince people that while the polit-ical system established in the name of socialism may not be what one might have wished for, one cannot look forward to another ('socialism with a human face' or something of the kind). The advantage of the term, however, is that it clearly indicates which historical reality we have in mind. To be sure, I will also use the words *communism* and *communist*, but only in reference to an ideological design and to the parties that embraced it – first out of conviction, then out of habit. Neither can I do without the term *post-communist*, which is rather widely used today. Its scope is clear, however, because the fall of real socialism precisely coincides with the renunciation by East European communists once and for all of their former ideological claims – even of sham claims.

and Alexis de Tocqueville as well as in the writings of Hayek are experiencing a true renaissance'.[2] This is Adam Michnik's opinion. 'In a short time, triumphant liberalism has completely dislodged the rickety and expiring ideology of late communism', writes another Polish author.[3] In Eastern Europe, a surprisingly large number of people confess to liberalism, sometimes even to its 'pure' form, which long since would have been forgotten in the West had it not been for the heroic efforts of a handful of theorists, who were rarely appreciated by men of practice or by most of their university colleagues. One year before the 'refolution', Jacques Rupnik, who was one of the first to note this strange phenomenon, wrote: 'Nowhere in Europe can one find more orthodox pupils of the free-market theories of Milton Friedman than in Poland, where the dramatic decline of state industry is combined with backward private agriculture.'[4]

On the other hand, for a surprisingly large number of people in Eastern Europe, succumbing to liberalism is the most serious charge they can level against their opponents; such critics seem to think that the word 'liberalism' not only means something really serious, but also that it has suddenly become sufficiently understandable to everyone for it to be included in the lexicon of our everyday disputes and employed on a mass scale to evoke the desired associations and emotional reactions. Already during the 1991 and 1993 election campaigns in Poland, it was a frequently used epithet. Since that time it has been used in this way ever more often.

To be a liberal has ceased to be the luxury or 'craziness'[5] of a few intel-

Another terminological difficulty is caused by the term *Eastern Europe*, which is far from explicit; it sometimes refers to geography, sometimes to history, sometimes even simply to the policy of the last several decades. For example, David S. Mason calls Eastern Europe the European countries under communist rule which after the fall of communism are now East-Central Europe. See his *Revolution in East-Central Europe* (Boulder CO: Westview Press, 1992), pp. 7–8. For Piotr S. Wandycz, on the other hand, *East-Central Europe* is nothing else but Poland, Hungary, and Czechoslovakia. See his *The Price of Freedom* (London: Routledge, 1992). Without going into a discussion on this subject, I use the term *Eastern Europe* in its most common sense; even though it is easily open to question, I have in mind the European post-communist countries, excluding the countries of the former Soviet Union.

[2] Adam Michnik, 'The Presence of Liberal Values', *East European Reporter*, vol. 4, no. 4, p. 70.

[3] Piotr Marciniak, 'Po neoliberalnym szoku', *Przegląd Społeczny* 1993, no. 9, p. 18.

[4] Jacques Rupnik, *The Other Europe* (New York: Pantheon Books, 1989), p. 18. The author quoted was also author (with Pierre Kende) of perhaps the first larger publication noting the nascent expansion of liberalism in Eastern Europe ('Libéralisme et crise du système communiste en Europe de l'Est', *L'Autre Europe* 1988, no. 15–16, pp. 3–12).

[5] In introducing the word 'craziness' I refer to the name Stefan Kisielewski and his friends gave themselves when they created a tiny 'party of crazy liberals'. See Andrzej Walicki, 'Liberalism in Poland', *Critical Review* 1988, vol. 2, no. 1, p. 10.

lectuals, as it was in Poland not so many years ago, when the word 'liberal' was associated mainly with Kisiel ('Kisielewski's one-man political party', Mirosław Dzielski wrote later) or, at most, with small groups of enthusiasts, most of whom did not appear until after 1981. A few years later, in many circles being a liberal began to be regarded as a sign of normality, European thinking, progressiveness, and other cardinal virtues marking the passage from real socialism and socialism *tout court*, a period which really got under way after 1989. The label 'liberals' began to be applied to (and by) people in respect to whom such a classification had never entered anyone's mind; and despite the fact that they had not fundamentally altered their views.[6] Before long, this category became one of the most important tools for arranging the political scene and discussions on the direction of the reform, a fact of which outside observers accustomed to viewing Poland through the prism of the pre-1989 situation are not always aware.[7]

In the eyes of its ever more numerous supporters, and even of people who would not define themselves in this way, liberalism is not only one of the many orientations that have sprung up like mushrooms on the ruins of the old order, but also something more: the harbinger of a new society that should be built as quickly as possible, or, in any case, a designation of its absolutely indispensable *foundations*, prior to whose erection a discussion on other solutions is rather pointless.[8] Discussions on some 'third', still unknown, path have waned; the direction seems clearly marked, and the debates are ever more often confined to *how* and *how quickly* to proceed in this direction.

From the point of view of many participants and observers, the breakthrough of 1989 was nothing else but the historical victory of *liberalism* over socialism and the start of the return of the countries of Eastern Europe to their natural path of development, as it were, from which they had been

[6] This applies to Adam Michnik, quoted earlier.

[7] None the less, this phenomenon has been noticed. In addition to the already cited publications of Rupnik and Walicki, it is worth mentioning Michael D. Kennedy's *Professionals, Power and Solidarity in Poland* (Cambridge: Cambridge University Press, 1991), pp. 181–4, 353–9; David Ost, *Shaping a New Politics in Poland: Interests and Politics in Post-Communist East Europe*. Harvard University: Program on Central and Eastern Europe Working Paper Series, 1992, no. 8.

[8] It is worth quoting the statement of Janusz Lewandowski, one of the leading theorists and practitioners of Polish liberalism: 'The real discussion on choice of the Social Democratic or liberal path can get started only after the foundations of the market are in place. . . . Before this happens, in Poland there is the objective time of liberals as organizers of the breakthrough', in *Kongres Liberalno-Demokratyczny. Biuletyn Informacyjny*, 1992, no. 3 (11), p. 13.

shoved aside many years ago by communism.[9] This point of view even has
its own philosophy of history, which was expounded most fully by Francis
Fukuyama in his 'The End of History': '. . . the complete exhaustion of the
vital forces of systemic alternatives to Western liberalism and its unabashed
victory'.[10] Almost everywhere it is taken for granted that 'the great ideological contest of our century is over. The once maligned market has, after all,
turned out to be materialist man's best friend.'[11] Even people who until
recently were declared supporters of socialism in one form or another (like
Robert Heilbronner) today not infrequently admit that 'the competition
between capitalism and socialism has ended: capitalism has won'.[12]
Scholars and politicians declare almost unanimously that today there is no
other path before Eastern Europe than 'liberal democracy and a free
market'.[13] As Gareth Stedman Jones sceptically observes, the defeat of
socialism is commonly regarded as irrefutable evidence of the 'intrinsic
strength of liberal capitalism as such'.[14]

This is not the place to ponder on how much wishful thinking there is in
these opinions and how much realism in the evaluation of a situation which
is strikingly new and urgently calls for a new definition. If anything could be
predicted on the basis of historical analogies, we would be warranted in
surmising that, once again, we have to do with the illusion of having found a
final solution – the *fallacy of the last revolution* – a dream characteristic of
historical watersheds. This is of no great importance in this context,
however; what is important is that this is the climate of opinion today and
probably will continue to be for a long time to come. This climate is more
prevalent in the East than in the West, where, in spite of everything, there is
more scepticism and uncertainty: people in the West already know that
liberal democracy and the free market are no panaceas, albeit, perhaps,
nothing better has ever been invented. For this reason, one sometimes finds
Western authors who expect encouragement and an example from the East,
because 'it is in the East that the fervent revolutionary enthusiasm for the

---

[9] See Jiři Musil, 'Czechoslovakia in the Middle of Transition', *Daedalus* 1992, vol.
121, no. 2, p. 175. See also *The Crisis of Leninism and the Decline of the Left: The
Revolutions of 1989*, ed. Daniel Chirot (Seattle and London: University of Washington
Press, 1991), Preface.

[10] Francis Fukuyama, 'The End of History', *National Interest* 1989, no. 16, p. 3.

[11] Stanley Sheinbaum (quoted by Seymour Martin Lipset), 'No Third Way: A
Comparative Perspective on the Left', in *The Crisis of Leninism*, op. cit., p. 215.

[12] Quoted after Lipset, op. cit., p. 215.

[13] See *Study Group on Central and Eastern Europe, United States Institute of Peace*,
Institute of Peace, Washington DC, May 1990, p. 1.

[14] Quoted after Krishan Kumar, 'The Revolutions of 1989: Socialism, Capitalism, and
Democracy', *Theory and Society* 1992, vol. 21/3, p. 315.

principles of liberal democracy and the free market has come to life once again'.[15]

2. *The actuality of liberalism*

'A Time and Place for Liberals' was the title of an article published in 1989 by an eminent Polish sociologist in one of the most popular Polish weeklies.[16] The title hit the bull's-eye, even though at that time the word 'liberal' meant something else than it would a few years later. Almost overnight, liberalism became an important factor of political life in Poland (and elsewhere as well). It really did become popular. Even a Catholic publicist in his still rather traditional criticism deems it proper not to oppose anti-liberalism to liberalism, as Catholic writers were wont to do, but to oppose two other, good, liberalisms, one of which is contained in a papal encyclical.[17] Indeed, it should be stressed from the outset that this unexpected popularity of liberalism is manifested in greater numbers not only of supporters of one kind of liberalism or another but of opponents of any form of liberalism as well. The latter are prone to blame liberalism for everything that is the worst,[18] especially for the fact that people today are supposedly living less well than under real socialism.[19] To be sure, so far liberalism is criticized more as a controversial economic strategy (justly or unjustly regarded as liberal *par excellence*) than as a grand design for the society that would emerge from the pursuit of this strategy.

We will deal with the critics of liberalism later, when the subject-matter of the debate is more precisely defined. For now, however, it suffices to say that even the growing number of attacks on liberals may be taken as evidence of its success: liked or not, praised or condemned, understood

[15] Thomas L. Pangle, *The Ennobling of Democracy: The Challenge of the Postmodern Era* (Baltimore: The Johns Hopkins University Press, 1992), pp. 84, 87–9.

[16] Jan Szczepański, 'Czas i miejsce dla liberałów', *Polityka*, 8 July 1989, no. 27 (1679).

[17] See Maciej Zięba OP, 'Dwa, a nawet trzy liberalizmy', *Tygodnik Powszechny* 1993, no. 2. See also Michael Novak, *The Catholic Ethic and the Spirit of Capitalism*, Part II (New York: The Free Press, 1993). On 'Christian liberalism' see Józef Tischner, 'Nieszczęsny dar wolności', *Znak* 1993 (Kraków), pp. 10–13.

[18] For instance, a Christian Democratic deputy to the Polish Diet referred to the growing number of suicides as 'victims of the liberal experiment'. See *Super-Express*, 29 January 1992, no. 20 (327).

[19] This is not the place for a substantive discussion of this issue, but it is worth mentioning that the popular statement on the *universal* pauperization of the society is not all that self-evident. What is most typical seems to be an increase of social inequalities combined with the impoverishment of some groups. Most striking is the lack of reliable data.

correctly or quite erroneously, liberalism has occupied an important place in the political scenes of Poland, Hungary, and Czechoslovakia (or rather, the Czech Republic). It is entirely possible that in the near future it will make a similar career in those post-communist countries in which there has been little mention of it until now. All the evidence suggests that, after the complete discreditation of real socialism, in which state control was magnified to an absurd, if not totalitarian, degree, the appearance of liberalism (and, I daresay, in its strong version) is a psychological and social necessity. As Vladimir Gligorov correctly noted, 'one has to experience conflict with socialism to see the natural beauties of liberalism'.[20] There is no doubt that 'the liberal doctrine of freedom is favoured since it appears to many people as the most decisive departure from the discredited ideology of Communism'.[21] Whatever might be said about the pluses and minuses of liberal economic recipes, the turn towards liberalism seems understandable, because in Eastern Europe it is perfectly suited to act as an *anti-doctrine* – to use the apt phrase of Józef Pajestka.[22] Bruce Ackerman[23] put it very well when he said that liberalism often appears as 'inverted Marxism', which differs from Marxism chiefly in that, instead of socialism, it sanctifies capitalism, permitting the use of the same established patterns of thinking alluding to 'the end of history'.

In all likelihood, another factor spurring the advances of liberalism in this part of the world is that, in many respects, liberalism in the West has recently experienced a genuine renaissance. Even though the present condition of liberalism is not as healthy as might be wished by its East European supporters,[24] who into the bargain have shown an exaggerated tendency to associate it chiefly with the really not so miraculous economic policies of Ronald Reagan and Margaret Thatcher, there is little doubt that in the last half-century in the West the climate of opinion has turned in favour of capitalism and the free market.[25] On the other hand, liberalism as a political

[20] Vladimir Gligorov, 'The Discovery of Liberalism in Yugoslavia', *East European Politics and Societies* 1991, vol. 5, no. 1, p. 20.

[21] Kazimierz Z. Poznański, 'Property Rights Perspective on Evolution of Communist Type Economies', in *Constructing Capitalism: The Reemergence of Civil Society and Liberal Economy in the Post-Communist World* (Boulder CO: Westview Press, 1992) p. 89.

[22] Józef Pajestka, *Polskie frustracje i wyzwania. Przesłanki postępu cywilizacjnego* (Warsaw: BGW, 1991), pp. 50–1.

[23] Bruce Ackerman, *The Future of Liberal Revolution* (New Haven CT: Yale University Press 1992), pp. 34–5.

[24] See 'Czy koniec ery liberalizmu?' Beata Polanowska-Sygulska interviews John Gray, *Znak* 1992, no. 444 (May), pp. 104–16.

[25] See Milton Friedman's preface to the last edition of *Capitalism and Freedom* (Chicago: The Chicago University Press, 1982), pp. 6–9.

philosophy arouses a lot more political interest today than years ago, when so much was written about its 'crisis' or 'end'. For someone who follows Western publications, especially Anglo-Saxon ones, it is no exaggeration to say that 'our *fin de siècle* has begun with a veritable "liberalizing" of political thought'.[26]

It is quite another matter whether and to what degree what happens in political thought is directly connected with political reality: much evidence points to the fact that the liberal political philosophy whose renaissance is so evident is a kind of art for art's sake.[27] Furthermore, a sizeable part of the new liberal writings seems to be characterized by an orientation that was clearly identified by Richard E. Flathman: 'Dissatisfied (as all self-conscious liberals are?) with the available formulations of liberal theory, in seeking to refashion it to my liking I increasingly look to sources outside and thought by many to be at odds with liberal doctrine and practice.'[28] This orientation makes the literature interesting, but hardly helps to make a synthesis that would reveal the 'essence' of liberalism. None the less, whatever the fate of liberalism in the West, one can be certain that for a good many years to come it will retain its present attractiveness for the post-communist countries; for liberalism best satisfies the strong need in these countries to oppose what recently had been and to some extent still is, while at the same time offering the hope of something much better in the future. Somewhat jokingly, one can add that, as usual, the creations of the liberal 'renaissance' will reach them after a delay, and so, later than elsewhere, these ideas will be seized upon as novelties and the last word of Western political thought.

[26] *Liberalism and the Moral Life*, ed. Nancy L. Rosenblum (Cambridge MA: Harvard University Press, 1989), Introduction, p. 3. See Thomas A. Spraegens Jr., 'Reconstructing Liberal Theory: Reason and Liberal Culture', in *Liberals on Liberalism*, ed. Alfonso J. Danico (Totowa NJ: Rowman & Littlefield, 1986), p. 34; and Norman P. Barry, *On Classical Liberalism and Libertarianism* (New York: St Martin's Press, 1987), p. 2.

[27] This thesis was put forward by Benjamin Barber in *The Conquest of Politics: Liberal Philosophy in Democratic Times* (Princeton NJ: Princeton University Press, 1988). According to Richard Bellamy, 'the striking feature of most liberal ideas is a combination of philosophical sophistication with political and social naiveté (*Liberalism and Modern Society: A Historical Argument* (University Park PA: The Pennsylvania State University Press, 1992), p. 217).

[28] Richard E. Flathman, *Willful Liberalism: Voluntarism and Individuality in Political Theory and Practice* (Ithaca NY: Cornell University Press, 1992), p. 1.

3. Has liberalism scored a victory?

However, I by no means contend that in Eastern Europe, where until a few years ago patently anti-liberal views and practices predominated, we are, or soon will be, witnesses to an unprecedented triumph of liberalism. Surely, never has liberalism gained as many supporters in so short a time as there; none the less, I hesitate to defend such a thesis for particular reasons.

First, no one really knows to what such a thesis could apply; for this liberalism, which is gaining recognition and importance like wildfire, is rarely clearly defined, and people who discourse on its subject-matter often have in mind entirely different things. This accounts for the confusion in matters of liberalism even among such unquestioned authorities as president of the Liberal International, Otto Lambsdorf, who in an interview declared: 'Today, I am unable to evaluate the Polish political scene; I have also lost my orientation as to what the word "liberalism" really means for Polish politicians.'[29] One can say that in Eastern Europe liberalism has already been discovered, but hardly anyone had a map of the new land in his hand or was even fully aware of the need for such a map. Even though there is no precise definition of liberalism anywhere (see Chapter II), where it has a longer history this lack is somewhat made up for by the existence of precedents and stereotypes, which prevent people from letting the concept of liberalism stand for anything they wish. In such places, there is less of a tendency to include within this concept everything that is not state socialism, or to reduce liberalism to an encomium of capitalism as such. In Eastern Europe there is exceptional conceptual confusion concerning liberalism; thus, it is best to avoid such categorical theses until what they refer to has been precisely defined.

Second, however we define East European liberalism, it cannot be asserted that it enjoys mass social support. Yet, it is still too early to speak of its 'fiasco',[30] and even less so to hold that 'the dark side of the process current in Eastern Europe is . . . the gradual retreat of the liberal-democratic tendency in the face of the growth of corporate populism with all of its elements'.[31] None the less, the movement in this direction is unmistakable. What is more, even where liberals are allotted their '15 minutes' (as was said in Poland when, after the presidential elections, the liberal Jan

---

[29] 'Liberał z krwi i kości'. An interview with Count Otto Lambsdorf, president of the Liberal International, chairman of FDP, *Wprost*, 15 December 1991, no. 15.

[30] See Jarosław Gowin, 'Nędza liberalizmu, czyli o perspektywach ładu liberalnego w Polsce', *Przegląd Polityczny* 1992, no. 4, p. 49.

[31] Slavoj Žižek, 'Eastern Europe's Republics of Gilead', *Dimensions of Radical Democracy. Pluralism, Citizenship, Community*, ed. Chantal Mouffle (London: Verso, 1992), p. 199.

Krzysztof Bielecki became prime minister), this does not necessarily suggest that liberalism is carrying the day; rather, the truth is that the necessity of taking practical decisions forces a retreat to the positions of 'practical liberalism', which means giving up solutions regarded as the best and as liberal in the full meaning of the word.[32] The outcome is a situation which J. M. Kovács appropriately described as follows: 'The pendulum has begun to swing in the liberal direction (especially in rhetorics), but – after leaving the point of suspension – it has not gone very far yet.'[33] While it is a fact that in the last few years the East European societies have experienced a 'neo-liberal shock',[34] becoming acquainted with various aspects of the market economy (and not always the most positive ones), it is very evident that no 'liberal revolution' has yet taken place there.

Third, there is the failure, more precisely partial success, of the economic reform programme, which is widely regarded as liberal (whether rightly so is unimportant); in other words, the understandable failure of an economic miracle to take place right after the first moves in the direction of a market economy makes a rapid expansion of liberal views most unlikely. The deepening frustration of large segments of the post-communist societies is manifested in one election after another; liberal candidates have a hard time explaining to voters that, in fact, no 'liberal revolution' has yet taken place, that the real trouble is that there is too little and not too much liberalism. Even if liberals manage to hold on to positions gained earlier or even strengthen them somewhat, they cannot gain a legislative majority to enable them to carry out their programme consistently in its unabridged form.

4. Response to the challenge

Thus, the importance of liberalism in the post-communist world is not necessarily due to its already visible political strength (though, as in the case of liberal parties in the West, it is perhaps greater than the support for liberals at the polls). Rather, its real source of strength seems to lie in that, in comparison with other more influential trends, it demonstrates quite a lot of

[32] See 'Liberalizm praktyczny'. Danuta Zagrodzka interviews Janusz Lewandowski, chairman of the Liberal-Democratic Congress and Minister of Ownership Changes in *Gazeta Wyborcza*, 13 April 1991; 'Nie mam konfliktów sumienia'. Marek Rudziński interviews Jan Krzysztof Bielecki in *Sztandar Młodych* 24–26 May 1991, no. 9.

[33] János Mátyás Kovács, 'Prologue: Crossing the Threshold', *Reform and Transformation in Eastern Europe: Soviet-type Economics on the Threshold of Change*, ed. J. M. Kovács and Marton Tardos (London: Routledge, 1991), p. xv.

[34] See P. Marciniak, *Po neoliberalnym szoku*, op. cit., pp. 18–24.

dynamism, initiative and determination in respect to the goals it wants to achieve. Even more important, liberalism seems to offer the most total response to the *challenge of the new historical situation* that came into being after the fall of real socialism; many other trends, on the other hand, confine themselves to spooking people with communists and employing conventional patterns of thinking that were in vogue long before the communists came on the scene. If the changes taking place in Eastern Europe embrace *renewal* and *restoration* simultaneously,[35] then the liberals certainly belong to those politicians for whom renewal is the essential matter. In other words, liberalism today seems to offer the most consistent blueprint for a new[36] political-social-economic order; in contrast, the supporters of other orientations are often content with criticizing this design in the name of conventional ways of thinking that appeal to sentiments and resentments and to 'supplementing' or 'correcting' this design; yet, when they gain control over the course of events, they unabashedly do more or less the same thing as liberals. It should also be remembered that certain tenets of the liberal *credo* are really questioned by no one – not even by the former communists, albeit in their role as today's 'Social Democrats' it behoves them to criticize liberalism. One can be against liberalism, but politics in Eastern Europe can no longer be carried on as though liberalism did not exist – at least, if one is aware that in the modern world an integral part of every valid political conception must be 'a conception of a sound economic policy that can reasonably hope to prove effective through time'.[37] Most probably, one of the main reasons for the present marginal status of the ideologists of civil society is that they were too principled in their approach and ignored economic matters (see Chapter IV).

Whether we like it or not, today's horizon of the discussion on the indispensable transformation of the political systems of the countries of Eastern Europe has been delimited in the main by liberals; of course, only in part is this their personal contribution, for, as it has turned out, numerous solutions

[35] See Andras Bozóki, 'The Hungarian Transition in a Comparative Perspective', in *Post-Communist Transition: Emerging Pluralism in Hungary*, eds Andras Bozóki, Andras Korosenyi and George Schöpflin (London: Pinter Publishers, 1992), p. 163.

[36] This newness is relative, of course. The 'Autumn of Peoples' in 1989 was not a revolution that 'shakes the world with novelty'. Its characteristic feature was the use of the rhetoric of a *return* to principles as old as the (Western) world. This rhetoric also played a big role in later discussions on the future of the East European societies; in these discussions it was often emphasized that this was not another experiment but the application of already *tried and tested* solutions. This motif is strikingly evident in the rhetoric of the East European liberals.

[37] See John Dunn, 'Capitalism, Socialism, and Democracy: Compatibilities and Contradictions', *The Economic Limits to Modern Politics*, ed. John Dunn (Cambridge: Cambridge University Press, 1990), p. 195.

proposed by them have gained prominence as a somewhat natural counter-proposal to the old order, which now must be replaced by a new one. This accounts for liberals' sometimes excessive self-assurance ('arrogance', as Jarosław Gowin writes critically and self-critically), which leads them to believe that 'the guarantee of the victory of liberal values is . . . reality itself'.[38] To quote Gligorov once again: 'The main ally of liberalism in a socialist country is the inefficiency of its economy.'[39] Liberalism had to appear, if only as the indispensable *frame of reference* of every serious discussion on the future path of countries ruined by the communist experiment. In fact, liberalism had appeared in this role even before its name consciously began to be widely used for a specific programme. This pre-history of liberalism was first and foremost a prolonged discussion on the necessity of introducing market mechanisms to the economy; this discussion was best exemplified by the book of Włodzimierz Brus and Kazimierz Łaski entitled *From Marx to the Market*.[40] The practical results of this discussion were rather meagre; and it would be unwarranted to maintain that economic liberalism in Eastern Europe today has its origins in this discussion. None the less, this debate clearly shows that the revision of socialist economic dogmas had to lead in the direction of liberalism.[41]

In speaking of the 'naturalness' of liberalism as an alternative position, I by no means wish to aver that it is an absolutely correct position. Ascertainment of the defeat of some position does not automatically make the opposite position true, even though now its viability must be seriously taken into consideration. This is all the more reason why liberalism is an exceptionally important idea in the post-communist countries, a proposal that cannot be ignored, irrespective of whether liberals are right in everything and whether they are able to gain social support for their views. If liberalism did not exist, it would have to be invented to ask the right questions about the future of these countries.

5. *The problem of the migration of ideas*

In taking up studies on liberalism in Eastern Europe, I was not motivated solely by the desire to investigate one of the most important ideologies which today are finding new applications and are, perhaps, entering into

[38] J. Gowin, op. cit.

[39] V. Gligorov, op. cit., p. 8.

[40] Włodzimierz Brus and Kazimierz Łaski, *From Marx to the Market* (Oxford: Clarendon Press, 1989).

[41] See especially *Reform and Transformation in Eastern Europe*, op. cit., and 'Rediscovery of Liberalism in Eastern Europe', *East European Politics and Societies*, ed. János Mátyás Kovács, 1991, no. 1 (special number devoted entirely to this subject).

their second youth. I also wanted to see what important changes otherwise familiar ideas undergo when they are transported to entirely different conditions from those in which they originated. Indeed, it can hardly be gainsaid that 'the acceptance of liberalism as the ideological foundation of political action in a communist country is an unprecedented experiment requiring an original interpretation and exceptional methods of action',[42] the future leader of the Liberal-Democratic Congress said a few years ago.[43] If this is so (which we have no reason to doubt), studies on liberalism in Eastern Europe may be interesting not only from the point of view of 'Sovietology', so to speak, but also for their contribution to our knowledge of liberalism in general, which suddenly finds itself in a new historical situation. This has given rise to new questions and difficulties, which cannot be addressed without going beyond the solutions tried out in the West. Liberalism is not merely a set of technical directives that can be applied with the same success in all conditions, despite what some Western economists may believe when they give advice to their colleagues from the East.

The transfer of ideas about social life from one set of conditions to others is an extremely complicated process, in whose course not only the geographical place in which they are applied changes. That is why it is worth pondering on what this nascent East European liberalism is and how it compares with that liberalism which so often has been referred to as 'the modern embodiment of all of the characteristic traditions of Western politics', 'the generalization of the centuries-long experience of Europe', or 'the inborn attitude of a normal civilized Westerner towards life'.[44] The

---

[42] Donald Tusk, 'Prawo do polityki', *Przegląd Polityczny* 1989, no. 12, p. 8.

[43] In this book I do not deal with the organizational aspects of the liberal movement, both on account of its nature and because this is a complicated matter. The problem is that in no country of Eastern Europe is liberalism confined to one party. In Poland, the Liberal-Democratic Congress is currently the most important party, because it is the most numerous and most influential. In addition, there is the Union for Realistic Politics, which represents a more orthodox neo-liberal position. What is interesting is that within parties that do not call themselves liberal (such as the Democratic Union), one can find people and groups whose liberalism is not open to question and, on the merits of the case, cannot be distinguished from the liberalism of the Congress, with which the Union plans to merge. The party system in the countries of East Europe is not yet fully shaped; and non-substantive (for example, biographical and social) matters have an important influence on how people form into groups. The system is so unstable that, quite possibly, when this book appears, the comments on specific organizations will have become outdated.

[44] F. M. Watkins, *The Political Tradition of the West* (Cambridge MA: Harvard, 1949), p. ix; Janusz Lewandowski, 'Liberalizm stosowany', a conversation between J. K. Bielecki, D. Filar, J. Kozłowski, J. Lewandowski and D. Tusk, *Przegląd Polityczny* 1991, no. 1 (13), p. 7; Thomas O. Neil, *The Rise and Decline of Liberalism* (Milwaukee: Bruce Publishing Company, 1953), p. 25.

appearance of liberalism in Eastern Europe is one of the real signs of a 'return to Europe', from which this region was artificially cut off half a century ago (leaving aside the fact that even before this it had been on the periphery of Europe); and even though East European liberalism owes almost everything to Western thinkers,[45] it is by no means merely an imitation of Western models. It may be convenient for East European liberals to stress their faithfulness to these models, because this makes it easier for them to present their programme as a tried and tested social policy and to ward off the charge of proposing yet another suspect experiment. None the less, liberals are quite aware that in social life there are no perfect imitations; and this is all the more true where a political philosophy that has evolved over centuries is supposed to come into existence virtually overnight as the result of a political fiat!

As Karl Mannheim argued, the very transfer of ideas to another social environment changes their meaning and function.[46] For a historian of ideas, such a change is a fascinating subject; for, unlike a philosopher, he is interested not so much in ideas *per se* as in their encounter with the life of specific societies and in the processes by which ideas are transformed in the search for answers to questions different from those to which they had originally provided an answer.

In no circumstance is liberalism a simple elementary idea whose vicissitudes may be rather easily traced by investigating changing contexts. Liberalism is a general name for a wide category of many different ideas, doctrines and practices, from among which people who come later make a selection. This selection, which is often made unconsciously, gives their views the stamp of originality; for much depends on what is accepted, what is rejected, what is combined with what. In the course of such processes the internal dilemmas of liberalism constantly reappear. In our case, what is most interesting is the dilemma: liberalism as the *design of a good society* to be realized unconditionally to reach a state close to selected Western models; and liberalism as a *method of political action* that excludes quasi-Bolshevik ways of realizing ideas, and hence does not permit haste and compulsion. In the countries of Eastern Europe, in which liberalism lacks a tradition and an infrastructure, there might be a strong temptation to 'grab people by the throat and impose liberalism',[47] following the example of General Pinochet. Apart from whether this is at

---

[45] As François Furet wrote: 'With all of the fuss and noise, not a single new idea has come out of Eastern Europe in 1989.' Quoted from K. Kumar, op. cit., p. 316.

[46] Karl Mannheim, 'The Problem of a Sociology of Knowledge', *Essays on the Sociology of Knowledge* (London: Routledge and Kegan Paul, 1952), p. 188.

[47] Words of Stefan Kisielewski quoted by Janusz Korwin-Mikke in an interview for *Życie Warszawy*. I quote from *Nowy Dziennik*, 1 December 1992.

all possible, the question arises whether this would be the same liberalism to which the West owes so much. And would this be liberalism at all? Perhaps there is no one liberalism?

6. *What is this book about?*

I do not regard this book as a 'report' on one of the new developments in Eastern Europe, but, rather, as the story of another adventure of liberal thought, whose history, as we can see, is far from concluded.

When I started work I naively believed that it would be a historical monograph on a fragment of most recent history. This turned out to be impossible for many reasons, especially because the sources are extremely rich as well as scattered. The liberalism dealt with here is not a philosophy expounded in books and journals available in every university library. It is something much more elusive. Sometimes it does not go beyond the spoken word, leaving a trace behind either only in the memory of the speakers or recorded in difficult to find places: minutes, notes, materials for discussion at some meeting or another, articles in the low-circulation press, etc. Very few journals have appeared that by assumption were liberal organs (like *Przegląd Polityczny* in Poland); the books can be counted on one's fingers. An additional source of difficulties is that in Eastern Europe liberalism was born in conditions of censorship and conspiracy; and it can be easily imagined that difficulties in reaching sources were even greater when I tried to deal with countries other than Poland.

As a result, my original idea unfortunately had to be delimited in two ways.

First, this is *de facto* a book about liberalism in Poland today, though it does contain some broader generalizations and, in so far as possible, utilizes materials from Hungary and Czechoslovakia (Chapter IV). This apparently serious limitation can be justified not only by the technical difficulties which I encountered. Poland is an exceptionally fruitful area for study. In dealing with earlier times, E. Garrison Walters wrote of Poland that 'her problems in the period reflect all the social, economic, and political dilemmas that plagued all Eastern Europe. A thorough exposition of Poland's situation provides a touchstone for analysing the specific concerns of the other nations as well as a framework for understanding the status of the region as a whole.'[48] Today, this opinion can be repeated without qualification, for the political and economic processes characteristic of contemporary Eastern

---

[48] E. Garrison Walters, *The Other Europe: Eastern Europe to 1945* (Syracuse NY: Syracuse University Press, 1988), p. 170.

Europe started in Poland and were the most visible there. From my point of view, it is especially important that precisely in Poland liberalism rather early reached a high level of articulation. It would be much better, of course, if I had more complete information about Hungary and Czechoslovakia.

Second, there is another reason why this book is not exactly what I would have liked it to have been. This is more a book *about ideas and problems* than about events, people, or organizations. A partial justification for this is the fact that the most recent history of the events of East European liberalism is replete with intricacies that do not seem very important for the development of ideas; for these intricacies stem not so much from real differences of views as from chance political alliances that may change at any time. The best evidence of this is that differences of positions within individual parties are often greater than differences among persons belonging to different parties; indeed, one can find liberals outside liberal political parties. To say the truth, I am even pleased with this forced return to the history of ideas, since this avenue of approach best suits my professional competencies and the logical order of the research tasks: before writing a monograph on a particular event, one should have a clear idea of what event we have in mind.

II Instead of a Definition of Liberalism

That is far from an empty idea. But it is not a program, and for that, thanks are due. [1]

1. The difficulty of defining liberalism

One of the scholars of liberalism wrote: 'In approaching anything to do with liberalism there is always an initial and irritating difficulty: What is liberalism? How shall we define it?' [2] While these questions are extremely important, I would like to devote as little space to them as possible; yet, since they concern delimitation of the subject-matter of this work, they cannot be avoided entirely. I am aware that the material was not adequately defined in the Introduction, which touched on many things united only by a common name. Unfortunately, neither will this chapter satisfy the reader's curiosity on that score, since it focuses mainly on explaining why such a definition is lacking.

Attempts to define liberalism are usually futile, since their result is either a catalogue of existing definitions, from which we gather only that they are different, incomplete and inconsistent; or still another arbitrary definition that merely lengthens this list without eliminating ambiguities and contradictions in approaching the same subject-matter, which by its nature is vague and replete with inherent contradictions.

'The word "liberalism" defies precise definition since its usage includes a variety of meanings in a number of different contexts' [3] – is how the entry 'liberalism' starts in one encyclopedia, and could very well serve as the

---

[1] Leslie W. Dunbar, *Reclaiming Liberalism* (New York-London: W. W. Norton, 1991), p. 39.

[2] Charles Frankel, 'Does Liberalism Have a Future?', in *The Relevance of Liberalism*, eds Zbigniew Brzeziński, Seweryn Bialer, Sophia Slusar and Robert Nurick (Boulder CO: Westview Press, 1978), p. 99.

[3] *New Catholic Encyclopedia* (New York: McGraw-Hill, 1967), vol. VIII, p. 701.

introduction to any work on liberalism that is concerned with the historical aspects of the problem and not with presenting one of its countless varieties as liberalism *tout court*. Only authors who give liberalism their own arbitrary definition without concern for how it relates to other definitions can be certain of what liberalism means. The terminological confusion is compounded by clear national peculiarities in the history of liberalism, with the result that what passes for liberalism in one country is often called by a different name in another. It also sometimes happens that liberal clothing is donned by politicians who have little in common with liberalism.

Neither the boundaries of liberal political philosophy nor those of liberal political and economic practice have ever been distinctly marked, and what was and/or is in their ambit strikes us with its diversity. 'Liberalism both as precept and practice has undergone changes so great that the term as currently used has come to have contradictory meanings',[4] is the commonly accepted opinion. There was not, is not and very likely never will be any orthodox liberalism, any *quintessential* liberalism, any consistency or inconsistency which could serve to determine whether someone's views are or are not liberalism, or are liberal to a greater or lesser extent. 'There is no catechism, no single authoritative document, no seminal thinker to whom to refer.'[5]

More cautious scholars have always been aware of these difficulties and have made it clear that – even when dealing with liberalism as a whole – they were disinclined to search for its 'pure essence'.[6] Scholars who are more sceptical about the unity of liberalism, like John Gray in his latest works, even question the legitimacy of using the word 'liberalism' in the singular; they argue that the historical legacy of liberalisms is 'a complex structure of practices and institutions' making up today's 'liberal civil society' and not some unified system of views over whose reconstruction historians and political philosophers have been toiling for ages. Gray, reputed to be the greatest contemporary scholar of the subject, is of the opinion that the result of the latest research has been 'to effect a historical deconstruction of liberalism as an intellectual tradition and to retrieve for us the discontinuities, accidents, variety, and historical concreteness of the thinkers indifferently lumped together under the label of "liberalism".'[7]

---

[4] Harry K. Girvetz, *The Evolution of Liberalism* (New York: Collier Books, 1963), p. 13.

[5] Michael Mandelbaum, 'The Long Life of Liberalism', in *The Relevance of Liberalism*, op. cit., p. 201.

[6] See Kenneth Minogue, *The Liberal Mind* (London: Methuen, 1963), p. 13.

[7] John Gray, *Liberalisms: Essays in Political Philosophy* (London: Routledge, 1989), p. 262. See Pawel Śpiewak, 'Ideologie i obywatele', *Więź* 1991, p. 31. Gray's earlier position may be found in his book *Liberalism* (Minneapolis: University of Minnesota Press, 1986).

Another contemporary author states that 'there never was a liberalism, only a family of liberalisms'.[8] Moreover, in addition to liberalisms as more or less theoretical constructs, the historian of the last two centuries constantly encounters practical liberalisms, so to say, which probably belong to the same family but whose similarity or unity is much more elusive.[9]

Isolating and defining liberalism are among the most difficult tasks of writing history. We are not always even in complete agreement that we are dealing with a *political* phenomenon, for, where liberalism is concerned, John Dunn notes 'extreme imprecision of reference', consisting in the fact that 'being a liberal is often a matter of broad cultural allegiance and not of politics at all – or certainly not of the major organizational issues of politics'.[10] Thus, in addition to political liberalisms, we have to do with economic and cultural liberalisms, which sometimes display a high degree of autonomy and are not necessarily associated with a liberal political orientation or even (in the case of economic liberalism) with traditionally antiliberal ones.

2. *Banalized liberalism*

It is hard to give a definition of liberalism in the world today; for what eventually might be regarded as the real and original accomplishment in their time of liberals of various shades and degrees has become the common property of all political 'schools' encompassed by the term *liberal democracy*, which has been called such not because it suits only liberals – and no one else. One can well imagine a liberal democracy without liberals or, in any case, one without a liberal political party. Guido de Ruggiero in his classical history of liberalism had already written that it is not the property of this or that government, but endures, despite changing governments and party colours.[11]

This opinion is even more firmly grounded than it was decades ago, for, as Kenneth Minogue stated, in time there arose 'an enlarged and somewhat

[8] Thomas A. Spraegens Jr, 'Reconstructing Liberal Theory: Reason and Liberal Culture', in *Liberals on Liberalism*, ed. Alfonso J. Damico (Totowa NJ: Rowman & Littlefield, 1986), p. 36.

[9] 'The liberal movement operated at two levels, the level of thought and the level of society. It consisted of a body of doctrines and a group of principles that underlay the functioning of . . . institutions' – J. G. Merquior, *Liberalism Old and New* (Boston: Twayne Publishers, 1991), p. 2.

[10] John Dunn, *Western Political Theory in the Face of the Future* (Cambridge: Cambridge University Press, 1993), p. 30.

[11] Guido de Ruggiero, *The History of European Liberalism* (Boston: Beacon Press, 1955), p. 363.

refurbished liberalism' which 'provides moral and political consensus and which unites virtually all of us, excepting only a few palpable eccentrics on the right and communists on the left'.[12] In recent decades, even communists have seemed reluctant to be exceptions, as evidenced by their transformation first into Eurocommunists, and after this, on a wider scale, into 'Social Democrats', 'Democratic Left', etc. Even if some duplicity may be suspected in such actions, these attempts are the best proof that participation in this 'moral and political consensus' is regarded as good form nowadays. Despite numerous critiques of liberal democracy still heard from the right and from the left, ever fewer politicians are willing to replace it with something entirely different, in contrast to the interwar period. Furthermore, the main tenets of the liberal creed have become part of international treaties recognized by all countries – even by those countries that do not respect these tenets in practice.

Who today would openly dare to make deletions on the list of liberties drawn up by John Stuart Mill and including: 'liberty of conscience . . . liberty of thought and feeling . . . absolute freedom of opinion and sentiment on all subjects . . . the liberty of expressing and publishing opinions . . . liberty of tastes and pursuits, of framing the plan of our life to suit our own character . . . liberty . . . of combination among individuals, freedom to unite for any purpose not involving harm to others'?[13] Of course, deletions are being made and probably will continue to be made, though in an atmosphere of ever greater hypocrisy that, while not questioning the principles themselves, permits exceptions to them in special and allegedly temporary circumstances.

It is also food for thought that the restriction of liberties is often made in the name of the liberal principle that the liberty of the individual may not bring harm to others. Liberty itself is no longer execrated; rather, it is praised as a good thing – but is not always possible. In other words, liberalism is criticized not for existing *per se*, but for not being such as it ought to be. The opinion that 'any human political order . . . must take with great seriousness the major concerns and ideals of this tradition'[14] has become threadbare.

In describing the situation right after the French Revolution, Karl Mannheim treated liberalism and conservatism as two opposite philosophies of life, not to mention the fact that their political antagonism was perfectly

---

[12] K. Minogue, *The Liberal Mind*, op. cit., p. vii.

[13] John Stuart Mill, 'On Liberty'. *The Philosophy of John Stuart Mill: Ethical, Political and Religious*, edited and with an Introduction by Marshall Cohen (New York: The Modern Library, 1961), p. 200.

[14] Thomas A. Spraegens, Jr, *The Irony of Liberal Reason* (Chicago: The University of Chicago Press, 1981), p. vii.

obvious to him.[15] Leo Strauss, who dealt with the situation a century and a half later, also defined liberalism by opposing it to conservatism, but he added that 'here and now liberalism and conservatism have a common basis: for both are based here and now on liberal democracy, and therefore are antagonistic to communism'.[16] A more or less similar change took place in the relation between liberalism and socialism, if we refer to socialism in the civilized Western version and not the socialism practised by communists under the name 'real socialism'.[17] That is why today one can say of liberalism that 'its concepts . . . are no longer confined to paid-up liberals or the Liberal Party, but are present within both social democracy and latter-day Conservatism'.[18]

It is of little consequence what role was played in these changes by metamorphoses within individual camps (including, of course, in the liberal camp itself, which, in the words of John Dunn, turned out to be 'distressingly plastic'[19]), namely, rejection by the conservatives of the idea of restoration, even their lack of any clear vision of the good society, and the abandonment by the socialists of the utopia of a brave new world that would be a negation of the capitalist world in every respect. More important were the broader processes shaping contemporary political systems, in which the fight between different orientations is losing the character of a holy ideological war to resolve the dilemma 'who will get the better of whom?'[20] Yet, it

[15] See Karl Mannheim, *Conservatism: A Contribution to the Sociology of Knowledge*, trans. David Kettler and Volker Meja (London: Routledge and Kegan Paul, 1986).

[16] Leo Strauss, *Liberalism, Ancient and Modern* (New York: Basic Books, 1968), p. vi.

[17] See Peter Clark, 'Liberals and Social Democrats in Historical Perspective', in *Liberal Party Politics*, ed. Vernon Bogdanor (Oxford: Clarendon Press, 1983), pp. 27–42; *Liberalizm i socjaldemokracja wobec wschniopeuropejskiego wyzwania*, ed. Piotr Marciniak and A. Stadler (Warsaw: Fundacja Polska Praca, 1991); Martin Krygier, 'In Praise of Conservative-Liberal-Social-Democracy', *Quadrant* 1992, vol. XXXVI, no. 5 (286), pp. 12–23.

[18] Stuart Hall, 'Variants of Liberalism', in *Politics and Ideology: A Reader*, ed. James Donald and Stuart Hall (Milton Keynes: Open University Press, 1986), p. 34.

[19] John Dunn, *Rethinking Modern Political Theory* (Cambridge: Cambridge University Press, 1985).

[20] I do not intend to repeat here the once fashionable thesis on the 'end of the age of ideology', which has turned out to be much too premature. I only speak of the growing consensus on the rules that should be observed by the contending sides and the boundaries that cannot be crossed. In other words, I am concerned with the end of what Kenneth Minogue called *a one-and-a-half party system*, consisting in the fact that only one side supports the existing political system with full conviction, while a larger or smaller part of the other side only waits for the opportunity to arrange everything the way it thinks best. (K. Minogue, 'Introduction: The Concept of Thatcherism', in *Thatcherism: Personality and Politics*, eds K. Minogue and Michael Biddis (New York: St Martin's Press, 1987), p. xii.)

is obvious that these two processes are difficult to separate from each other.

In any case, as C. Wright Mills wrote, 'as a kind of political rhetoric liberalism has been banalized: now it is commonly used by everyone who talks in public for every divergent and contradictory purpose'.[21] Liberalism has sunk, so to speak, into the wide background of liberal democracy, thereby losing much of its former relatively clear identity.

This signified, on the one hand, a resounding triumph of its principles, a victory which, on the other hand, caused what not without reason has been called the 'crisis of liberalism'. As more of the substance of liberalism entered into the 'moral and political consensus' of the Western world, the more difficult it became for liberalism to retain its former separateness and attractiveness – at least in those places where the main dangers opposed by it had been averted. In time, liberals did discover new dangers and put forward new postulates that did not belong to the repertoire of 'classic' liberalism, but this only attested to the fact that their heroic epoch was over. They began to demand various things ever more often in contradiction with the letter and spirit of the old liberalism; yet, they no longer were and could no longer be the sole, or even main, embodiment of the idea of liberty, for liberty had become a universally recognized principle. The greatest threat to freedom in the twentieth century, the appearance of the 'totalitarian temptation', mobilized a broad front of defenders of freedom rather than revived liberalism as a separate political orientation, notwithstanding the fact that the works of Aron, Berlin, and Popper – so important for our theoretical self-knowledge – were born in the latter historical context.

Alain Besançon, by way of digression, distinguished liberalism as a 'doctrine' from liberalism as the 'form taken by Western society'.[22] This is a very appropriate formula. Here is the source of the semantic paradox consisting in the fact that – as Giovanni Sartori put it – 'while an unnamed liberalism has represented . . . the most fundamental experience of Western man, "liberalism" as a rightful denomination for this experience has been applied in most countries only for a few decades'.[23] Hence, although liberalism made a great contribution to the political culture of the Western world, it paid for this with a crisis of its identity, which for a long time has been confirmed by theorists rather than by political practitioners. 'Much of what

[21] C. Wright Mills, 'Liberal Values in the Modern World', in *Power Politics and People: The Collected Essays of C. Wright Mills*, ed. Irving Louis Horowitz (New York: Ballantine Books, 1963), p. 189.

[22] Alain Besançon, 'Kościół, liberalizm, komunizm'. An interview conducted by Wojciech Karpiński, *Zeszyty Literackie*, winter 1984, no. 5, p. 113.

[23] Giovanni Sartori, 'The Relevance of Liberalism in Retrospect', *The Relevance of Liberalism*, op. cit, p. 3.

survives of liberalism today is not identified as such.'[24] Moreover, what could be regarded as typically liberal practical solutions does not necessarily come from liberals.

All of this creates a strong temptation to accept the view that liberalism is not, as Jerzy Jedlicki wrote, 'a ready and complete ideology but at most a minimum programme, a *preface* to an ideology'. This preface would consist of a relatively few simple principles which, though genetically linked with liberalism as a separate and, so to say, party orientation, can be accepted by almost everybody, since 'a person . . . who says he is a liberal only speaks the first word about himself'.[25]

All of this also discourages one from searching for some constant 'essence' of liberalism, some 'integral' liberalism,[26] and from constructing definitions of liberalism that would enable one to say what is and what is not 'true' liberalism, what is liberalism in the strict sense, and what is liberalism only in the loose, metaphorical, sense. Consequently, I would be in favour of a situational[27] definition of liberalism, one that would focus more on its functions in specific but very different historical situations than on such or another system of specific justifications and substantiations that ideologists, philosophers and politicians have created and still are creating in such great numbers. I would not put much effort into reconciling these justifications and substantiations and in culling out some common core. This hardly means that I am inclined to disregard ideological and philosophical discussions on liberalism; yet, I do not believe that such discussions are very useful when we are dealing with any *specific* liberalism, for as a rule they treat of what liberalism could and should be and not of what it was or is. It should also be remembered that the liberalism which is the subject-matter of this book is not theoretically refined, and it would be a waste of time to try to find in it any traces of the great discussions on the 'essence' of liberalism.

[24] Ibid., p. 14.

[25] Jerzy Jedlicki, 'Antynomie liberalnej koncepcji wolności', in *Źle urodzeni czyli o doświadczeniu historycznym. Scripta i postscripta* (London-Warsaw: Aneks i Polityka, 1993), p. 43.

[26] A concept used by John H. Hallowell in *The Decline of Liberalism as an Ideology with Particular Reference to German Politico-Legal Thought* (Berkeley: University of California Press, 1943), which even argues that one should begin with a 'description of the idea of liberalism in the Platonic sense' (p. ix). See especially Chapters I and II.

[27] I refer to the classic study of Samuel O. Huntington, 'Conservatism as an Ideology', *American Political Science Review* 1957, vol. LI, pp. 454–73.

3. *Who is a liberal in Eastern Europe?*

In my reflections on liberalism in Eastern Europe I will be guided mainly by who calls himself a liberal and is defined as a liberal by others, even though it may turn out that the people identified in this way are not very much alike and in certain respects completely unlike the generally recognized classics of liberal thought and their contemporary continuators in the West, to whom they tend to refer. Such a procedure seems more sound than starting from a more or less arbitrary definition and then seeing what fits the definition and what does not. A similar strategy has been adopted by many other authors who have dealt with liberalism. This approach was favoured by Anthony Arblaster, when he argued that the subject 'requires a historical rather than a purely conceptual and inherently static type of analysis'.[28] J. G. Merquior took a similar position when he wrote: 'It is far easier – and wiser – to *describe* liberalism than to attempt a short definition. To support a theory of liberalism, old and new, one ought to proceed by a comparative description of its historical manifestations.'[29]

And yet, the strategy pursued by historians to extricate liberalism from the declarations of its supporters and their reputation cannot eliminate the necessity of some 'conceptual' analysis, in which some knowledge about different varieties of liberalism and a personal view on liberalism in general are required. There are two reasons for this.

First, in certain historical situations the liberals distinguished in this way constitute too large and heterogeneous a body to be studied as a whole. In countries living under a dictatorship or just liberated from dictatorship, it usually does not take much to regard oneself as a liberal and to pass for a liberal for quite a long time. In effect, some 'liberals' can sometimes even be found in the ranks of the party wielding dictatorial power. In such a situation, all of the critics of this dictatorship are usually classified as 'liberals', irrespective of their views and of what political system they want to replace dictatorship with. In the liberal democracies the words 'liberalism' and 'liberal' are used sparingly, but in countries on the opposite pole to liberal democracy these words are unquestionably overused.[30] In order to declare

[28] Anthony Arblaster, *The Rise and Decline of Western Liberalism* (Oxford: Blackwell, 1984), p. 8.

[29] J. G. Merquior, *Liberalism Old and New*, op. cit., p. 1.

[30] Jakub Karpiński wrote ironically about the successive First Secretaries of the Communist Party of the Soviet Union, each of whom was more of a 'liberal'. (Entry 'Liberalism', in J. Karpiński, *Polska, komunizm, opozycja, Słownik* (London: Polonia, 1985).) See György Konrad, *Antipolitics: An Essay* (San Diego, New York, London: Harcourt, Brace, Jovanovich, 1984), p. 136. Western political commentators, who tended to use the word to designate even the slightest 'loosening' of controls, contributed to this devaluation of the word 'liberalism'.

oneself as a liberal in England, France or the USA, one has to have special reasons; in today's post-communist countries, until recently it sufficed to be dissatisfied with the status quo and to pine for some, even the most vaguely defined, liberty, or 'greater liberty'.

This accounts for the false impression of many observers, as mentioned in the introduction, that in 1989 liberalism scored a great victory in Eastern Europe, whereas, in fact, only the communist dictatorship had been overthrown, which is not necessarily the same thing. However we define liberalism, we should assume that this word would be completely superfluous were it to stand for everything that is not communist dictatorship (or any other kind of dictatorship). The words 'liberalism' and 'liberalization' are closely related, but they refer to two entirely different political orders that should not be confused with each other. Liberalism is one of many possible options after the collapse of a dictatorship; under dictatorship, liberalization is the only option of all of the opponents of dictatorship.

It is easy to understand why those people in Eastern Europe who regarded themselves as liberals for their characteristic and quite distinctive political, economic or other views sometimes showed a certain irritation with overuse of the word 'liberalism' and tried to prevent being swallowed up in the crowd celebrating the fall of dictatorship and the supposed 'triumph of liberalism'. Czech liberals like Václav Klaus and Tomaš Ježek fought against the 'false liberalism' which everyone started to espouse after the 'velvet revolution': 'Liberalism in its European meaning is not a loose body of ideas that one may use to describe as liberal anything one likes – even attitudes, practices, and policies which are in fact quite opposite to it . . . Liberalism is a closely tied set of ideas: it is a clearly distinct and quite unambiguous set of several dominant principles.'[31]

We already know how difficult it is to reconstruct this 'closely tied set of ideas' if one is a historian and not an ideologist who puts forward his own proposition of liberalism. None the less, only after it has been narrowed down does the term 'liberalism' become a useful tool of political analysis, a field in which, on account of specific historical circumstances, it has acquired too broad a meaning. Even if we are unable to construct a satisfactory definition of liberalism, in each specific case we should be able to show in what respect liberal views differ from other views. Since 1989 this is becoming easier because, as under dictatorship, the word 'liberalism' is ever more often differentiating and dividing people rather than uniting them. Consequently, it is becoming filled with more concrete and hence more controversial political, social and economic content.

---

[31] Václav Klaus and Tomaš Ježek, 'False Liberalism and Recent Changes in Czechoslovakia', *East European Politics and Societies* 1991, vol. 5, no. 1, p. 28.

4.   *A temperament or a philosophy of life?*

Subsequent chapters will discuss in detail the emergence in Eastern Europe, especially in Poland, of liberals who are no longer satisfied with 'liberalism' as the 'first word' of every opponent of dictatorship. Here a longer digression seems in order on how the copious literature on liberalism can help to identify the liberal orientation wherever it appears.

From what was said previously about the difficulties of defining liberalism, it can hardly be concluded that liberalism has lost its identity completely or that it never had any identity. Even authors who are the most sceptical about the possibility of discovering some 'essence' of liberalism by no means contend that expatiations on liberalism, or admitting to liberalism, are a misunderstanding in the sense that they bring to life something that does not exist in reality. All the same, it is widely believed that some real unity lies hidden behind the multiplicity of liberalisms. The trouble is that this unity cannot be expressed in the form of interrelated assertions which are accepted by all liberals without reservations and rejected by all non-liberals. The question is, how to search for this unity; on what level is it to be found? The existing literature of the subject seems to provide some useful guidelines.

Two basic tendencies manifest themselves in this literature. The first relegates to the background what liberals have proclaimed and/or are proclaiming, and accents their *attitude* towards life. Though highly distinctive, this attitude hardly leads to the acceptance of common views on what the world is like and what it should be like. In other words, *how* liberals think and act is more important than any specific results of their thought and actions. Such an approach frees the researcher from distress caused by the notorious inconsistency of the views of people who today and in the past have regarded themselves and been regarded by others as liberals, though it immediately raises doubts whether any durable political community may be based exclusively on a method.

The second tendency appears in renewed efforts to find some distinctive liberal *Weltanschauung*, some philosophy of life of which liberals themselves are not fully aware, but which manifests itself repeatedly in their pronouncements and actions. Such a philosophy may be reconstructed from the so-called 'canonical' texts to which liberals are wont to refer.[32] Liberals may be divided into those who accentuate the exceptionality of the liberal *attitude* (in method, temperament, sensitivity, etc.) and those who feel an

---

[32] One of the most important texts is John Stuart Mill's *On Liberty*, though its successive interpretations (like those of all of Mill's works) raise doubts whether it means the same thing to everyone. See John Gray, 'Mill and Other Liberalisms', *Liberalisms*, op. cit., Chapter 12.

irresistible urge to construct a liberal *theory*, a body of ideas leaving as little doubt as possible as to what assumptions liberalism holds, what it asserts and postulates.

An example of the first tendency is the anthology, popular years ago, compiled by J. Salwyn Shapiro, who stated that liberalism is simply 'an attitude towards life – sceptical, experimental, rational, free' and mentioned Socrates and Abelard as the first liberals.[33] At first glance, this is a naive position and difficult to defend, but one may insist that it expresses a sound intuition. We find this intuition in a different form in many other authors. Without going into the substance of liberalism they boil it down to the absolute minimum, in keeping with the view of Harold Laski that liberalism is 'hardly less a habit of mind than a body of doctrine'.[34] In this vein, Judith N. Shklar wrote that 'apart from prohibiting interference with the freedom of others, liberalism does not have any particular doctrines about how people are to conduct their lives or what personal choices they are to make'.[35] One of the most famous representatives of liberalism, Bertrand Russell, articulated a similar point of view most clearly when he wrote that 'the essence of the Liberal outlook lies not in *what* opinions are held, but in *how* they are held: instead of being held dogmatically, they are held tentatively, and with consciousness that new evidence may at any moment lead to their abandonment'.[36]

Consequently, the liberal attitude rather often has been compared to the 'scientific view of the world', which, Russell asserted, was to be 'the intellectual counterpart of what is, in the practical sphere, the outlook of liberalism'.[37] In fact, more than any other political *famille spirituelle* liberals remind one of 'enlightened rationalist fundamentalists', as Ernest Gellner called them, stressing that while they reject all claims to absolute truth, they have absolute faith in method; while they relativize all assertions, they absolutize the procedures of arriving at them and their justifications.[38]

Another possible way of approaching liberalism, but one which leads to similar results, is to accent not its intellectual predilections but its special brand of emotionality or sensitivity. Thus, it is sometimes assumed that liberalism 'does not refer to a formal tradition of thought; its coherence is

[33] J. Salwyn Shapiro, *Liberalism: Its Meaning and History* (Princeton NJ: van Nostrand, 1958), p. 14.

[34] Harold J. Laski, *The Rise of European Liberalism* (London: Allen & Unwin, 1936), p. 15.

[35] Judith N. Shklar, 'The Liberalism of Fear', in *Liberalism and the Moral Life*, ed. Nancy L. Rosenblum (Cambridge MA: Harvard University Press, 1989), p. 21.

[36] Bertrand Russell, *Philosophy and Politics*, quoted from A. Arblaster, *Rise and Fall of Western Liberalism*, op. cit, p. 26.

[37] Ibid.

[38] Ernest Gellner, *Postmodernism, Reason and Religion* (London: Routledge, 1992).

psychological, and not a matter of intellectual history'.[39] J. M. Keynes's *bon mot* may serve as a perfect illustration of this approach: 'A Whig is a perfectly sensible Conservative. A Radical is a perfectly sensible Labourite. A Liberal is anyone who is perfectly sensible.'[40] To be sure, one may also regard liberalism as 'the amalgam of a sensibility and a technique'.[41] From this point of view, liberalism has neither its own philosophy nor its utopia, and hence one would have to agree entirely with Bruce Ackerman, who, from the position of a liberal, professed that 'liberalism does not depend on the truth of any single metaphysical or epistemological system . . . In order to accept liberalism, you need not take a position on a host of Big Questions of a highly controversial character.'[42] The critics of liberalism often make the same point when they argue that, preoccupied with improving the formal, procedural or technical forms of social life, liberalism has strayed dangerously far away from the Aristotelian conception of politics, which associated politics with a certain notion of the common good.[43] The author of perhaps the best book on the liberal way of thinking, Kenneth Minogue, stated that 'liberalism . . . has come more and more to see politics simply as a technical activity like any other'.[44] In any case, these are not isolated opinions. What is interesting, however, is that they lead to widely divergent views on liberalism: what is a great advantage of liberalism for some, is an unforgivable sin for others.

The characterization of liberalism as really the only political orientation that in disputes on justice places 'stress on procedural rather than substantive

[39] Nancy L. Rosenblum, *Another Liberalism: Romanticism and the Reconstruction of Liberal Thought* (Cambridge MA: Harvard University Press, 1987), p. 3.

[40] Quoted as the motto in *Liberal Party Politics*, ed. V. Bogdanor, op. cit., p. v.

[41] K. Minogue, *The Liberal Mind*, op. cit., p. 7.

[42] Bruce Ackerman, *Social Justice and the Liberal State* (New Haven CT: Yale University Press, 1981), p. 361. The background of such views is the concept of *reasonable pluralism* of John Rawls, who holds that the characteristic feature of modern society is the joint appearance of not only various philosophical, moral, religious, etc. doctrines but also of various doctrines that are irreconcilable but justifiable. The problem, therefore, is not to determine which of them is absolutely true, but to find a *modus vivendi* among them. (See John Rawls, *Political Liberalism* (New York: Columbia University Press, 1993), Introduction.

[43] See Alasdair MacIntyre, *After Virtue* (London: Duckworth, 1986), p. 156; Kirk F. Koerner, *Liberalism and Its Critics* (New York: St Martin's Press, 1985), Chapter 4. See Marcin Król, who praises liberalism for 'technique' but reproaches it for its inability to get to the *sacrum* and to address the problem of man's spiritual life ('Dylematy liberalizmu', *Aneks* 1981, no. 24/25, pp. 7, 14). See William M. Sullivan, *Reconstructing Public Philosophy* (Berkeley: University of California Press, 1982), p. 58.

[44] K. Minogue, *The Liberal Mind*, op. cit., p. 5. Jürgen Habermas likewise maintained that liberal policy is directed 'not towards the solution of practical goals . . . but towards the solution of technical problems' (*Towards a Rational Society* (London: Heinemann, 1971), pp. 102–3).

justice'[45] and declines defining social *goals*, being content with establishing formal rules that can at most minimize the harm coming from lack of agreement on this basic question, in the opinion of others unquestionably has its merits (as does the formula of 'neutrality' used ever more often in descriptions of liberalism), but it does not go far enough. Neither do I think anyone would be satisfied with a description that lacked a substantive illustration of the trend. The tendency to describe liberalism as a distinctive *Weltanschauung* or, in any event, as a political orientation rooted in a particular *Weltanschauung* continues to find numerous proponents. Indeed, for some time now even liberals themselves have become more zealous in presenting liberalism as a system of assertions and have been creating a liberal social philosophy whose range of interests does not differ significantly from philosophies with other orientations. Nor is it true that only liberalism is incapable of formulating its own utopias.

In the latest literature, Anthony Arblaster, who took an extremely critical stance, was most consistent in applying the strategy of reconstructing liberalism as a philosophy of life. He tried to show that what we are dealing with is a 'coherent' and 'comprehensive view of the world', one that has both certain 'metaphysical and ontological' assumptions and a relatively wide-ranging philosophy of man and society whose essence is individualism.[46] Arblaster's line of argumentation is questionable, however; he seems to have laid too much stress on 'typically' liberal views that fit his hypothesis and not enough on opposite examples, of which the history of liberalism is replete. None the less, the inaccuracies of one author or another in and of themselves do not negate the contention that liberalism is something more than an attitude, technique, 'way of thinking' or some kind of sensitivity that at most can generate purely formal rules of social conduct.

In the profuse literature on the subject, the thesis that the substance of liberalism can be defined is often upheld. This viewpoint is supported both by advocates of liberalism and by its enemies, who are still numerous despite the success of the liberal 'minimum programme'. The most heated debates in recent times over liberalism (such as the debate between liberals

---

[45] See David Spitz, *The Real World of Liberalism* (Chicago: The University of Chicago Press, 1982), p. 2.

[46] A. Arblaster, *The Rise and Decline of Western Liberalism*, op. cit., Part 1. See John H. Hallowell, who, after attempting to reconstruct 'integral' liberalism, concludes that it is 'premised upon the individualistic *Weltanschauung*' (*The Decline of Liberalism*, op. cit., pp. 3, 12, 21). For the time being, how individualism may be defined is less important. For difficulties encountered here see Steven Lukes, *Individualism* (New York: Harper & Row, 1973).

and communitarians[47]) would have been simply impossible had both sides not shared the view that liberals are definitely *asserting* something. If liberalism were only a method or an attitude, the increasing efforts to provide it with a philosophical foundation and make it a coherent *system* of views on basic questions of social philosophy would serve no purpose. Anyone who undertakes such an effort must agree at least in part with Benedetto Croce, who emphatically stated that liberalism 'goes beyond the formal theory of politics' and 'coincides with a complete idea of the world and of reality'.[48]

While these efforts have not produced a reconstruction of liberalism, their persistence shows that professing liberalism by no means precludes searching for answers to the Big Questions of social philosophy. Moreover, it might even be possible to demonstrate that all of these efforts are distributed along a certain segment of the scale of conceivable positions. Although no specific philosophy comes into play, neither can liberalism appeal to every philosophy. Consequently, it seems that the question of the manifest and tacit assumptions of liberalism cannot be avoided.

The only caveat is not to go too far in a description of the substance of liberalism. Otherwise, one would ascribe to all liberals views which, though typical of some or even a large number of liberals, in the light of available information are not shared by every prominent liberal. Such a designation should be avoided not only because many liberals have said nothing about issues of fundamental importance for others, but also because many of them have explicitly gainsaid what others have asserted. Thus, while a goodly number of liberals have been indifferent to religion, one cannot take this for a characteristic feature of liberalism in general, since an equal number of liberals have espoused religion. For the same reason one should be wary of associating liberalism with an apologia of the free market and free competition. Likewise, 'atomism', with which liberalism has been rebuked since the times of Hegel,[49] cannot be laid at the door of every liberal, since among liberals there are some who use the following argumentation: 'The liberal view is sensitive to the way our individual lives and our moral considerations are related to, and situated in, a shared social context. The individualism that underlies liberalism isn't valued at the expense of our social nature or our shared community. It is an

---

[47] See Stephen Mulhall and Adam Swift, *Liberals and Communitarians* (Oxford: Blackwell, 1992).

[48] Benedetto Croce, *Politics and Morals*, trans. Salvatore Castiglione (New York: Philosophical Library, 1945), p. 112.

[49] See S. B. Smith, *Hegel's Critique of Liberalism: Rights in Context* (Chicago: The University of Chicago Press, 1989), p. 7.

individualism that accords with, rather than opposes, the undeniable importance to us of our social world.'[50]

To put it in a nutshell, whatever is asserted about views supposedly
characteristic of liberalism, it should be remembered that in its long history
liberalism has served various goals and interests, has adapted to various
local traditions, and has used various theoretical languages. For this reason,
every description that goes beyond a very high level of generality will
inevitably be untrue. The same thing can be said for all -isms, with the
exception of those that have created their own dogmatic systems, which the
programme of liberalism definitely precludes.

5. The language of the rights of the individual

So what can be said about liberalism in general that would not be at variance
with its self-evident multiplicity of forms and changeability, which none the
less are of assistance in distinguishing liberals from non-liberals and
'liberals' in the sense that the latter to some degree share a love of freedom
and sympathize with the institutions of liberal democracies? One can spare
oneself such generalities as 'a liberal is a man who believes in liberty'[51] or
'liberalism is the belief in and commitment to a set of methods that have as
their common aim greater freedom for individual men'.[52] Only the last five
words of the second quoted statement give us really important information
that goes beyond the etymology of the words 'liberal' and 'liberalism',
namely, that this orientation treats people as *individuals* and not as cogs of
some Great Machine or as cells of some 'social organism', whose own goals
and needs might not be reducible to the needs of individuals and might even
be in conflict with them.[53]

The core of liberal social philosophy doubtlessly is to be found here, if
one can speak of any philosophy at all. From here comes the opinion reiterated rather unanimously, which I quote as expressed by Judith Shklar:

[50] Will Kymlicka, *Liberalism, Community and Culture* (Oxford: Oxford University
Press, 1989), pp. 2–3. See Bruce Ackerman, *The Future of Liberal Revolution* (New
Haven CT: Yale University Press, 1992), pp. 20–1.
[51] The entry 'Liberalism' in *The Encyclopedia of Philosophy* (New York: The Free
Press, 1967), vol. IV, p. 458.
[52] The entry 'Liberalism' in *New Catholic Encyclopedia* (New York: McGraw-Hill,
1967), vol. VIII, p. 701.
[53] I refer here to the classic statement of Thomas Paine: 'Public good is not a term
opposed to the good of every individual collected. It is the good of all, because it is the
good of everyone; for as the public body is every individual collected, so the public good
is the collected good of those individuals' (quoted from S. Lukes, *Individualism*, op. cit,
p. 49).

'Every adult should be able to make as many effective decisions without fear or favor about as many aspects of her or his life as is compatible with the like freedom of every other adult. *That belief is the original and only defensible meaning of liberalism.*'[54]

Although on the surface pedestrian and presenting innumerable difficulties in applying it to specific situations, this opinion unquestionably touches upon the heart of the matter. If a liberal social philosophy exists, it is a philosophy that speaks in the language of the *rights of the individual*. This individual may be conceived in various ways, that is more or less 'atomistically', but *he or she* and *his or her* natural rights, which are vested in *him or her* irrespective of the social conventions and the provisions of positive law in effect in various times and places, are always in the centre of our attention. This is the Archimedean point of liberalism. The philosophy that liberalism has sought and is still seeking should begin from this point, and no preparation or justification of this philosophy is necessary. Here liberalism differs from numerous other conceptions, which evoke human rights understood in one way or another, but treat them as a category subsumed under a particular theological or philosophical idea.

In this respect, there seems to be no essential difference between 'old' and 'new', 'classic' and 'revisionist', 'individualistic' and 'collectivist' liberalism, despite the fact that these rights of the individual have been defined in different ways and various means have been employed to guarantee them – from the famous principle *laissez-faire et laissez-passer, le monde va de lui-měme*, with which every liberalism sometimes has been quite wrongly identified,[55] up to and including the *welfare state*, which, although associated by some of its critics with socialism, none the less owes at least as much to the liberal absolutization of the rights of the individual as to the socialist idea of equality.

The emphasis on individual rights clearly distinguishes liberalism from

---

[54] Judith N. Shklar, 'The Liberalism of Fear', op. cit., p. 21 (italics, Jerzy Szacki). Steven B. Smith rightly notes that in contemporary political thought 'the rehabilitation of human rights has gone hand in hand with revival of the philosophy of liberalism. Indeed, it is probably not too much to say that the idea of rights forms the core of the Western liberal tradition' (*Hegel's Critique of Liberalism*, op. cit., p. 99).

[55] This is done repeatedly on the one hand by some liberals (so-called 'classic', 'neoliberal', 'libertarian' liberals) and on the other by numerous critics of liberalism from the left and from the traditional right. Such an identification, however, requires a rather loose approach to the history of liberalism, one that would leave out the essential ingredients of J. S. Mill's conception and his elimination as cryptosocialism of everything that is called 'new', 'social', etc. liberalism. These tendencies, which are dominant in the twentieth century and are challenged by neoliberals more in theory than in practice, already appeared in the last century. J. M. Keynes's *The End of Laissez-faire* (1926) became a sort of manifesto of the new stage in the development of liberalism.

those great 'schools' of social philosophy whose starting point is the needs of the *community*, which are understood in one way or another – those of the nation, class, people, or any other social collectivity. For this reason, the concept of 'collectivist' liberalism, which is sometimes used, is inherently contradictory, though some liberals labelled in this way differ in many respects from the rest. A liberal may be perfectly aware of the necessity of contributing to the community, but he does not elevate this obligation to the status of a 'cult' or to something that takes precedence over individuals.

One can say that, to some extent, what we are really dealing with is the specific *language* in which liberals put forward their design of the good society. Their explicit proposals in this respect need not always differ from those of the nationalists, socialists or populists. A scrutiny of the programmes of European liberal parties reveals a simply astonishing gamut of possible combinations,[56] as does an analysis of North American liberalism, in which one finds enough conceptions and programmes coexisting with each other to provide the platforms for a dozen or more parties, and not necessarily liberal ones, at odds with one another.

As a rule, more is involved than the manner of formulating and justifying postulates. There is a strong belief that nothing can be gained for society by ignoring what is due to the individual. 'Each enlargement of the authority and functions of the State must justify itself as an enlargement of personal liberty',[57] wrote J. A. Hobson, one of the first ideologists of the 'socialization' of liberalism. This 'new' liberalism may have been poorly conceived, but it cannot be criticized for consciously moving away from values that are fundamental for liberalism. Irrespective of the wide differences among them, past and present liberals have always championed a society which in principle takes the rights of the individual for granted. From each point of view of liberalism, these rights are a *given* that politicians must take into consideration. Individuals are the only source of energy and initiative in society. It follows, therefore, that even the most protective state can have no other goal but to liberate this energy and initiative where, for some reason, they have been suppressed or put to sleep. It is quite another matter whether such *affirmative actions* really do lead to the desired goal, which critics of 'social' liberalism rightly point out.

In a certain sense, the absurd and anachronistic conception of the state as a 'night watchman', which has been regarded as a distinctive characteristic of 'old' and 'classic' liberalism, in fact 'does capture the spirit of the liberal

---

[56] See *Liberal Parties in Western Europe*, ed. Emil Joseph Kirchner (Cambridge: Cambridge University Press, 1988).

[57] J. A. Hobson, 'The Crisis of Liberalism', 1909, quoted from the anthology *The Liberal Tradition from Fox to Keynes*, ed. Alan Bullock and Maurice Shock (New York: New York University Press, 1957), p. 197.

Weltanschauung',[58] because what is most important in social life takes place without the participation and initiative of the state. Although a strong tendency appeared in 'social' liberalism to assist and guide these spontaneous processes, its starting assumption remained unshaken. 'Social' liberals continued to believe that the sole aim of liberal social engineering is to set in motion something that already exists, something that would need no help were it not for artificial barriers that have to be removed. Using the old metaphor, one can say that the night watchman sometimes has a lot of work, but it is never really creative work and it would be better if it were not needed. Hobhouse, also one of the first 'social' liberals, made this point as follows: 'The heart of liberalism is the understanding that progress is not a matter of mechanical contrivance, but of liberation of living spiritual energy.'[59] Since individuals are the source of this energy, they should be allowed to act as freely as is feasible in the expectation that the general outcome will be better than what can be achieved through interdictions and restrictions. From this conviction 'social' liberals derive the principle of 'interfering with individuals only in order to set free new and larger opportunities'.[60] It is something else entirely whether this principle has always been observed and what are the side effects of interventions that in principle were supposed to be of limited scope and duration. Here I am not drawing up a balance sheet of the achievements and failures of liberalism, but only trying to educe its basic *intention*, which determines its ideological identity.

Thus, one can state that, despite its narrowing scope of application over time, the principle of laissez-faire has never been abandoned by liberals as the most general principle of social engineering. In a certain sense, this principle has defined and still does define the position of liberalism in a world swayed by ideologies. In contrast to liberalism, these ideologies, even when they recognize the *Declaration of the Rights of Man and the Citizen* without reservations, are disposed primarily towards disciplining citizens by assimilating them into such or another Great Community, one whose supposed needs would dictate what the individual may and may not do. These ideologies often have good arguments in their favour. They can point to the signs of the moral and social crisis of Western societies in the wake of progress. For liberals, however, these ideologies threaten to squander the unquestioned achievements of these societies, especially by their call to limit the liberty of the individual and to restrict the freedom of actions of the institutions that guarantee this freedom.

---

[58] Gordon Smith, 'Between Left and Right: The Ambivalence of European Liberalism', in *Liberal Parties in Western Europe*, op. cit., p. 20.

[59] Quoted from D. J. Manning, *Liberalism* (London: Dent, 1976), p. 18.

[60] J. A. Hobson, 'The Crisis of Liberalism', op. cit., p. 192.

The response of liberals to the crisis was not to search for the lost community or to construct some new community in which the individual would be more or less incapacitated. Rather, it was to formulate ever more suitable *rules of the game* for a society that has been irreversibly individualized. Without restricting the rights of the individual in any major way, such rules could preserve social equilibrium and prevent a society divested of the old authorities from plunging into anarchy and from succumbing to an authoritarian ruler promising order for the price of escape from freedom. These rules, of course, varied widely and embraced larger or smaller areas of social life. The disputes among liberals, which cause deep divisions and antagonisms, are precisely over this question. For liberals, however, it goes without saying that the greatest good is the liberty of the individual; for them this tenet is self-evident and needs no justification, whereas all attempts to restrict it are debatable from the very nature of things and can be questioned at any time.

No specific political programme automatically springs from the views discussed above. Neither are they necessarily linked with such and not another philosophical position. Yet, it is worth noting that the liberal who wishes to construct a theory leans towards nominalism rather than towards sociological realism; he is more likely to embrace the Kantian than the Hegelian tradition. None the less, liberalism in this sense seems to be specific enough so that one can distinguish it, at least roughly, from other orientations, even if these orientations accept such or other liberal postulates and the institutions that have originated from the implementation of these postulates in liberal democracies.

Perhaps it would be more fitting to call liberalism not a social philosophy or philosophy of life, but a *style of thinking* in the sense used by Karl Mannheim in his work on conservatism.[61] The choice of words is not the most important thing, however; what is important is that liberals are *different* not only because they are, let us assume, less dogmatic and more tolerant than conservatives, nationalists or socialists. To what has been said above obviously could be added that the recognition of individual rights without reservations goes hand-in-hand with closing off a rather extensive *private* sphere, in which the sovereignty of the individual would be completely unrestricted, and an as narrow as possible *public* sphere, in which the individual would participate, theoretically, of his own free volition as a part of the whole. This subject will not be developed here and many themes that could be taken up are left out, since all possible developments would be the consequences of applying the language of the rights of the individual.

[61] Karl Mannheim, 'Conservative Thought', in *Essays on Sociology and Social Psychology* (London: Routledge and Kegan Paul, 1953), pp. 5–8.

6. *The problem of economic liberalism*

The question that must be addressed, however, is whether, according to the widely held stereotype, so-called *economic* liberalism should be included in the general characterization of liberalism as one of its essential elements. There is no dearth of authors who contend that true liberals are, of necessity, *Prophets of Freedom and Enterprise*,[62] people who believe that private ownership and a free market are the foundation of any other liberty.

Weighty historical and logical arguments can be put forward in support of this thesis. On the one hand, economists who are advocates of a free market have played an enormous role in the history of liberalism, and even much of today's invigoration of liberal thought may be laid to them; on the other hand, it is hard to imagine a consistent defence of the rights of the individual that would leave out the sphere of economic activities or hold that, for some reasons, the postulate of maximum freedom should not apply especially to this area.

Even if every liberal is not absolutely convinced as to the old philosophical thesis that private ownership is a simple and necessary extension of the rights of the individual to control his own personal destiny, he will be hard put to refute the argument that repudiation of the principles of economic liberalism seriously restricts freedom in all areas, enough evidence in support of which has been supplied by the communist experiment of the twentieth century. Thus, to say the truth, every liberal will surely agree with the opinion that 'upholding the liberal rights of individuals is incompatible with the abandonment of all private-property rights',[63] even though many a person ponders the fact that ownership also means a sort of *power* over other people. This power, vested in some, of necessity limits the rights of others, especially when groups of small owners are not involved, groups in which, theoretically, every small owner would have enough strength to defend himself. No matter what liberals themselves think of this, it can be argued that the market writ large most appropriately reflects the rough outlines of the liberal vision of the good society, a society that upholds free choice and risk.

However, there seems to be no necessary connection between any kind of liberalism and economic liberalism, especially between economic liberalism in its extreme form, which by assumption excludes interference of the state in the economy and any restrictions on the freedom of individuals in this area.

---

[62] The title of an anthology of writings of liberal thinkers, which was issued in 1975 by Kogan Page for Aims of Industry. A more detailed justification of linking all liberalism with economic liberalism is put forward by Ludwig Mises in *Liberalism in the Classic Tradition* (San Francisco: Cobden Press, 1985). See also Milton Friedman, *Capitalism and Freedom* (Chicago: The University of Chicago Press, 1982).

[63] D. A. Lloyd Thomas, *In Defense of Liberalism* (Oxford: Blackwell, 1988), p. 89.

On the one hand, it is not hard to find dyed-in-the-wool liberals who (unjustifiably, perhaps) have attached no importance to economic matters or, even worse, have openly sinned against the credo of economic liberalism. It is also worth remembering that, as Giovanni Sartori stressed, political liberalism originated much earlier than economic liberalism (in the author's terminology, *liberism*).[64] On the other hand, there have been outstanding practitioners of economic liberalism (General Pinochet, for example) who were not liberals in any sense of the word.[65] Norberto Bobbio remarked that 'neoliberalism today refers primarily to a widely supported economic doctrine, while political liberalism is regarded as no more than a means to its realization; or else it represents an uncompromising commitment to an economic liberty of which political liberty is viewed as no more than a corollary'.[66] This affranchisement of economic liberalism, so to speak, is nothing really new. In some countries this happened as early as the nineteenth century, a process that was sometimes marked by resignation from the aspiration for non-economic freedoms and sometimes by a tactic based on the belief that somehow other freedoms would follow in the wake of economic freedom and that, consequently, for the time being it was not worth making the effort to secure these other freedoms. It goes without saying that the latter position requires making many additional assumptions which are hardly self-evident for every liberal.

There is no evidence that economic liberals have ever been a majority among liberals. On the contrary, economic liberals are so different from most other liberals that they often use special names to set themselves apart from them: 'classical' liberals, 'neoliberals', 'libertarians', or even 'conservatives', as in the United States.[67] Yet, sometimes economic liberals continue

[64] Giovanni Sartori, *The Theory of Democracy Revisited* (Chatham NJ: Chatham House Publishers, 1987), p. 379.

[65] G. Sartori wrote in this regard that 'we must carefully distinguish liberalism from *laissez-faire*, the market economy' ('The Relevance of Liberalism in Retrospect', op. cit., p. 8). Bruce Ackerman showed how liberals 'have been trying to put the market in its place – as one, but only one, of a series of fundamental commitments' (*The Future of Liberal Revolution*, op. cit., pp. 9–10). For John Rawls – see *Political Liberalism* (New York: Columbia University Press, 1993, p. 338) – the connection of political with economic liberalism is even looser.

[66] Norberto Bobbio, *Liberalism and Democracy* (London: Verso, 1990), p. 81.

[67] Especially noteworthy seems the popularization of the term *libertarianism* as the name for all those conceptions that preclude any departures whatsoever from free market principles and call for limiting the influence of the state on social life to the maximum extent. This terminological innovation does not resolve the issue, however, for it is limited to those cases in which pertinent views are in this and not some other way. See Norman P. Barry, *On Classical Liberalism and Libertarianism* (New York: St Martin's Press, 1987), p. 18; Will Kymlicka, *Contemporary Political Philosophy: An Introduction* (Oxford: Clarendon Press, 1990, pp. 95–6). In the Polish literature, a book on such ideologists was written by Ryszard Legutko, who uses the term *laissez-faireism* as a philosophical category. See his *Dylematy kapitalizmu* (Paris: Editions Spotkania, 1986).

to emphasize that they and only they are liberals in the best meaning of the word, whereas all the others are, at bottom, 'socialists'.

When economic liberalism is examined against the broad canvas of the history of liberalism, one is inclined to treat it as one of many possible aspects of the liberal orientation and as only one of its possible practical manifestations, but not as an integral and necessary part of liberalism in general. If all those who do not share the views of economic liberalism were to be regarded as not 'true' liberals, there would be no reason not to regard as a liberal someone who, for instance, extols dictatorship only because he or she expects it to provide conditions for unrestricted economic activity. It must be remembered, of course, that among the most radical supporters of economic liberalism were thinkers who personified the liberal mind (such as Friedrich von Hayek).[68] Thus, I believe, they owe such an opinion not so much to their economic views as to the context in which these views originated. One can even defend the thesis that liberalism would have remained an orientation of marginal importance had its core been economic liberalism.[69]

I reiterate, however, that this hardly means that a liberal who observes the rules of logic can remain neutral, let alone hostile, to private ownership. Between socialism (or, even more so, communism) and 'libertarianism' there is a range of other positions; and, historically speaking, most theoreticians and practitioners of liberalism are distributed along this rather wide spectrum. These liberals need not be state socialists *à rebours*, who thereby sin against the earlier quoted opinion of Bertrand Russell that a liberal holds his opinions conditionally and not dogmatically. The terms *pre-market liberal* and *post-market liberal*, introduced by Steven B. Smith in his analysis of Hegel's views,[70] make sense if they refer to liberals who are not radical supporters of a free market. I lean towards David Spitz's opinion that 'liberalism is not wedded to any particular economic order and is able to countenance a wide assortment of property rights'. It stands to reason, of course, that liberals must accept private property 'as a bulwark against government, as a source of power perhaps necessary to counteract an overwhelming or otherwise unchallengeable amount of authority amassed by bureaucrats'.[71]

---

[68] See especially John Gray, *Hayek on Liberty* (Oxford: Blackwell, 1984).

[69] The best, though indirect, justification of this view is the celebrated book of Karl Polanyi, *The Great Transformation* (Boston: Beacon Press, 1957). Support for this conviction may also be found in economic liberals themselves, who – like Ludwig von Mises – have often stated that nearly all 'liberals' do not share their views; *Liberalism in the Classic Tradition*, op. cit, p. 172.

[70] S. B. Smith, *Hegel's Critique of Liberalism*, op. cit., p. 172.

[71] D. Spitz, *The Real World of Liberalism*, op. cit., pp. 149–50.

7. *A multitude of liberalisms*

After this rather long digression on the 'essence' of liberalism, it is time to return to the main drift of the argument and move on to the next question. Here, when dealing with Eastern Europe, one cannot confine oneself to what liberals and so-called 'liberals' say about themselves. The reason is that their consciousness is, or for a long time has been, false. In the special conditions of Eastern Europe, we see not only a miraculous multiplication of liberals but also an effacement of differences among them, which at the outset were naturally minor in comparison with the differences that separated all of them from real socialism. Thus, even when we are somehow able to distinguish 'real' liberalism, so to speak, from 'liberalism' characterized mainly by rebellion against dictatorship or by slogans in support of liberty, we may well wonder whether we are dealing with one or with many liberalisms. In my opinion, at the outset it will be expedient to put forward the hypothesis of a *multiplicity of liberalisms*. There are arguments in its favour both in what we know about liberalism in general and in the fact that this hypothesis is the least risky one for a researcher. Such an approach avoids the errors that could result from assuming that we have to do with liberalism *per se* and that the sole task is to describe it as a certain whole. The odds are that the internal differentiation of liberalism referred to repeatedly above is now taking place in Eastern Europe. It is an interesting question to what extent this process is a result of borrowing inspiration from various sources and to what extent it is a consequence of the effort to cope with dilemmas arising from local conditions.

In referring to our general knowledge of liberalism, I have in mind not only those scholars cited earlier who have questioned the existence of one liberal tradition, but also the much larger number of those who, without ceasing to treat of one tradition, in their works have introduced countless differentiations into 'old' and 'new', 'earlier' and 'later', 'classic' and 'revisionist', 'conservative' and 'radical', 'individualistic' and 'collectivistic', 'British' and 'continental', 'European' and 'American', etc. liberalism. The literature also speaks of neoliberalism, but this term should not be confused with new liberalism, which is 'old' as opposed to neoliberalism; and post-liberalism, since post-modernism has made all other post-trends and post-problems fashionable. Some of these distinctions have already been used in our discussion, though the main focus thus far has been on what seems common to various ostensibly contrasting liberalisms.

Perhaps the most important distinction was introduced (or most clearly formulated) by C. B. Macpherson in his book on liberal democracy, a concept which, in his opinion, usually refers to 'a society striving to ensure that all its members are equally free to realize their capacities' or simply to 'the democracy of a capitalist market society'.[72] It is of little importance here that Macpherson himself too closely linked liberalism as such with the second possibility, as did the Marxists on the one hand and the ideologists of economic liberalism on the other, who are remarkably similar to the Marxists in certain respects. Macpherson's distinction correctly identifies the substratum from which innumerable varieties of 'new', 'social', 'revisionist' and 'protective' liberalism sprang up at one end;[73] and at the other, rather numerous reaffirmations (especially in recent decades) of the thesis that all freedom is the daughter of the free market, and consequently to be for liberty is more or less the same as to be for capitalism without reservations. The first tendency, which results in an expansion of the welfare state, brings liberalism close to the Social Democratic Party; the second one, however, leads to implacable hostility towards anything that even in the least smacks of socialism. During the past century, liberal thought oscillated between these two poles, in certain countries and at certain times moving closer to the former than the latter.

It would be a waste of time to ponder over which of these two liberalisms is 'better', more 'true' or 'authentic', for in the final analysis this is a matter of taste, over which there is no disputing. Both of them are rooted in the liberal tradition. Both of them speak in the same language of individual rights. Both of them strive to realize the same postulate of the greatest possible amount of freedom. It is extremely important, however, to be aware that these are two *different* and, in many respects, antagonistic liberalisms. Where liberty does not exist and the matter concerns gaining basic freedoms, these liberalisms might not manifest their differences; they might even seem very similar, especially since the *pars destruens* of all liberalism is basically the same. For instance, under real socialism the dispute referred to is really pointless. However, when conditions change or at least the hope of an imminent change appears, this dispute can and even must erupt. So in dealing with the development of liberalism, we must always have this controversy in mind. There is no reason to believe that liberalism in Eastern Europe will be able to avoid this conflict. If we look at Western liberalism, we may conclude that Eastern liberalism is fated to inherit all of the inherent dilemmas of the former.

[72] C. B. Macpherson, *The Life and Times of Liberal Democracy* (Oxford: Oxford University Press, 1977), pp. 1–3. For more information about the views of this author on liberalism see *The Political Theory of Possessive Individualism: Hobbes to Locke* (Oxford: Oxford University Press, 1962); Kirk F. Koerner, *Liberalism and Its Critics*, op. cit., Chapter 2.

[73] A representative survey of the classic writings of 'new liberalism' is contained in the anthology of Bullock and Shock, *The Liberal Tradition*, op. cit., pp. v and vi. See also *Sozialer Liberalismus*, ed. Karl Holl (Göttingen: Gunter Trautmann and Hans Vorlander, Vandenhoeck & Rupert, 1986).

In brief, a study of the first manifestations of liberal thought cannot stop at the surface of general declarations; rather, it must attempt to discover what lies behind them and whether the word 'liberalism' means the same thing every time it is uttered. It goes without saying that we may be dealing with hidden differences or with ones that will appear only in time, when it becomes necessary to take positions on issues that were of no practical importance as long as real socialism existed. For at stake under real socialism was the achievement through a common effort of the liberal or liberal-democratic minimum, which reduced itself to matters over which it was indecorous to argue in polite company.

In Poland, at least three different circles of liberal ideas have arisen. These circles must be distinguished as clearly as possible from each other and will be discussed in separate chapters (IV, V, and VI). The first one, which in essence boils down to a truncated version of the minimum liberal programme, I call *protoliberalism*.[74] It seems important to me because it contains an affirmation of certain values characteristic of liberalism, despite the fact that neither the catchword 'liberalism' nor ideas that would allow us to speak of liberalism in the full meaning of the word appear in it. A study of this circle will reveal the sources of the attractiveness of liberal ideas under real socialism on the one hand, and on the other will expose why they are hard to accept. The second circle is *economic liberalism*, an orientation with a pro-capitalist programme. It emerged in the 1980s as an alternative both to communism and to anti-communism in the form of the protoliberal democratic opposition. The third and final circle is still not fully shaped *integral liberalism*, which is attempting to overcome the limitations of economic liberalism and to formulate a position whose main, or even sole, feature would not be a justification of capitalism. What we are dealing with here is not so much (or not only) a particular economic doctrine that could coexist with non-liberal views on matters outside economics such as the idea of a liberal culture, in which the postulates of the rule of law, the philosophical neutrality of the state, respect for the rights of minorities of all kinds, tolerance, etc. would become a reality.

The liberal circles outlined above are certain ideal types, and it is hardly my intention to divide up the nascent liberal movement into clearly distinct trends. Rather, it is to show the possible ways of transformation of what Bertrand Russell called *the diffuse liberal sentiment*[75] as a reaction to socialism in the expanded and consciously accepted liberal position. In

---

[74] Some authors use this term in reference of those ideas and practices which others simply called liberalism, only pointing out that they have in mind liberalism *avant la lettre* (see J. G. Merquior, *Liberalism Old and New*, op. cit., p. 2). The reader will see that I use this term in a different sense.

[75] Bertrand Russell, *Unpopular Essays* (London: Unwin, 1988), p. 308.

specific cases the differences among these paths may be difficult to grasp. It is not entirely clear whether the two liberalisms I have distinguished are exact counterparts of the two orientations mentioned by Macpherson, which requires separate analysis. In any case, in this book it seems necessary to ask once again about what *kind* of liberalism we are dealing with. The question is all the more important in view of the fact that positions have not yet crystallized and party divisions are not distinct enough when we look for essential ideological differences.

III Historical Background

The people of Central Europe . . . cannot be separated from
European history, they cannot exist outside it; but they represent
the wrong side of history: they are victims and outsiders.[1]

1. *Eastern Europe vis-à-vis the West*

Before I take up the development of liberalism in today's Eastern or Central
Europe,[2] some introductory remarks need to be made about the historical
context of our subject. This is necessary because the development of liberalism depends not only on the present demand for liberal ideas on the part of
politicians or on the supply of these ideas on the world marketplace of ideas,
but also on the *historical underpinning* upon which this exchange takes
place. I have in mind the historical substratum in the sense used by Ludwik
Krzywicki, who called attention to the obstacles encountered by every
innovation, even when a given society desperately needs it. 'We live girdled
and fettered by past centuries',[3] wrote Krzywicki, who in his studies tried to
show the influence of this factor on the spread of new ideas, a process
whose pace depends not only on whether they provide an effective solution

---

[1] Milan Kundera, 'The Tragedy of Central Europe', in *From Stalinism to Pluralism: A Documentary History of Eastern Europe since 1945*, ed. Gale Stokes (New York: Oxford University Press, 1991), p. 221.

[2] In footnote 1 to the 'Introduction' I explain the sense in which I use the term 'Eastern Europe'. Here it should be added that 'Eastern Europe has evolved not in four decades but over the centuries.' (See Ivan T. Berend, 'The Historical Evolution of Eastern Europe as a Region', *International Organization* 1986, vol. 40, no. 2, p. 329.) See Jeno Szucs, 'Three Historical Regions of Europe', in *Civil Society and the State*, ed. John Keane (London: Verso, 1988), pp. 291–331; also Piotr S. Wandycz, *The Price of Freedom: A History of East Central Europe from the Middle Ages to the Present* (London: Routledge, 1992), pp. 1–2. In other words, I assume that the countries covered under the name 'Eastern Europe' have many common features that distinguish them from Western Europe on the one hand and from Russia on the other. On account of this dual distinction a strong argument can be made for using the term 'Central-Eastern Europe'.

[3] Ludwik Krzywicki, *Studia socjologiczne* (Warsaw: PIW, 1951), p. 141.

to the tasks faced by a given collectivity, but also on whether this collectivity is capable of accepting these ideas, on whether it has such and not other experiences, institutions and customs.

In other words, I have in mind the kind of historical and sociological analysis exemplified in Ralf Dahrendorf's book *Gesellschaft und Demokratie in Deutschland*, which appeared only a few years after the downfall of Hitlerism and exposed the foundations on which the construction of German liberal democracy was started.

Although liberals sometimes express the conviction that what they really want is a return to the 'natural conditions of mankind',[4] the opposite view seems more warranted – namely, that such conditions exist (or perhaps have existed) in relatively few countries and since a rather short time ago.[5] However liberalism is understood, it cannot be regarded as common to all cultures or as the destiny of all mankind. The chances are that it is a phenomenon limited in time and space and that its manifestation outside certain boundaries was and remains only a possibility. To put it as briefly as possible, liberalism is a phenomenon of the so-called Western world of the last few centuries; even if it appears elsewhere, it is as a more or less successful *transplant*. It is hardly surprising that in their own countries liberals, as a rule, have a pro-Western orientation and show the least fears of the possibility that modern innovations will threaten native values; their opponents, on the other hand, are wont to appeal to local values and to condemn modern Western culture. This is so even today. Whether some country or region is capable of assimilating liberalism apparently depends on whether it belongs to the Western world at least in some respects. Making efforts in this direction is always based on the conviction that the Western 'process of civilization' is always beneficial and, at least potentially, universal. Quite obviously, the word 'West' refers not only to a geographical region but also to a type of culture.

From this point of view, the situation of the countries of Eastern Europe was and is rather unclear. Some of them (especially Poland, Hungary and Czechoslovakia) have had very strong ties with the West and an even stronger feeling of these ties. In spite of this, these countries, firstly, were on the periphery of the West; secondly, their ties with the West were often weakened and sometimes for a long time; thirdly, for the last several decades these countries have lived in rather deep isolation, which without completely destroying the feeling of ties with the West nevertheless did rupture many real ties. In Poland only the tie through the Roman Catholic

[4] See Bernard Wheaton and Zdének Kavan, *The Velvet Revolution* (Boulder CO: Westview Press, 1992), p. 162.

[5] See Karl Polanyi, *The Great Transformation: The Political and Economic Origins of Our Time* (Boston: Beacon Press, 1957), p. 43.

Church remained strong, a tie with only one tradition of Western culture.

Consequently, one cannot say that these countries of Eastern Europe definitely *belong* to the Western world without introducing many reservations, which seem in order not only because of these countries' recent communist past but also because of their more distant past. Ken Jowitt was correct when he wrote that 'in a curious, unintended, and highly consequential way, Leninist rule reinforced many of the most salient features of traditional culture throughout Eastern Europe'.[6] For this reason, today's Eastern European liberalism finds itself in opposition not only to communism but also – in no small measure – to the legacy of the more remote past. The 1991 election platform of the Liberal-Democratic Congress in Poland stated that liberals are trying to overcome both the 'post-communist collapse' and the 'backwardness that has increased for at least two centuries'.

The catchphrase 'return to Europe', which became fashionable after 1989, unavoidably has a metaphorical sense. In any case, if it is taken literally, it does not refer (except for Czechoslovakia, perhaps) to those things that today's liberals most often have in mind: rights of the individual, liberal democracy, the free market economy, etc. It was this that I meant when in the Introduction I wrote of the absence of a liberal tradition. In fact, 'the category "liberal" may seem like an empty one for many of the countries of Eastern Europe, except Czechoslovakia'.[7] The thesis on the absence of a liberal tradition must be expanded and made more precise, however, for in its general wording it may raise doubts.

2. The myth of the 'golden freedom' of old Poland

In the case of Poland, this thesis is at variance with the deeply rooted stereotype of Poland as a country of individualists, of a nation which in the past not only kept up with the West but even outpaced it in the development of liberal institutions. During his stay in the United States in the summer of 1925, ambassador Aleksander Skrzyński uttered the following words about noblemen's Poland: 'Poland possessed, without question, the most liberal political system that Europe up to that time had produced.'[8] Aleksander

---

[6] Ken Jowitt, 'The Leninist Legacy', in *Eastern Europe in Revolution*, ed. Ivo Banac (Ithaca NY: Cornell University Press, 1992), p. 209.

[7] Daniel Chirot, 'Ideology, Reality and Competing Models of Development in Eastern Europe Between the Two World Wars', *East European Politics and Societies* 1989, vol. 3, no. 2, p. 401. See Paweł Śpiewak, 'Wolność jako wyzwanie', *Przegląd Polityczny* 1993, no. 19/20, pp. 6–10.

[8] Aleksander Skrzyński in *For Your Freedom and Ours: Polish Progressive Spirit from the 14th Century to the Present*, ed. Krystyna M. Olszer, second enlarged edition (New York: Frederick Ungar Publishing Company, 1981), p. 204.

Świętochowski, on the other hand, wrote as follows: 'If from the deeds of the Polish nobility we took away excesses and the exclusiveness of caste, we would be left with what is contained in Mill's splendid treatise *On Liberty*.'[9]

Despite the mostly bad press that the 'golden freedom' of the nobility had, the viewpoint expressed above was not uncommon. One of its first manifestations was the positive mention of Poland in *Vindiciae contra tyrannos* (1579), one of the publications that belongs to the pre-history of European liberalism. Recently, this view was repeated in more subtle form by Norman Davies, who in his popular history of Poland wrote of 'the specific values of individualism and liberty that have marked the Polish spirit across the ages'[10] and gave this assessment of the democracy of the nobility:

> Oddly enough the ideals of the Polish nobility possess an air of striking modernity. In the age when most Europeans were lauding the benefits of Monarchism, Absolutism, or of state power, the noble citizens of Poland-Lithuania were praising their 'Golden Freedom', the right to resistance, the social contract, the liberty of the individual, the principle of government by consent, the value of self-reliance. These concepts feature widely in the ideologies of modern, liberal democracies . . . The coincidence of view between the Polish nobleman of the seventeenth or eighteenth century with the liberal democrat of the nineteenth and twentieth centuries is not purely fortuitous. It is caused by their common concern to combat the powers of the state. The one opposed the initial manifestations of the phenomenon, the other opposes its modern excesses, but their enemy is the same.[11]

'The aversion of noblemen's Poland to the authoritarian state', as Tadeusz Łepkowski phrased it,[12] became part of the enduring stereotype of the Polish national character. Sometimes, certain characteristics of contemporary Poles that made it hard or impossible for them to adapt to the 'Byzantine' communist system are associated with the legacy of 'golden freedom' of the nobility. Two Polish economists recently wrote that 'the Polish national tradition provided a particularly unreceptive soil for the Soviet-type

---

[9] Quoted from Zbigniew Ogonowski, *Filozofia polityczna w Polsce XVII wieku i tradycje demokracji europejskiej* (Warsaw: IFiS, 1992), p. 25.

[10] Norman Davies, *God's Playground: A History of Poland* (New York: Columbia University Press, 1982), vol. II, p. 640.

[11] N. Davies, op. cit., vol. I, pp. 489–90. See Ogonowski, op. cit., pp. 98–100.

[12] Tadeusz Łepkowski, *Uparte trwanie polskości* (London: Aneks, 1989), p. 16.

economic administration'.[13] The context of this statement leaves no doubts that the authors had in mind precisely the 'liberal institutions' of pre-partition Poland. It was very likely that Stalin also had this tradition in mind when he uttered his famous statement that 'communism fits Poland like a saddle fits a cow'.[14]

Indeed, in comparison with the history of Russia, Polish history abounds in facts which seem to confirm the truth of this stereotype. In Eastern Europe not only Poles have cause to remind the world of their love for freedom and to believe that for this reason they belong to a different civilization than do the former subjects of the Russian empire.[15] In any case, it is hard to disagree with the Polish historian who charges Western historians with 'the tendency to ignore the libertarian traditions of Poland and to stress, instead, her economic and social backwardness'.[16]

When we go back to the past, these traditions of freedom do indeed appear rich, and some of the privileges of the nobility (*habeas corpus*, *neminem captivabimus*, etc.) really do look like precursors of later Western solutions that have entered into the liberal canon. This is why so many Polish thinkers of the nineteenth century felt that Poland does not have to learn freedom from the West, because freedom is an inseparable part of Poland's national heritage. One of the pamphleteers of the November Insurrection of 1830–1 wrote as follows: 'The fatherland of political freedom is our land, Poland, . . . in liberal principles and institutions we are ahead of all the nations of Europe. . . . We must revive these institutions and extend them to all citizens, we do not have to imitate anything.'[17] So in the face of the above arguments, perhaps there is a liberal tradition in Eastern Europe, or at least in Poland, and the assertion that it is lacking needs major revision? It would seem that such a revision is not required for the following reasons.

First, we should not pay too much heed to formal similarities. The freedom to which the Polish nobility was so strongly attached was an entirely different kind of freedom from the one professed by modern liberalism. Andrzej Walicki wrote that the freedom of the Polish nobility was

[13] Wiktor Herer and Władysław Sadowski, 'The Incompatibility of System and Culture and the Polish Crisis', in *Polish Paradoxes*, ed. Stanisław Gomułka and Antony Polonsky (London: Routledge, 1990), p. 128. See also N. Davies on 'Solidarity' as a return to the political traditions of noblemen's democracy (*God's Playground*, op. cit., vol. II, p. 797).

[14] Quoted from D. S. Mason, *Revolution in East-Central Europe* (Boulder CO: Westview Press, 1992), p. 40.

[15] See M. Kundera, *The Tragedy of Central Europe*, op. cit., pp. 218, 222.

[16] Andrzej Walicki, *Philosophy and Romantic Nationalism: The Case of Poland* (Oxford: Clarendon Press, 1982), p. 12.

[17] J. B. Ostrowski, 'Przyszły król', *Nowa Polska* 1831, no. 20.

'freedom conceived as participation in group sovereignty and not as a defense of the rights of the individual to pursue his individual life goals'.[18] The famous *liberum veto*, which has been regarded as a typification of the unconstrained individualism of the nobility was, as the same author remarked, 'more an ethos of archaic collectivism, for it was the reverse side of the belief that decisions affecting the community should be taken unanimously'.[19] It is also worth bearing in mind that the ideological justification of the 'golden freedom' of the nobility was a belief in the common origin of the members of this estate rather than the belief that certain rights are vested in them as *individuals*. It has often been argued that, since the Polish nobility was very numerous, its democracy was not less limited in the class sense than in the liberal democracies of the beginning of the nineteenth century, in which an even smaller percentage of citizens enjoyed full political rights. None the less, this argument is not convincing, because the Polish nobility was a closed group (apart from a few exceptions, many of which were contrary to the law), in which membership was inherited.

Second, this 'liberalism' of the nobility not only did not open the way for new kinds of activities. On the contrary, it promoted sluggishness, and thwarted adaptation to changing internal and external circumstances. For a long time, the ideology of the nobility was an obstacle to modernization of the economy; this ideology was, so to speak, the Polish variety of the economic traditionalism described in Max Weber's famous treatise.[20] It is an uncontested fact that the 'liberalism' of the nobility was easily exploited by the local magnates and foreign despots. For this reason, in his copious history of liberalism Guido de Ruggiero makes only one short mention of Poland; moreover, it is highly critical, for it names Poland as an exemplification of a false conception of freedom.[21] The complete silence of other historians of liberalism should be attributed not so much to their ignorance of East European affairs – which is widespread in the West – as to the fact that, in many respects, the 'golden freedom' of the Polish nobility lay outside their sphere of interests.

Third, even if we admit that the legacy of noblemen's democracy was an important beginning and an advance payment, we must be aware that we

[18] Andrzej Walicki, 'Trzy patriotyzmy', Warsaw *Res Publica*, 1991, p. 32.
[19] Ibid., p. 20.
[20] See Władysław Smoleński, 'Szlachta w świetle własnych opinii', *Wybór pism* (Warsaw: KiW, 1954), pp. 16–21. The best study of the ancient Polish 'political economics' is Janina Rosicka's book, *O wyobraźni ekonomicznej Polaków* (Kraków: Universitas, 1991).
[21] Guido de Ruggiero, *The History of European Liberalism*, trans. R. G. Collingwood (Boston: Beacon Press, 1959), p. 263.

have to do with an *interrupted* history, since 'ruled as it was by autocratic and feudal powers, Poland did not have the opportunity to develop the early constitutional tradition into a modern political culture'.[22] In the period of the Partitions of Poland, this tradition certainly had great symbolic importance. However, it did not become the starting point of the democratic thought of the nineteenth and twentieth centuries; rather, it often served as a negative example. The view unquestionably prevailed that '*Polish* democracy must be distinguished from *noblemen's democracy*.'[23]

Fourth, and finally, when I speak of the absence of a liberal tradition, I have in mind not so much what historians can find and interpret as what Michael Oakeshott likes to refer to as *practical* history,[24] that is, most briefly, what really influences the attitudes of people today, irrespective of whether they are particularly interested in the past and whether they have any understanding of it. From this angle, it does not seem that the 'golden freedom' of the nobility may be regarded as a part of such history. I lean towards the view that the interpretations which gained popularity in 1981, according to which 'the Polish working class can be seen as reviving the political traditions of the Noble Democracy – traditions which appear to survive almost two centuries of suppression',[25] have more rhetoric in them than substance. If the continuity of some tradition of *fighting for independence* is involved here, this hardly means that this is a *liberal* tradition. It has already been argued that these very well could be two entirely different things. There is absolutely no reason at all to associate every fight for freedom with liberalism, especially in cases of conquest and foreign domination.

No matter how glorious a tradition such or another country of Eastern Europe has in fighting for liberty, it cannot be claimed that liberalism in the West European or North American meaning really became an important experience of political man in any of the East European countries. This does not mean, of course, that liberal ideas were entirely absent there. Individual liberal ideas may have taken root there, but – as Rett R. Ludwikowski wrote – 'the liberal framework was far from complete'.[26] These ideas permeated various ideological contexts in which it is sometimes hard to identify them.

---

[22] S. Gomułka and A. Polonsky, 'Introduction' to *Polish Paradoxes*, op. cit., p. 4.

[23] Jan Czyński, 'Co to jest demokracja?', in *700 lat myśli polskiej: Filozofia i myśl społeczna w latach 1831–1864*, comp. A. Walicki (Warsaw: PWN, 1977), p. 847.

[24] Michael Oakeshott, 'The Activity of Being an Historian', *Rationalism and Other Essays* (London: Methuen, 1962), pp. 153–5.

[25] N. Davies, *God's Playground*, op. cit., vol. II, pp. 797–8.

[26] Rett R. Ludwikowski, *Continuity and Change in Poland: Conservatism in Polish Political Thought* (Washington DC: The Catholic University of America Press, 1991), p. 80.

Liberalism as such, however, never became the starting point of enduring and influential schools of political thought inspiring wide social circles and having a noticeable influence on the life of these countries. 'For decades Polish liberalism was a weak trend, a secondary, if not an outright marginal one.'[27] The absence of modern liberalism becomes even more evident in not very successful efforts to revive liberal traditions.

It is hardly any exaggeration to say that while individual liberals, even outstanding ones, have existed in Eastern Europe, liberalism did not exist there as a constantly present orientation that would have to be included in even a general description of the political landscape of the region in the nineteenth and twentieth centuries.[28] Any historian who undertakes to reconstruct liberal thought encounters enormous difficulties. If he defines liberalism too narrowly, the subject vanishes almost completely, for hardly anyone is left who would meet all of the criteria of the definition; if he defines it too broadly, however, it becomes even less visible, for the boundaries between liberal and other systems become erased.[29] Such a historian constantly runs the risk of describing as a liberal 'anybody who wrote or spoke about progress, abolishment of absolutism, and self-determination of nations'.[30] It is no wonder that the history of liberalism in Eastern Europe has not yet been written and that all we have is the history of individual *episodes*.[31]

[27] Preface by Piotr Winczorek to Wojciech Sadurski, *Racje liberała: Eseje o państwie liberalno-demokratycznym* (Warsaw: Presspublica, 1992), p. 5.

[28] While we find out one thing or another about liberalism in Michał Śliwa's latest book, this really isn't much, and he has more to say about 'weaknesses'. See *Polska myśl polityczna w pierwszej połowie XX wieku* (Wrocław: Ossolineum, 1993), pp. 17–22.

[29] This difficulty is best shown by R. R. Ludwikowski in *Continuity and Change in Poland*, op. cit. (see especially pp. 82–4, 144–6, 192–6, 259–63).

[30] Ludwikowski, op. cit., p. 80. See the same author's 'Liberal Traditions in Polish Political Thought', *Journal of Libertarian Studies* 1981, no. 3, pp. 255–61; and 'Kim są 'polscy' liberałowie?', *Widzieć mądrość w wolności: Księga pamięci Mirosława Dzielskiego*, a collection edited by Bogusław Chrabota (Kraków: Krakowskie Towarzystwo Przemysłowe, 1991), pp. 131–44.

[31] See Helena Więckowska, *Opozycja liberalna w Królestwie Kongresowym 1815–1830* (Warsaw, 1925); Piotr Chmielowski, *Liberalizm i obskurantyzm na Litwie i Rusi: 1815–1822* (Warsaw, 1898); Tadeusz Stegner, *Liberałowie Królestwa Polskiego: 1904–1915* (Gdańsk 1990). More synthetic approaches may be found in Jerzy Jedlicki, 'Obozy ideowe Królestwa wobec zmian społecznych', *Przemiany społeczne w Królestwie Polskim 1815–1864*, collective work ed. Witold Kula and Janina Leskiewiczowa (Wrocław, 1979), pp. 463–96; and Maciej Janowski, 'Liberalizm polski w XIX wieku' (manuscript). In November 1992 a conference was held in Konstancin (near Warsaw) entitled 'Liberal Traditions in Poland', at which many interesting papers were read. See *Tradycje liberalne w Polsce* (Warsaw: Wydawnictwo DiG, 1993).

3. *Economic backwardness and the absence of a liberal tradition*

This poverty of the liberal tradition may be rather easily explained if we bear in mind how greatly the Eastern European societies differed from those societies in which liberalism was born and grew rankly in the last two centuries.

Here I do not intend to put forward the Marxist argument that liberalism is just an ideological superstructure of the capitalist base or 'simply the political form . . . of capitalist production',[32] but it is hard to deny – as Anthony Arblaster wrote – that 'liberalism grew up together with Western capitalism and even today liberal-democratic systems only flourish in advanced capitalist societies'.[33] The belief in the close link between liberalism and capitalism is also held by many liberals. The thesis on the *historical* connection of liberalism with capitalism is not even questioned by authors who would prefer to separate these two concepts. There are strong arguments in support of C. B. Macpherson's thesis on the connection of liberalism with 'possessive market society', but critics have succeeded in undermining many links of the argumentation leading to it.[34] This thesis does not have to be put in a very strong form. It suffices if we accept, firstly, that liberals are characterized by 'a relatively welcoming attitude toward commercial society',[35] and, secondly, that their characteristic style of thinking may become spread only with the advance of individualization and alienation of the individual from traditional communities in the wake of the development of capitalism.[36] This hardly means that liberalism as such is only an apologia for capitalism.

[32] See John Dunn, *Western Political Theory in the Face of the Future* (Cambridge: Cambridge University Press, 1993), p. 36.

[33] Anthony Arblaster, *The Rise and Decline of Western Liberalism* (Oxford: Blackwell, 1984), p. 84. See Gordon Smith, 'Between Left and Right: The Ambivalence of European Liberalism', in *Liberal Parties in Western Europe*, ed. Emil Joseph Kirchner (Cambridge: Cambridge University Press, 1988), p. 17.

[34] See especially C. B. Macpherson, *The Political Theory of Possessive Individualism: Hobbes to Locke* (Oxford and New York: Oxford University Press, 1962). The critical literature is reviewed by Kirk F. Koerner, *Liberalism and Its Critics* (New York: St Martin's Press, 1985), Chapter 2. Paradoxically, Macpherson's 'Marxist-oriented' argumentation is strengthened most effectively by wholehearted liberals such as Milton Friedman in *Capitalism and Freedom* (Chicago: The University of Chicago Press, 1962).

[35] See Stephen Holmes, 'The Permanent Structure of Antiliberal Thought', in *Liberalism and the Moral Life*, ed. Nancy L. Rosenblum (Cambridge MA: Harvard University Press, 1989), p. 237.

[36] John H. Hallowell, *The Decline of Liberalism as an Ideology with Particular Reference to German Politico-Legal Thought* (Berkeley: University of California Press, 1943), pp. 12–14.

There is an obvious discordance between liberalism as the theory and practice of civil society arising in the West under capitalism and the reality of the backward East European societies with their semifeudal socio-economic structure, small and rather weak middle class, and the dominance of an illiterate peasantry, a class which in the times of B. Constant and J. S. Mill still did villein service and remained largely within the confines of a natural economy. These generalizations are obviously simplifications that leave out the enclaves of capitalist progress springing up here and there. None the less, I can take the liberty of making such generalizations, for these enclaves did not determine the face of the region. Similarly, in treating of the West in general terms, we do not have to dwell on Portugal or Ireland. While it is a truism that there are no uniform regions, yet these regions can be distinguished from one another in a sensible way and contrasted with each other in many respects.

In the socio-economic conditions that prevailed in Eastern Europe during the period of the rapid development of liberalism in the West, liberalism, if anyone in Eastern Europe had even heard of it, was the outlook of a relatively small number of individuals, of persons who had read a lot about it in books and newspapers published in Western countries and who believed that liberalism provided the best blueprint for achievement of the liberty and prosperity of mankind. Most of these individuals, it should be added, were intellectuals who had little influence on practical affairs. The other proponents of liberal ideas were scattered members of the landed aristocracy in favour of modernization of their society. Jerzy Jedlicki on this question wrote about the 'domestication of liberalism by intellectuals from the landed aristocracy' and at the same time showed that this consisted in bending the 'slogans of freedom, equality, and property to the interests of large landed estates'.[37] Robin Okey ponders on the unusual phenomenon, in his opinion, of 'liberalism emanating from the nobility and for some time dominated by it'.[38]

Liberalism could be neither a generalization of accumulated experiences nor even a macro-political programme for the immediate future. When attempts were made to turn it into such a programme, it either became a utopia or was reduced to individual slogans and postulates, thereby losing its original identity and becoming a seasoning for other ideological dishes – for example, for conservatism, which thanks to liberalism became more modern and palatable to persons searching for something other than a way of salvaging the traditional system of social relationships. Due to the lack of a suitable foundation – as Ludwikowski remarked – 'even firm supporters of this ideological trend did not see any chance of creating an independent

[37] Jerzy Jedlicki, 'Obozy ideowe', op. cit., pp. 474, 483.

[38] Robin Okey, *Eastern Europe 1740-1985: Feudalism to Communism* (London: Hutchinson, 1986), p. 69.

liberal political movement. In this situation, popular liberal slogans started to permeate kindred ideological movements, which was typical in Polish conditions.'[39] The possibilities of forming political movements were seriously limited, or for decades did not exist at all. This accounts for the vicissitudes of the writing of history, which either completely lost sight of liberalism or turned it into a huge sack that could contain everything that was not revolutionary or extremely traditional.

4. *Non-economic reasons for the weakness of liberalism*

It goes without saying that everything should not be reduced to socio-economic conditions. For the historical destinies of ideas are full of surprises (for example, who could have imagined that Marxism would make the greatest career in non-industrialized countries!), and in the countries of Eastern Europe other factors appeared that were an impediment to the progress of liberalism. Let us see what factors of this kind were present in Poland.

First, long years of the 'golden freedom' of the nobility before the loss of statehood at the end of the eighteenth century had instilled in enlightened Poles the conviction that modernization of the country as well as effective defence against the mounting external danger must and would result in a strengthening of the state. While during this time in the West efforts were being made to limit the authority of the state over citizens and, soon there-after, to protect citizens against the tyranny of the majority, in Poland, on the other hand, reformers were mostly engaged in trying to strengthen the authority of the state and only after this to create something like a demo-cratic majority. The reason for this was that most informed Poles, not without reason, saw one of the main causes of the national catastrophe in the excessive privileges of individuals and of a privileged minority.

These were not the only catchwords of the reform movement during the Enlightenment period, but in many other matters it was completely in accord with the aspirations prevalent in the West, from which it drew its ideas and examples (the strengthening of the state was to be achieved through its major reform largely in line with Western experiences); none the less, the difference was not minor. This is perhaps best illustrated by the example of Stanisław Staszic, who as one of the chief and most consistent supporters of modernization and advocate of many liberal values, at the same time became involved in opposing certain liberal trends because he associated them with the 'anarchy' of the gentry he wished to combat.[40] Even the viewpoint that

[39] R. R. Ludwikowski, 'Liberal Traditions', op. cit., p. 257.
[40] See Barbara Szacka, *Stanisław Staszic* (Warsaw: PIW, 1966), p. 179.

Poland should be brought up to Western standards as quickly as possible did not necessarily imply receptiveness to political liberalism. While attractive in some respects, in others political liberalism seemed to threaten the order the Polish reformers wanted to create. When they spoke of 'freedom', they had in mind the abolition of estate privileges rather than rights of the citizen as an individual who was to be given as much independence as possible. What they wanted was that every individual, irrespective of origin or the estate to which he or she belonged, would feel part of the whole, a participant in the public weal, a member of the nation. The greatest evil in their view was the pursuit of private interests and anarchy, which was commonly associated with the former Commonwealth of the Gentry, a tradition to which the opponents of democratic reforms, though not they alone, went back.

Second, one of the consequences of the failure of the reform efforts and Poland's loss of independence was that Polish political thought in the nineteenth century concentrated on how Poland could once again *be* as a nation-state rather than on worrying about *how to be* from the standpoint of specific political solutions. In other words, they were more interested in 'whether Poles could regain independence' than in how Poles would organize themselves after achieving this goal. In this context, how they would organize themselves now was subordinated completely to the fight for independence. According to Maurycy Mochnacki, who consciously postulated such a hierarchy of questions, to appeal to liberalism in a country like Poland shows a tendency to reprehensible doctrinairism and lack of understanding for really important matters. He wrote as follows of the so-called Kalisz liberals: 'What will we gain from this and what benefit accrue to the country that the advocates of the Kalisz faith are willing to die for their delusions and principles? We need independence and unity, not doctrinairism and adamant stubbornness in theoretical prejudices. Our old Poland will not arise from theory . . . . An entire book of Benjamin Constant's guarantees and all of the dogmas of his admirers will not give us half a troop of cavalry.'[41]

This way of thinking turned out to be very durable in Poland. More than a hundred years later we find it in Ignacy Paderewski's speech at the inaugural meeting of the National Council of the Polish Republic in Paris: 'We are not fighting for a noblemen's, people's or workers' Poland, for a capitalist or a socialist Poland, for a Poland of lords or a Poland of peasants. We are fighting for a complete Poland, the only Poland, great and independent.'[42]

[41] Maurycy Mochnacki, 'O stronnictwie tzw. Kaliskim', in *Dzieła Maurycego Mochnackiego* (Poznań: J. K. Żupański, 1963), vol. IV, p. 273.

[42] *Wizje Polski: Programy polityczne lat wojny i okupacji 1939–1944*, introduction, selection and elaboration by Kazimierz Przybysz (Warsaw: Elipsa, 1992), motto.

Historical circumstances decreed that the imperative to fight for Poland pushed into the background the question of what kind of Poland this was to be. One also gets the impression that renouncement of politicizing by many 'Solidarity' activists and the Citizens' Committees that arose from this movement was based on the same thinking.

I do not maintain, of course, that the fight for independence is by nature lacking in political colour, since Polish historical experience also contradicts such a view. On the other hand, the fight for independence creates a situation in which classic divisions often become blurred and the chances of various political orientations are not the same as in 'normal' countries, where there is no problem of collective subjugation. To put it briefly, such a situation favours *nationalism* and reduces the attractiveness of *par excellence* individualistic liberalism. The nation takes the place of civil society in the social consciousness.[43]

When I use the word 'nationalism', I do not make a value judgment. I simply have in mind all conceptions, good and bad, splendid and sinister, whose centre is the concept of the *nation* as a community absolutely primary in respect to individuals and to all associations originating from the will of individuals. In the centre of interest of nationalists, whatever they are like, are the collective rights of the *nation* and not the rights of individuals. Nationalists by no means necessarily have to negate the rights of individuals, as sometimes has happened, but these rights are secondary for them. In their view, restitution of the rights of the nation will somehow automatically result in an affirmation of the rights of the individual, who is enslaved because the nation is not free; but not the reverse, namely, that affirmation of the rights of the individual will restore the freedom of the nation.

From the nationalist point of view, as Heltai and Rau rightly note, 'every individual belongs to a nation, and the characteristics of his nation determine the essence of his existence and the most important features of his personality. Because the individual is defined as a part of and derives his meaning from the nation, he cannot properly be considered independent of it . . . In other words, the doctrine of nationalism removes the rights of individuals from the political scene and replaces them with those of the nation.'[44]

In every one of its varieties, nationalism requires the assumption that the most important social bonds and duties of the individual to the collectivity are in no way a matter of his free choice. It requires the assumption that society is a supraindividual whole, to which individuals should be absolutely

[43] I refer here to the words of Kazimierz Z. Sowa stated in 'Polski kryzys i polska reforma', *Socjologia–społeczeństwo–polityka* (Rzeszów: WSP, 1992), p. 114.

[44] Peter Andras Heltai and Zbigniew Rau, 'From National to Civil Society and Tolerance', in *The Reemergence of Civil Society in Eastern Europe and the Soviet Union*, ed. Z. Rau (Boulder CO: Westview Press, 1991), p. 134.

subordinated as its parts. It requires the assumption that the acceptance by the individual of such or other convictions and patterns of behaviour must depend not so much on their conformity with some universal criteria as on whether they satisfy the values, interests, traditions, etc. of his or her group.[45] It is not my intention to give a detailed description of nationalism here. My sole aim is to point out that nationalism is an ideology which, if not fundamentally in opposition to liberalism, in any case contains many elements that are hard to reconcile with liberalism. The result is that even when there exists good will to arrive at a synthesis or an understanding, a conflict can easily take place.

The divergence or even opposition of liberalism and nationalism as ideologies in their 'pure' forms obviously did not prevent them from coming close to each other in certain historical situations. The best known example of this is Mazzini, who holds a prominent place in the history of both ideologies. Generally speaking, before 1848, especially in the dependent countries, the intermingling of nationalist and liberal ideas was rather common. It was the rise of so-called integral nationalism at the end of the nineteenth century that completely laid bare their opposition. Guido de Ruggiero could write that 'during the nineteenth century liberalism and national feeling arose and developed together'.[46] The same thing was pointed out by Stanisław Ossowski, who distinguished 'the Old and New Testament national ideologies' and stated that in the former 'the words "nation" and "country" were closely linked with the word "freedom"'.[47]

In his history of Poland, Czechoslovakia and Hungary, Piotr S. Wandycz uses the expression *liberal nationalism* in reference to the nineteenth century, asserting correctly that in this part of Europe nationalism at the beginning of the nineteenth century was 'almost by definition liberal', though 'a potential contradiction' existed between the nationalistic and liberal conceptions of society.[48] In fact, there is no doubt that in these countries, earlier nationalism had embraced many slogans of Western liberalism, while at the same time often criticizing Western societies for their 'individualism' and 'hucksterism'.

It may be suspected, however, that the presence of liberal slogans was a

---

[45] See Isaiah Berlin, 'Nationalism: Past Neglect and Present Power', *Against the Current: Essays in the History of Ideas* (Oxford: Oxford University Press, 1981), pp. 341–4.

[46] Guido de Ruggiero, *History of European Liberalism*, op. cit., p. 407. See J. H. Hallowell, *The Decline of Liberalism*, op. cit., p. 47 ('Nationalism, as it was originally conceived by men like Fichte, Herder and Mazzini, rather than being opposed to liberalism was its direct counterpart').

[47] Stanisław Ossowski, *O ojczyźnie i narodzie* (Warsaw: PWN, 1984), p. 65. See also his *Dzieła*, vol. III (Warsaw: PWN, 1967).

[48] Piotr S. Wandycz, *The Price of Freedom*, op. cit., p. 138.

consequence not so much of deeper spiritual affinity as of the fact that, first, nationalism often had to do with the same enemy as liberalism and, second, that it was rather simple to adapt these slogans by applying them to the nation rather than to the individual. Obviously, in this context their sense was largely changed, and they often retain only a verbal connection with their liberal prototypes. In any case, their presence on the political scene in and of itself is no evidence of the expansion of liberalism as such.

Historians of liberalism are generally in accord that there were few liberals in the area that interests me here and that 'many – too many [of them] – were also committed to illiberal nationalism'.[49] It could not have been otherwise, for the situation of countries subjected to foreign rule imposed a certain hierarchy of priorities, pushing into the background the freedom of the individual as an *individual* and not a member of the community. An important role here was unquestionably played by the illusion that liberation from foreign domination would automatically solve all problems.

Friedrich von Hayek correctly pointed to 'the constant but uneasy alliance between the liberal and the national movements during the nineteenth century', but at the same time he emphasized that 'though the concept of national freedom is analogous to that of individual freedom, it is not the same; and the striving for the first has not always enhanced the second. It has sometimes led people to prefer a despot of their own race to the liberal government of an alien majority; and sometimes it has often provided the pretext for ruthless restrictions of the individual liberty of the members of minorities.'[50]

Third, in Poland *Catholicism*, which played a vital role in public life, was unquestionably an important non-economic factor impeding the reception of liberalism. There is no room here to delve into the reasons for this or to explain in what this role consisted or still consists. To a certain extent, the reasons are obvious. For nearly two centuries the Catholic Church was really the only large national institution which had considerable freedom. In this situation, it performed numerous ancillary functions unknown to the Church in places where a civil society could develop freely. Neither can we comment here on the relations between Catholicism and liberalism in general, though it is a fascinating subject and not irrelevant to a description of contemporary Polish liberalism.

It suffices to say that Catholicism – incomparably more collectivist and authoritarian than Protestantism – could not forward the progress of liberal ideas. For a long time representatives of the Catholic Church had been

[49] Massimo Savadori, *The Liberal Heresy: Origins and Historical Development* (New York: St Martin's Press, 1977), p. 143.
[50] Friedrich von Hayek, *The Constitution of Liberty* (Chicago: The University of Chicago Press, 1960), pp. 14–15.

uncompromising and very active enemies of liberalism as a false and immoral, materialistic and anti-social philosophy.[51] Today, the attitude of Catholics towards liberalism is often different and one even finds Catholic liberals,[52] but this hardly means that the ancient hostility has disappeared.

For now, it is less important to what extent this hostility was due to the incompatibility of Catholicism and liberalism as styles of thinking and systems of values. Many misunderstandings (common among old-fashioned Catholics) arose from equating all liberalism with atheism or free-thinking and with capitalism viewed as contrary to the social teaching of the Church. Finally, historical circumstances at one time (and sometimes even today) were such that the realization of liberal postulates had to take place at the cost of the Church by limiting its influence and political role. In any case, in a country like Poland in the nineteenth century Catholicism was a serious obstacle to liberalism. To be sure, the underdevelopment of liberalism in other countries of Eastern Europe in which Catholicism was not the dominant religion or not nearly as influential as in Poland suggests that this was not the most important barrier. Moreover, it should be noted that the resistance of the Church did not prevent the spread of socialism and sometimes even of ideas far-removed from orthodox Catholicism.

Due to all of these factors,[53] neither in Poland nor in any of the other countries of Eastern Europe did liberalism become a popular way of thinking, a widely accepted practical programme for modernization of the country, either in the nineteenth century or later. No matter which of the numerous varieties of liberalism we take into consideration, it turns out to be unsuited to the needs and habits of the societies of this region during the period when liberalism was scoring its greatest triumphs in the West. So it is not surprising that in this region liberalism appeared mainly as a set of

---

[51] One of the best examples of the Catholic criticism of liberalism in contained in Emmet John Hughes, *The Church and the Liberal Society* (Princeton NJ: Princeton University Press, 1944).

[52] See *Democracy and Mediating Structures: A Theological Inquiry*, ed. Michael Novak (Washington DC: American Enterprise Institute for Public Policy Research, 1980); and numerous other works by Novak, especially *The Catholic Ethic and the Spirit of Capitalism* (New York: Free Press, 1993). The relationship between liberalism and Catholicism will be discussed in more detail in Chapter VI of this book.

[53] One important factor has been omitted here. For the more than one hundred years in which Poland lacked sovereignty and was divided among three occupying powers, the condition of Polish society was greatly influenced by the policies of these countries, which were hardly liberal. This was not only a serious impediment to the flow of ideas and political activities, but also led politically active members of society to believe that liberalism was a rather impractical programme – even less practical than the fight for independence. Of necessity reduced to purely economic and/or cultural activity, this was obviously a minimal programme.

abstract principles borrowed from somewhere else, principles which taken literally did not and could not have any practical application as any single idea or as a set of ideas taken out of their original context and incorporated into some new whole that cannot be called liberalism or, in any case, liberalism *tout court*.

In the political sphere, an example of such a bowdlerized liberalism, so to speak, is the aforementioned 'liberal nationalism', in the economic sphere – liberalism reduced to the postulate of modernizing landed estates of the gentry and to abstract praise of the free market, easily reconcilable with very illiberal views on all other matters. This was illustrated perfectly by Ludwikowski in his earlier quoted book on conservatism in Polish political thought, which on the one hand revealed the presence of many liberal ideas, but on the other, the striking absence of 'a full-fledged exposition of liberal doctrine'.[54] Thus, when historians write about Polish liberalism they do not necessarily have in mind the local counterpart of what is called liberalism in France or England; they often mean that such or another thinker or activist reminds one of Western liberals in some *fragment* of his or her convictions.

In the history of Poland of the last two centuries one can find quite a few such *fragments*. Indeed, at least in the sphere of ideas and postulates, there are many *elements* of liberal political doctrine, even more *elements* of economic liberalism,[55] and still more *elements* of liberalism that is sometimes called cultural and is regarded as the opposite of 'obscurantism', without reflecting whether – apart from praising progress and enlightenment – it has anything in common with liberalism as a political or economic doctrine. During the Congress Kingdom, such elements of political liberalism are most visible in the activities of Bonawentura and Wincenty Niemojowski, we find elements of economic liberalism in Fryderyk Skarbek, and Stanisław Kostka Potocki was regarded as an outstanding representative of cultural liberalism for his book *Podróż do Ciemnogrodu*. Yet, these various liberals belonged to different social worlds, so to say. The Niemojowskis protested against the decree on censorship prepared when Potocki was minister, while the economist Skarbek was clearly hardly interested in this matter. It was the same in other periods. Quite often, all it took to earn the title of liberal was to display a shade of criticism of traditional views and practices or to express support for 'civilizing' the country through education, modernization of the landed proprietors' economy and industrialization.

[54] R. R. Ludwikowski, *Continuity and Change in Poland*, op. cit., pp. 138–9.

[55] Ferdynand Zweig even argued that from the end of the eighteenth century liberalism was the dominant tendency in Polish economic thought (*Liberalizm w polskiej myśli ekonomicznej*, Kraków, 1937). To be sure, he used a very broad definition of liberalism, which in fact included all ideas favouring *greater* economic freedom.

It is striking that we have to do precisely with *elements*, and more or less isolated ones at that. These elements do not appear in the same conceptions of the same people, and neither do they combine into one whole in the programmes of particular groupings. Nor did various liberals and 'liberals' necessarily regard themselves as defenders of the same cause. There was no liberal *camp*, and the liberal parties that came into being at the beginning of the twentieth century (Progressive-Democratic Union, Polish Progressive Party and others) turned out to be ephemera of narrow scope.[56] Even if liberalism in this or another sense always seems to be present in Polish thought, this is an interrupted, partial and one-sided presence, a *dispersed* presence, one can say.

What is more, in comparison with the West, this fragmentary or 'incomplete' liberalism has a feature I would call *utopian*, accepting Mannheim's definition that a utopian way of thinking is one that is 'incongruous with the state of reality within which it occurs'.[57] In other words, liberal views in Poland, as elsewhere in Eastern Europe, were usually summoned up as counterproposals to what existed; they served in efforts to gain liberties that did not exist rather than to defend or consolidate freedom that already existed. To be sure, liberalism in the West also was often quite utopian, but as time went on, to an ever greater degree it acted to legitimize existing relationships, which might still be imperfect from the standpoint of such or another 'pure' liberal doctrine but were ever less in basic contradiction with it. For centuries it could be said of Western liberalism that 'it is . . . the property of no particular group, but . . . it is carried in the hearts of citizens, written into the laws, and practiced in the political institutions of existing, functioning political communities'.[58] This feature of liberalism seems more important than its undiminished capacity to generate systems of political philosophy as theoretical justifications of liberalism or, what happens ever less often, of specifically liberal political programmes. To this day, liberalism in Eastern Europe remains largely the 'property of a particular group', for which the main and still far from resolved problem is *passing from ideas to reality*, from postulates to facts. This perforce must have an influence on the way of thinking and behaviour of liberals, who, metaphorically, must 'plant' and 'build' rather than 'tend' and 'protect'.

It is not my intention to demonstrate that Poland or some other country of Eastern Europe does not have any liberal tradition at all. Despite everything,

[56] See Tadeusz Stegner, *Liberałowie Królestwa Polskiego* (Gdańsk, 1990).

[57] Karl Mannheim, *Ideology and Utopia: An Introduction to the Sociology of Knowledge* (London: Routledge and Kegan Paul, 1954), p. 173.

[58] Maurice Mandelbaum, 'The Long Life of Liberalism', in *The Relevance of Liberalism*, ed. Zbigniew Brzeziński, Seweryn Bialer, Sophia Slusar and Robert Nurick (Boulder CO: Westview Press, 1978), p. 203.

the ties of this region with the West were too strong, and the West was too attractive for liberalism to be completely unknown and unwanted. Since the appearance in *Pamiętnik Warszawski* (1816) of the article 'What Do Liberal Ideas Mean?',[59] access to them – presented in this form or another – has been declared by numerous people. However, the liberal tradition remains weak, marginal, incomparably poorer than the tradition of nationalism, populist democracy, social Catholicism or socialism. What is more, the liberal tradition is autonomous only to a minimal extent. The historian who wished to reconstruct it in full would have to study various intellectual trends in an effort to discover in them elements that deserve to be called liberal according to such or other criteria. The final conclusion would surely be the same as Ludwikowski's: 'Although liberalism has its own representatives and has infiltrated neighboring currents, it had never gained primacy in Poland.'[60]

None the less, such a reconstruction is worth the effort, since it could bring interesting discoveries in specific matters on both liberal *episodes* in Polish thought and on how the classics of Western liberalism were interpreted in Eastern Europe. The career of Herbert Spencer in the age of Polish positivism is an extremely interesting phenomenon.[61] What from the message of the author of *The Man versus the State* reached the Polish reader? Did Spencer's anti-statism have the same meaning for him as for English liberals, or did it overlap with the Polish idea of a 'nation without a state', which had nothing in common with liberalism, but grew out of the feeling that the existing state was predatory and alien? It might turn out that in Polish conditions even ideas unquestionably derived from classic liberalism underwent a fundamental reinterpretation. Ludwikowski refers to this when he writes that 'a Polish liberal put stronger emphasis on individuals' public duties, and often contradicting the individualistic character of liberalism, was inclined to claim the priority of communal and public values'.[62] We have to do with similar changes in other countries. For instance, during the interwar period Romanian *neoliberalismul* would be characterized by a protectionist policy as the way to a free market.[63] I leave off with hypotheses, but they do not seem unwarranted.

---

[59] See *Przemiany społeczne i gospodarcze w Królestwie Polskim: 1815–1830* (Warsaw: KiW, 1957), pp. 129–32.

[60] R. R. Ludwikowski, 'Liberal Traditions', op. cit., p. 260.

[61] Some authors even believe that positivism was 'a variety of liberalism created by Polish intellectuals in specifically Polish conditions'. See Andrzej Jaszczuk, *Spór pozytywistów z konserwatystami a przyszłość Polski 1870–1903* (Warsaw: PWN, 1986).

[62] R. R. Ludwikowski, *Continuity and Change in Poland*, op. cit., pp. 144–5.

[63] See D. Chirot, 'Ideology, Reality and Competing Models', op. cit., p. 379.

5. *Liberal ideas in interwar Poland*

Although the lack of success of liberalism in Poland was to some extent
linked with the situation of a conquered country, which inclined theorists
and men of action to concentrate on matters which were of marginal significance in Western liberalism, it cannot be said that much changed when
Poland regained its independence. While it is true that Poland was reborn as
a state that, with only a few reservations, may be called *liberal-democratic*,
after only a few years it started to lose this character (that is, from the *coup
d'état* of Józef Piłsudski in 1926) and evolved in the direction of an autocracy; moreover, from the very outset the system of liberal-democratic institutions established by the constitution of 1921 lacked a strong political base,
for none of the major parties fully identified with it. Paradoxically, the few
Polish liberals are easier to find in Piłsudski's camp than in the dominant
parties of the 'Sejmocracy' disbanded by him.[64] Furthermore, the difficult
situation of the new state inclined politicians to revert to centralist and statist
solutions, to which, in fact, interwar Poland owed much of its economic
successes.[65] Observing the history of the Second Republic, one can say that
Poland experienced the crisis of liberalism before liberalism was born there.
The same can be said of all the countries of this region with the exception of
Czechoslovakia.[66]

It is not my intention to discount this liberal-democratic episode from the
beginnings of the second Polish statehood. This episode left visible marks
in political culture and was responsible for the fact that at least some principles belonging to the essential core of liberalism entered into the language
of political discourse. It also seems that in Poland during the interwar
period individuals and groups appeared whose association with liberalism
was not entirely fortuitous.[67] There was still no liberal political party,
however, and very few people defined themselves as liberals, though some

[64] See Andrzej Friszke, *O kształt niepodległości* (Warsaw: Biblioteka 'Więzi', 1989),
pp. 233 ff; Władysław T. Kulesza, *Koncepcje ideowo-polityczne obozu rządzącego w
Polsce w latach 1926–1935* (Wrocław: Ossolineum, 1985), chapter III (on the restrictions of this liberalism see pp. 76–8).
[65] See Kazimierz Dziewulski, *Spór o etatyzm: Dyskusja wokół sektora państwowego w
Polsce międzywojennej. 1919–1939* (Warsaw: PWN, 1981); Jan Kofman, *Nacjonalizm
gospodarczy – szansa czy bariera rozwoju: Przypadek Europy Środkowo-Wschodniej*
(Warsaw: PWN, 1992).
[66] It seems that Romania may also be included among the exceptions, though in that
country there existed a rather strong liberal party (which even ruled for a certain time),
since Romanian liberalism was a phenomenon of a very special kind.
[67] I have in mind so-called 'intellectuals' liberalism', whose perhaps best exposition
can be found in Tadeusz Kotarbiński's *Idei wolności* (1936). See his *Wybór pism*
(Warsaw: PWN, 1957), vol. I, pp. 483–507.

contemporary economists did (Adam Krzyżanowski, Ferdynand Zweig and others). These liberals remained scattered and on the whole did not go much beyond defending the liberal core which could unite people of different political orientations in so far as they were interested in establishing, preserving and, afterwards, restoring liberal democracy. In no sense was this a political force. As in the past, liberalism manifested itself chiefly as a conglomeration of views and values that could be found in various segments of the political spectrum, with the exception of the extreme nationalist right and the extreme communist left. It was much easier to find someone who defended the general principles of liberal democracy; someone who was in favour (not without reservations) of the free market; and finally someone who fought against contemporary 'obscurantism', saving the ideas of enlightenment and tolerance, than someone who presented himself as a liberal *tout court* and made use of a specifically liberal programme for ruling the country. In short, the liberals of that day constituted a heterogeneous group and lacked a clear vision of a Polish *liberal* society. They had more of an impact on the general cultural atmosphere than on the direction of political or social development. One may surmise that this liberalism appeared mainly in intellectual circles and called forth little response outside of them. The collapse of the Second Commonwealth made it the object of severe and often unjust criticism from various points of view and spurred intensive searches to find a better order for postwar Poland. Liberals could not be heard in the chorus of voices on this subject. The wish to return to political democracy was expressed, but the programmes formulated during the war are conspicuous mainly for their tendency to promote anything but liberal solutions: nationalist, socialist or both of them at the same time, and Christian ones, of course. The declaration of the representative Council of National Unity of 15 March 1944 contained the promise that the national economy in all of its sectors 'would be conducted in accordance with the rules of a planned economy'[68] as well as many other equally non-liberal promises. It is really astonishing that some programmes contained a direct criticism of liberalism as allegedly one of the integral parts of the bad past. The most significant thing, however, is that, apart from a few general catchwords that hardly any would have dared to reject in the time of the struggle against fascism, liberalism as a position is virtually non-existent in this panorama of Polish political thought from the time of the last war. It is also interesting that catchwords of this kind tend to appear on the left rather than on the right. But that is another story that we will not go into here.

In a certain sense, this was of very little importance for the future of

---

[68] See *Wizje Polski*, op. cit., p. 346.

liberalism in Poland; even if liberalism had been well developed before the war, it would have been destroyed in the postwar period when the communists came to power.

6. *Communism versus liberalism*

Although the thesis on the anti-liberal nature of communism seems self-evident, it is worth dwelling somewhat longer on the problem of *communism versus liberalism* so as not to leave any doubts about the matter. Today's East European liberalism originates largely from the confrontation with communism, and hence we must have as clear an understanding as possible of the nature of the conflict between these two ideologies. As a matter of fact, this question is much more important for the rest of my argument than the problems of the history of Poland we have considered heretofore. The present status of liberalism in Eastern Europe was determined not only by specific features of the development of this region in the past but also, if not primarily, by the fact that for nearly half a century it was subjected to communist policy. This policy not only suppressed all manifestations of liberalism as an ideology, but it also systematically extirpated all potential mainstays of the citizen's independence from state authority from social life, all props to which the supporters of liberalism could appeal in the future.

The rule of communists is not a military occupation or simply an autocracy which, even when it uses the most inhuman forms of terror, leaves most fields of life largely unchanged and confines itself rather to suppressing manifestations of hostility than to rooting it out. Communist rule consists not in quashing demonstrations of something that, as such, must not be eliminated, but in transforming the entire social fabric. As Claude Lefort correctly wrote, 'it is not, therefore, so much a monstrous outgrowth of political power in society as a metamorphosis of society itself'.[69] The effects of such rule are naturally incomparably more far-reaching and lasting than the effects of any traditional dictatorship, if one can speak of such.[70] The problem consists not so much in the fact that communism destroyed the influences of liberalism as an ideology in Eastern Europe, for there was not much to destroy (one can even say, paradoxically, that in spite of itself communism helped to popularize liberalism as its complete negation); rather, the problem is that

[69] Claude Lefort, *The Political Forms of Modern Society: Bureaucracy, Democracy, Totalitarianism* (Cambridge: Polity Press, 1986), p. 79.

[70] See the comments of Edward Mokrzycki on the 'organic' changes that took place in Polish society after 1994 ('Społeczne granice wschodnioeuropejskich reform ekonomicznych', *Krytyka* 1991, no. 36, p. 64).

communism made barren the soil on which this ideology could grow. I have in mind the destruction of non-state sectors of the economy on the one hand, and on the other circumscribing the initiatives of individuals and liquidating all associations, organizations, self-administration, etc. independent of the state – that is, everything which today is usually called the 'civil society'. By all accounts, this destructive activity stemmed not only from actual imperatives of the fight for power but also from the very nature of communism as a long-range ideological social design. It was not that liberalism stood in the way in any specific situation, but that liberalism was fundamentally inconsistent with this design. Whether liberalism at that time was a real political force was beside the point.

The position of communist theory and practice towards liberalism was and had to be decidedly negative – in contrast to the position towards nationalism, which, however implacably negative in theory, in practice became more and more positive with the waning of the Leninist revolutionary sympathy for world revolution and especially with the drying up of the sources of legitimation (meagre to begin with) of the existing countries of the 'dictatorship of the proletariat'. This evolution obviously took place only in so far as nationalism allowed itself to be brought to heel and exploited as an instrument of communist strategy and tactics, which on a larger scale turned out to be impossible, of course, especially in the countries dependent on the former USSR. None the less, starting from the 1950s, signs of this evolution were clearly visible.

A similar evolution was inconceivable in the case of liberalism – in any case, until the last days of real socialism in some countries (Hungary and Poland), where under the influence of a severe economic crisis part of the ruling elite was willing to opt for a limited liberal economic programme. Yet, this was a time when hardly anyone doubted that communism as an ideology was living out its final days. As long as it continued to hold on as such, any 'liberalization' was a question not of revising ideological principles but purely and simply of the incapacity of realizing any policy consistent with them in a given period. Furthermore, it was quite apparent that as a rule the 'interstices' that appeared were in fields marginal to the wielding of power, and the communists saw to it that the nature of power was not seriously altered. Greater liberties ran the risk of conjuring up the spectre of the 'restoration of capitalism'. Tolerance for nationalism was incomparably greater: Ceaucescu's Romania never stopped being 'socialist', but Dubček's Czechoslovakia became 'anti-socialist' after only a few months.

The sources of communist anti-liberalism have deep roots. They are both theoretical and practical. One may wonder whether the philosophical opposition of Marxian communism and liberalism has not been exaggerated in certain respects and argue convincingly that 'though Marxian theory challenges liberalism, it also affirms and extends certain ethical claims which are at the heart of liberalism'.[71] At the same time, however, one cannot overlook the fact that here in many points we have to do with a really fundamental opposition, and the Marxian idea of the emancipation of man has little in common with the liberal conception.[72] The author of *Das Kapital* was quite explicit on this point, when in *The Jewish Question* he criticized the liberal conception of the rights of the individual from collectivist positions. 'The so-called *rights of man*, the *droits de l'homme* as distinct from the *droits du citoyen*, are nothing but the rights of a *member of civil society*, i.e., of egoistic man, of man separated from other men and from the community.'[73] To be sure, this was collectivism of a specific kind, opposed in some respects to the collectivism of earlier communism, since it grew out of the conviction that the individualism of liberal society impedes or even completely rules out a full realization of the potential of the individual.[74] None the less, this was still *collectivism* directed against liberal individualism and ruling out the prospect of creating a good society based on individuals as *individuals*.

It was not only the philosophical anthropology of Marx that separated him from liberalism. One could argue about whether the Marxian critique of liberalism for its individualism applies equally to all kinds of liberalism, and whether liberalism of necessity must be 'atomistic'.[75] However, even if the views of Marxians and liberals on the relationship of the individual to the society could be reconciled (a direction taken by some reinterpretations of Marx), enough differences would remain to speak of opposite philosophies of society.[76]

In the first place, they differ fundamentally in their approach to the problem of social change and the ways of reaching a good social organization. Liberals have been accustomed to the idea of a *spontaneous social order*, whereas from the outset the obsession of communists has been the

[71] Adam Gilbert, article in *Marxism and Liberalism*, ed. Ellen Frankel Paul et al. (Oxford, 1986), p. 19.

[72] See Andrzej Walicki, 'The Marxian Conception of Freedom', in *Conceptions of Liberty in Political Philosophy*, ed. Zbigniew Brzeziński and John Gray (New York: St Martin's Press, 1984), pp. 217–42.

[73] Quoted according to C. Lefort, *Political Forms of Modern Society*, op. cit., p. 245.

[74] D. F. B. Tucker, *Marxism and Individualism* (New York: St Martin's Press, 1980), p. 65. See also Adam Schaff, *Marxism and the Human Individual* (New York: McGraw-Hill, 1970).

[75] See especially Will Kymlicka, *Liberalism, Community and Culture* (Oxford: Clarendon Press, 1989).

[76] See Gang Ke, 'A Comparative Study of the Representational Paradigms Between Liberalism and Socialism', *Philosophy and the Social Sciences* 1990, vol. 20, no. 1, pp. 5–34.

planned organization of social life and, in so far as possible, the elimination from it of all 'spontaneity'. The opposition of these two approaches was best depicted by Karl R. Popper, who in his *The Open Society* described two kinds of social engineering.[77] Not much can be added to this, apart from the fact that in its decadent phase communism almost completely abandoned its utopian ideas, but in social practice continued to use utopian engineering, which postulates that the social system as a whole is shaped in accordance with something that is first conceived, then decided upon and acted upon.

The historical materialism of Marx and Engels obviously has little to do with this view, but it is not my concern whether communists have ever been good Marxists. It is also of little importance whether Marx's dreams of a leap to the 'kingdom of freedom' ever had anything in common with his theory of historical processes. In any case, communist practice was above all one of rampant voluntarism, which brings to mind Smith's description of the 'system man', who 'seems to imagine that he can arrange the different members of a great society with as much ease as the hand arranges the different pieces upon a chess-board. He does not consider that the pieces upon the chess-board have no other principle of motion besides that which the hand impresses upon them; but that, in the great chess-board of human society, every single piece has a principle of motion of its own, altogether from that which the legislature might choose to impress upon it.'[78]

There is also an obvious difference between communism and liberalism in approach to class. Whether we agree or not with the interpretation so popular among Marxians of liberalism as the ideology of a particular class of modern society,[79] it is hard to deny that liberalism addressed its message chiefly to the *middle class*, however defined, whereas communism placed its hopes in the gradual decline of this class, which along with other processes would open up the way to the final confrontation between the two 'main' classes and the unquestioned historical triumph of the proletariat.

The Marxian vision of modern society looked at from the angle of the Marxian philosophy of history inclined supporters of the latter to believe that the liberals might be right in the early stages of the development of capitalism, when the 'historical task' was the liquidation of feudalism; but liberals inexorably ceased to be right as capitalism 'matured' and the most

[77] Karl R. Popper, *The Open Society and Its Enemies* (Princeton NJ: Princeton University Press, 1971), vol. I, pp. 22–5, 157–68.

[78] Adam Smith, *The Theory of Moral Sentiments*, ed. D. D. Raphael and A. L. Macfie (Oxford: Oxford University Press, 1976), p. 234.

[79] See Edward S. Greenberg, 'Liberal Culture and Capitalistic Hegemony', *Liberalism and Modern Polity: Essays in Contemporary Political Theory* (New York: Marcel Dekker, 1978), pp. 251–71.

advanced societies approached the decisive moment of the socialist revolution. The growth of state interventionism and the crisis of liberal democracy in the twentieth century, as manifested in the expansion of authoritarian and fascist ideas, also confirmed leftist circles in the belief that liberalism is an anachronistic and unrealistic ideology.[80]

It is interesting that – as Irving Howe noted – the criticism of liberalism within Marxism was conducted from two entirely different positions: 'one that disdained liberalism for its failure to live up to its claims and one that disdained liberalism for its success in living up to its claims'.[81] On the one hand, liberalism was reproved for not realizing the ideal of liberty and really guaranteeing human and civic rights; on the other, it was criticized for bringing about disastrous social consequences. On the one hand, liberalism was taken to task in the name of its own principles, while on the other these principles were attacked as false or inadequate. All of the lines of criticism of liberalism came together in communism, and sometimes this criticism became very vitriolic. Paradoxically, this was the case especially in those countries in which dyed-in-the-wool liberals played a rather marginal role, for example in Russia or China.

This is a paradox only on the surface. In countries with a rich liberal tradition and well advanced on the way to modernization, the revolutionary left could contend that liberals had exhausted their possibilities and that it was time to go further by overcoming the obvious limitations of 'bourgeois' liberal democracy. This required casting aside the liberal programme: it could be regarded as simply inadequate, though not bad as far as it went. It was quite another matter that – as Michael Levin wrote – 'the critique of bourgeois freedoms all too often led backwards, to contempt for limited freedoms, rather than forward to the removal of such limitations'.[82] In any case, in developed Western countries the left could pose as continuators of liberalism and sometimes did so, while at the same time obviously disassociating itself from economic liberalism and embracing many of the catchwords of political and cultural liberalism which already had come to be taken largely for granted. One could only benefit from demonstrating one's attachment to these slogans, especially during the period of the fight against fascism.

---

[80] This view was echoed in C. Wright Mill's statement that '"free enterprise" today may mean freedom *for* a handful *in* the economic sphere of action. But it means dependence upon this handful for the mass of working men, and constant fear of being engulfed by them for the smaller businessmen' ('Collectivism and the "Mixed-up" Economy', *Power Politics and People* (New York: Ballantine Books), 1963, p. 181).

[81] Irving Howe, 'Socialism and Liberalism: Articles of Conciliation', *The Relevance of Liberalism*, ed. Zbigniew Brzeziński, op. cit., pp. 34 ff.

[82] Michael Levin, *Marx, Engels and Liberal Democracy* (New York: St Martin's Press, 1989), p. 141.

In backward countries, on the other hand, in which communism scored the greatest successes, liberalism was a much greater threat to communism, for liberalism openly advocated a *competitive* modernization programme. Where the 'tasks of the bourgeois-democratic revolution' were still a question of the future, the chance of the left depended greatly on whether it could appear as the only proponent of progress, pushing aside its less radical spokesmen. In Bolshevik rhetoric the label of 'liberals' was pinned on the latter. The Bolsheviks did their utmost to discredit them in the eyes of their potential followers, correctly assuming that in this way they were fighting for their own position in the reform movement. The discussion on the stages of the Russian Revolution, especially the debate on whether a bourgeois-democratic revolution must precede the revolution of the proletariat, indirectly concerned liberalism. The negative answer to this question, especially in Lenin's *Two Tactics of the Russian Social Democratic Party*, made it necessary to shove supporters of liberalism to the side, since only at their cost could Bolsheviks become the dominant spokesmen of the entire democratic movement.

I express no opinion here on whether these liberals or 'liberals' slighted by Bolshevik propaganda would have been able to modernize Russia. That is not important here; the point is that as potential modernizers they aroused such fury on the revolutionary left, which, if it had recognized them as 'progressive' politicians, perhaps may not have had to capitulate but would have had to wait for its time. Perhaps we can generalize and say that liberalism appeared most dangerous to the communists where and when liberalism put forward proposals for far-reaching political reforms to solve the same problems that the communists wished to solve through a revolution.

Like every revolutionary party, the communists really strove to fan social conflicts, whereas liberal reforms, if successful, would have assuaged conflicts and thus weakened arguments in favour of revolution. For this reason, the supporters of the Great Revolution preferred to deal with even the most extreme reactionaries rather than with politicians whose programme coincided to some extent with their own, but who recommended actions of an entirely different kind. That is why liberalism had to be combated by the communists as a dangerous political opponent and competitor. Paradoxically, in countries where it was stronger and more deeply rooted in public life, it was easier to ignore liberalism as one of many traditional movements.

These hypotheses are confirmed by the kinds of arguments most often used by communists in their dispute with liberalism. They most frequently argued that liberals minimized the importance of the class struggle and the revolution and also diverted the attention of the 'people' away from matters that were really important.[83] It is really farcical that these charges were always true, for 'liberals' by definition were people to whom they applied. Lenin's definition of 'liberalism' is little more than a political epithet with hardly any informational value. On the other hand, it has a strong emotional tone, often intensified even further by adding the adjective 'rotten' to the noun 'liberalism'.

So, one can say that, in the communist tradition, the dispute with liberalism has two completely different dimensions: theoretical and practical. We find the first one in Marx, when he criticizes the liberal understanding of the rights of the individual or when he presents his own conception of freedom as an alternative to the liberal one; the second one was represented by Lenin, when he combated his political opponents for their policy of conciliation and compromise. The first dimension was open to philosophical discussion, which did not have to be unfruitful; as regards the second one, any discussion was out of the question.

When we speak of communism in its practical applications, it is unimportant what Marx and his most sophisticated commentators thought, who could point out the real weaknesses of liberalism and address vital problems of political philosophy; what really matters were the strategy and tactics of communist political parties. Although at the beginning the communist movement was conceived as the 'material force' of philosophy, in time it become almost completely independent of this philosophy and began to be governed to an ever greater extent by its own political and propaganda imperatives. Depending on them, freedom was now a beautiful idea which liberalism, unfortunately, had been unable to carry into effect on account of its class limitations, now an empty phrase used by the bourgeoisie to deceive the people, and, finally, an instrument of political struggle that should be used in certain situations and rejected in others when no longer expedient.

Irrespective of these transitory about-faces in its approach to the idea of freedom, communism consistently cut itself off from liberalism, viewing it as an ideology basically hostile to itself and which, at most, could be credited with some historical accomplishments. This traditional aversion to liberalism became even stronger wherever communists succeeded in becoming the ruling party. There are probably several reasons for this.

1. Even those liberal or near-liberal slogans which communists had sometimes used during the fight for power to give themselves the best opportunities for expansion (such as freedom of speech and assembly) lost all instrumental value for them; what is more, these principles stood in the way of establishing the authoritarian regimes for which they struggled either

---

[83] See especially V. I. Lenin, *Przemówienie o oszukiwaniu ludu hasłami wolności i równości* (Warsaw: KiW, 1952); and Mao Tse-tung, *Combat Liberalism* (Peking: Foreign Languages Press, nd).

with heart and soul or out of necessity. For them, these slogans now simply became 'counter-revolutionary'. The only exception might be anti-clerical and free-thinking slogans in some countries belonging to the same tradition, since these slogans were still useful in fighting religion, which was a more powerful opponent for communism than liberalism; but in such cases pains were taken to replace the 'bourgeois' criticism with the 'Marxian' criticism (whatever that meant).

2. In the long run, the concept of the 'dictatorship of the proletariat' accepted by the communists ruled out tolerance for any ideas other than their own, and before long even the latter became subjected to strict control. The upshot was that the lack of freedom in fact was extended not only to the real and suspected enemies of communism but also to its sincere supporters. The restrictions introduced under the 'dictatorship of the proletariat' applied all the more to all kinds of public activity taking place without prior consent or encouragement by the one-party state, or conducted by politically 'suspect' persons. It is not important here whether we call this kind of system totalitarianism or not; this term has the undeniable advantage that it suggests control of the state over *everything*, towards which the communistic state worked during its Stalinist heyday.

3. Tactical considerations which in the past had led communists to court the favours of such or other 'non-proletarian' strata and groupings by promising to introduce or retain 'democracy', personal liberties, respect for law, etc. became ever less relevant when the communists assumed and then strengthened power. Utopian social engineering could be launched on a full scale only when power seemed to be consolidated and threatened by nothing and no one. Thus, in Poland the first years after the Second World War were a period of relative liberty, despite the clear hegemony of the communists and their control of the most important positions in the machine of government. The symbolic expression of this was going back to the liberal-democratic constitution of 1921 as fundamentally better than the supposedly 'fascist' constitution of 1935. Of course, this honeymoon was brief and consisted largely in a game of make-believe. International considerations, which during the Cold War became less significant, were still important at this time.

4. Since from the standpoint of the philosophy of history the communists, after gaining power, classified their social and economic order as more 'progressive', they had to treat the ideological 'relics' of previous social movements as anachronisms whose continued existence would be evidence that the revolution had not gone far enough. So the communists spared no effort to liquidate the social 'base' of these movements, an endeavour in which they succeeded quite well; it became harder and harder to find social forces to which such or another 'pre-revolutionary' ideology could appeal.

This, of course, did not reduce the moral and logical value of the arguments contained in these ideologies, but it did greatly diminish their social importance – which, even without this, was minimized on account of the strict limitation, if not ban, on the possibility of articulating them publicly.

Hence, one can say that even if a powerful liberal movement had existed in Eastern Europe, it would have had little chance of surviving the decades during which communism was carrying out its programme. Even the strongest political parties and most popular ideologies of half a century ago survived the period of real socialism only in vestigial form, and to this day efforts to resuscitate them usually end in a fiasco. It is an open question to what extent the communists succeeded in their unremitting effort to instil their own views and values in the population of the countries controlled by them; however, there is no question that they were very successful in destroying the influence of other ideological systems – at least, of those which until not long ago had been rooted in 'superstition' of the people and therefore more resistant to both ideological persuasion and police compulsion. To be sure, certain general convictions survived, but everything that could become a programme fell to pieces. This explains the strange career of communist revisionism when people started to look for some alternative to communism. It also seems to account for the also highly unconventional nature of the later democratic opposition. The communists succeeded in creating a social order without clear political alternatives – an order generating dissatisfaction and rebellion but not political thought.

Until the emergence of 'Solidarity', revolt had been episodic and rather spontaneous; dissatisfaction had been expressed primarily in the tendency of people to withdraw from public life or to participate in it only to the extent this was absolutely necessary or was deemed as such (participating in ritualistic elections, belonging to mass organizations, etc.). People were more inclined to retreat to the cellar of private life than to think about what a public life that would suit them should look like. In a certain sense, there was a concordance between this main line of self-defence and the evolutionary direction of the system itself, which, after the period of unsuccessful attempts to create a 'new man', concentrated more on keeping society in a state of apathy to enable governments lacking legitimacy to wield power.

IV   Protoliberalism: Autonomy of the Individual and Civil Society

The autonomy and solidarity of human beings are the two basic and mutually complementary values to which the democratic movement relates other values.[1]

1. *Liberalism as communism à rebours*

Paradoxically, the contrast between communism and liberalism in the countries of real socialism favoured the survival and reception of certain liberal ideas as well as rediscovering them on one's own. Precisely because these two paradigms of modern political thought were each other's negation, the triumph of one of them did not make the other one irrelevant, because it remained the source of arguments for those who were dissatisfied with this triumph.

I hardly maintain that these arguments were and are used consciously; it is very likely that they occur to people at times when they want to criticize certain arrangements created in accordance with the opposite paradigm. Thus, it was impossible to take a firm stance against communism without at the same time reaffirming at least part of the 'liberal canon'. In their fight against communism, even people of traditionally anti-liberal structures (such as the Roman Catholic Church) manifested clearly liberal tendencies by sometimes defending principles which they probably would have rejected in other circumstances. David Ost correctly observed that in this special context 'the heart of the problem was state control as such: the state's subsumption of society. When the enemy became the state, the opposition became liberal.'[2]

The negation of communism and the search for some alternative proposal were the natural source of liberal sympathies, because liberalism was ideally suited for this role. Independently of its starting point, any critical thinking about communism revitalized the classic subjects of liberal thought, even if the critic knew little about liberalism and/or was biased against it.

[1] György Konrad, *Antipolitics: An Essay* (San Diego, New York, London: Harcourt, Brace, Jovanovich, 1984), p. 123.
[2] David Ost, 'The Limits of Liberalism in Poland', *Telos* 1991, no. 89, p. 91.

One can say that in the countries of real socialism liberalism appeared first as a sort of communism *à rebours*, that is, primarily as a set of principles which argued against the official ideology and essentially were its reversal: freedom as the opposite of the omnipresent prohibitions and restrictions, human and civic rights as the opposite of unlimited state power, freedom of assembly as the opposite of rampant state control, the market as the opposite of the command economy and unrealistic economic plans, the rule of law as the opposite of lawlessness and licence, the right to have one's own opinion as the opposite of conformism and censorship, etc. One did not have to study the classics of liberal thought to discover these principles.

In perhaps the first article on liberalism in Eastern Europe, Jacques Rupnik and Pierre Kende wrote that after decades of the communistic principle of 'everything for the state', liberal solutions suggested themselves spontaneously, so to speak.[3] A mechanism which Max Sheler called *resentment* could often be observed at work here. According to him, 'the formal structure of resentment expression is always the same: some A is affirmed, valued and praised not for its own intrinsic quality but with the unverbalized intention of denying, devaluating and denigrating B. A is played off against B.'[4]

This attractiveness of liberalism-as-contrast increased as hopes faded for some meaningful reform of real socialism and of giving it a 'human face'. The renewal of socialism was to consist in adding to it some elements of the liberal tradition: on the one hand, civil liberties allowing citizens to control their government; on the other, the free market, which would act as a counterpoise to the bureaucratic plan and provide greater economic efficiency. The growing chorus of voices in the 1970s stating that real socialism was 'unreformable' paved the way for the appearance of a holistic model of the 'open society' that would have none of its drawbacks and all of its advantages – a model based, more or less openly, on the Western liberal democracies.

2. A question about the 'liberalism' of the democratic opposition

The birth of this model was a relatively long process, whose first stage was the *democratic opposition*,[5] which is the main topic of this chapter. The

---

[3] Jacques Rupnik and Pierre Kende, 'Libéralisme en crise du systeme communiste en Europe de l'Est', *L'Autre Europe* 1988, no. 15–16, p. 8.

[4] Max Sheler, *Resentment*, trans. William W. Holdheim (New York, 1961), p. 68.

[5] It is debatable whether the term 'opposition' should be used in this case, for in no way was this opposition in the sense this word is used in parliamentary systems. Objections can also be raised to the term 'dissidentism', which from the outset was been used interchangeably. For a discussion of these terminological difficulties see Knud Erik Jörgensen, 'The End of Anti-Politics in Central Europe', in *Democracy and Civil Society in Eastern Europe*, ed. Paul G. Lewis (New York: St Martin's Press, 1992).

leading question is whether we really have to do with liberalism, as might be assumed from some of the ideas which became popular at this time. This question is posed at the outset in a milder form by introducing the concept *protoliberalism*. The stronger form seems inappropriate for the reasons previously mentioned (see Chapter II) and because it would require a negative answer straight away.

First, because the idea of a 'third way' was prominent in circles of the democratic opposition, a way leading to a society that would be both post-communist and post-capitalist.[6] Second, because the issue of building a new social order was not yet on the agenda, while the a priori construction of something that would not acquire practical importance until sometime in the unforeseeable future seemed, not without reason, a waste of time. The more so as the programmatic slogans of the democratic opposition called for a turn away 'from abstract political unions of the future towards concrete human beings and ways of defending them effectively in the here and now'.[7] Since communism had come into existence from a utopia and a long-range plan, its opponents avoided planning to exaggeration,[8] assuming that everything concerning the future is premature, even if it is self-evident. For them the really important problem was how to oppose communism and save the values threatened by it. Moreover, they hated labels identifying them with such or another ideological or political *system*.

Some people may object to use of the term *protoliberalism* to characterize the views of the East European opposition. In fact, such a characterization of these views is neither necessary nor self-evident. Thus, it is hardly surprising that the term has been used rarely, with emphasis more often laid on the fact that this is something without precedent in earlier political thought. While the word 'liberalism' was uttered time and again in political commentaries, it was used unthinkingly in the very broad sense in which people always speak of liberalism in cases of a revolt against dictatorship combined, as is common, with a revindication of such or other elements of the liberal minimum programme, especially human and civic rights. Such use of the word 'liberalism' is not necessarily without sense, but it provides little help in better understanding the views described, whose meaning went

---

[6] See G. Konrad, *Antipolitics*, op. cit., p. 140. Václav Havel wrote in the same vein, though less clearly, about the crisis of technical civilization as a whole and imagined that the post-communist society would also be 'post-democratic' (V. Havel et al., *The Power of the Powerless: Citizens Against the State in Central-Eastern Europe*, ed. John Keane and trans. Paul Wilson (Armonk NY: M. E. Sharpe Inc., 1985), pp. 85–9. See Jacek Kuroń, *Polityka i odpowiedzialność* (London: Aneks, 1984), p. 54.

[7] V. Havel, op. cit., p. 79.

[8] See Michael Burawoy and János Lucaćs, *The Radiant Past: Ideology and Reality in Hungary's Road to Capitalism* (Chicago: The University of Chicago Press, 1992), pp. 150–1.

beyond the fact that they were simply 'liberal'.

The same thing can be said of all other '-isms', and, consequently, commentators must either assert the syncretism of these views or conclude that the classification scheme does not apply to them. In the main, textbook labels are useless, because before 1989 the articulation of political positions in Eastern Europe had not yet attained the level to which these labels apply, that is, the level of *multiparty* Western democracy.

One can argue whether this 'syncretism' was the strength or weakness of East European communists; or whether, as was believed at times, it opened the way to overcoming the traditional dilemmas of political thought; or whether it was just an expression of a more specific and, by nature, transitory situation, whose change would result in the split-up of a unique whole into parts reminding one, for better or worse, of well-known and easily identifiable '-isms'. If we take the second of these opinions as correct, as has been proven by the subsequent course of events and the present alignment of forces on the political scene, then we are justified in attempting to distinguish within this recent whole (or 'synthesis', as some deceived themselves) individual, relatively uniform elements and to treat them as embryos of present orientations whose separateness no one doubts.

It is worth asking whether the beginnings of contemporary liberalism (liberalisms) can be found within the East European democratic opposition, and if so, how strong these beginnings are. In other words, it is worth pondering whether this liberalism is (or these liberalisms are) only the result of a shift in the frame of mind and views, or whether it is also a continuation and concretization of motifs that were present earlier in the thinking of people emancipating themselves from communism. Of course, questions of this kind only to a limited degree apply to the *political* programme in the ordinary sense of this word, for the democratic opposition did not have and did not want to have such a programme. Thus, our attention will be directed not only to the political postulates of the democratic opposition but also to the set of *values* often expressed in these postulates.

A comprehensive analysis of the system of values of the East European democratic opposition would go beyond the scope of this book, and so it will not be attempted here. I restrict myself to two matters which, in my opinion, are crucial to an understanding of its general nature and to what I call protoliberalism. The first of these matters is the autonomy of the *individual*, the second is *civil society*.

In the first case the matter concerns – just to spite the communist tradition – the formation of the *individualistic* tradition, according to which the individual has the unlimited right to bring the existing political order before the tribunal of his or her own conscience and reason. The second is development by individuals of public life that would be both an expression of their genuine needs and independent of the government. Free individuals and their freedom of assembly – these are the two main issues to be discussed. These matters are closely related. As Adam Seligman writes, 'it is after all the very existence of a free and equal citizenry – of that autonomous, agentic individual – that makes civil society possible at all'.[9] It is very plain that here we have to do with subjects which, in the past, were of cardinal importance for the development of liberal thought.[10]

3. 'Anti-political' politics

An analysis of texts from the circle of East European democratic opposition encounters great difficulties, especially when we try to relate them to historically familiar paradigms of political thought. The question even arises whether we should do this, since the authors of these texts have stubbornly emphasized the *anti-political* nature of their position and have refused to identify themselves with any traditional orientation. Václav Havel said that people should 'shed the burden of traditional political categories and habits'.[11] In his *Antipolitics* György Konrad wrote that 'a society does not become politically conscious when it shares some political philosophy, but rather when it refuses to be fooled by any of them'.[12] The dissident movement did not offer another policy in opposition to communism, but tried to create a new morality, a different view of the world, a different life style. Such was the theory and such was the practice – in any case, for as long as the movement's representatives were only dissidents whose scope of actions was limited.

The simplest explanation for this shunning of politics is that it was a *tactical* necessity. A realistic assessment of the situation in effect led to the conclusion that, albeit highly desirable, no change of the political system would be possible in the foreseeable future, and thus efforts should be focused on those areas in which something can be achieved here and now. In the existing geopolitical situation, the political system could not be reformed or replaced by another one. Hence, strictly political actions were doomed to failure, while creating a programme of such actions for tomorrow could easily become a pure pipe-dream. In view of this, the dissidents argued,

[9] Adam Seligman, *The Idea of Civil Society* (New York: Free Press), p. 5. See *Liberalism, Citizenship and Autonomy*, ed. David Milligan and William Watts Miller (Aldershot: Avebury, 1992).

[10] See John Gray, *Liberalism* (Minneapolis: University of Minnesota Press, 1986), Part 1.

[11] Václav Havel, *The Power of the Powerless*, op. cit., p. 66.

[12] G. Konrad, *Antipolitics*, op. cit., p. 66.

what can be done should be done: influencing people's way of thinking and developing their self-organization skills, thereby indirectly preparing for the Great Change that unquestionably someday would be possible. This programme, which Adam Michnik called 'new evolutionism',[13] was very radical without a doubt, for it rejected real socialism outright and called for the creation from the 'grass roots' of the widest possible enclaves of independence. Yet, it contained nothing that would turn it into a political programme: there was no mention of taking power away from communists or of transforming the existing political institutions. During the times of 'Solidarity', the idea of 'new evolutionism' was replaced by the idea of the 'self-limiting revolution', whose basic content was essentially the same, except that the scope of political aspirations was considerably expanded with the weakening of the argument that the opponents of communism had no real power at their command, an argument which had been used to support the anti-political attitude.

However convincing the above anti-political interpretation, it cannot be regarded as sufficient, for it ignores the originality of a conception that was not just another version of the 'organic work' programme; it fails to appreciate its hidden radicalism and the fact that its architects were not seeking to withdraw from politics but rather to find a way of engaging in it that would be adequate to the situation of the 'post-totalitarian' society, in which – as Havel said – 'all political life in the traditional sense has been eliminated'.[14] What is more, even if the 'new evolutionism' resulted from a wrong diagnosis of the situation, a considerable part of the anti-political argument would have remained valid, for it was based not only on the conviction that for the time being nothing could be done with the political order but also, if not primarily, on the discovery that established patterns of political thinking from the past or borrowed from Western societies would not work in the conditions of real socialism. This explains the paradoxical assertion of Havel that the idea of political revolution is unacceptable to the dissidents not because it is too radical but because it is not radical enough.[15]

Václav Havel's *The Power of the Powerless* is easily the best presentation of this position. It clearly expresses the thought that 'the post-totalitarian system . . . is not the manifestation of a particular political line followed by a particular government. It is something radically different . . . To oppose it

[13] Adam Michnik, 'Nowy ewolucjonizm (1978)', in *Ugoda, praca organiczna, myśl zaprzeczna* (Warsaw: Biblioteka Krytyki, 1983), pp. 140–8.

[14] V. Havel, *The Power of the Powerless*, op. cit., p. 49. Adam Michnik wrote: 'In the communist countries there was no independent political thought – there were manipulations on the part of the authorities and outbursts of social anger' (*Szanse polskiej demokracji* (London: Aneks, 1984), p. 100).

[15] V. Havel, *The Power of the Powerless*, op. cit., pp. 79–80.

merely by establishing a different political line and then striving for a change in government would not only be unrealistic, it would be utterly inadequate, for it would never come near to touching the root of the matter.'[16] In the conditions created by this system, the parties to the conflict are not different political lines opposing each other in so-called normal societies. Here something much more elementary is involved: the fight between 'life' and the system, whose nature was to suppress everything that was unrestrained, spontaneous and eluding control.[17] The stakes in this struggle are not such or another political arrangement, whatever its merits, but the chance for a real human existence, which is denied to the subjects of the communistic state. This is not a political revolution but an 'existential and moral' one,[18] thanks to which people will learn to 'live within the truth' and cooperate voluntarily in really elementary and, at least on the surface, not political things.

The Czech 'chartists' Martin Hybler and Jiři Němec made the following perceptive observation: 'If a political element is present it is far closer to the classical meaning of the word than it is to the modern idea of parliamentary government. That is, it is more an elementary interest in the affairs of human society – in the *polis* – which is proving to be a vital human need and necessity.'[19]

Here, it seems, we have to do with a well-thought-out conception of the social world and its changes, a conception quite different from those that politicians ordinarily use. Its best summary is the following quotation from *The Power of the Powerless*:

A genuine, profound, and lasting change for the better can no longer result from the victory (were such a victory possible) of any particular traditional political conception. More than ever before, such a change will have to derive from human existence, from the fundamental reconstruction of the position of people in the world, their relationships to themselves and to each other, and to the universe. If a better economic and political model is to be created, then perhaps more than ever before it must derive from profound existential and moral changes in society. This is not something that can be designed and introduced like a new car. It is to be more than just a new variation on the old degeneration, it must above all be an expression of life in the process of transforming

[16] Ibid., p. 68.
[17] Ibid., pp. 29–30, 48.
[18] Ibid., pp. 49–53.
[19] See *Charter 77 and Human Rights in Czechoslovakia*, ed. M. Gordon Skilling (London: George Allen & Unwin, 1981), p. 325.

itself. A better system will not automatically ensure a better life. In fact, the opposite is true: only by creating a better life can a better system be developed.[20]

David Ost was right when he stated that 'the opposition turned to civil society not just because there was no other sphere in which it could immerse itself, but also because there was no other in which it wanted to immerse itself'.[21] It is also hard to disagree with the same author that anti-politics was 'part of a new world view that felt that the state was not all-important',[22] while a political change alone, even a seemingly profound one, may easily fail to touch the most important things on the 'prepolitical' level.

The slogans of anti-politics should not be taken too literally, however, of which the communist authorities were well aware. They treated the dissidents as *political* opponents and did not take seriously their repudiations of politics. And there were good reasons for treating the dissidents in this way.

First, the boundary line between the political and non-political is fluid,[23] and communism politicized even those areas which in other systems have little to do with politics. As Havel noted: 'If the suppression of the aims of life is a complex process, and if it is based on the multifaceted manipulation of all expression of life, then, by the same token, every free expression of life indirectly threatens the post-totalitarian system politically.'[24] Second, dissidents hardly concealed the fact that, in their opinion, the communist system is essentially evil, and they untiringly criticized both how it works and the principles on which it is based. Third, they were aware that in the existing conditions what they were saying, for example about morality, had 'an unambiguous political dimension'.[25] In fact, in the communistic state the very catchphrase 'to live within the truth' was nothing else but a call for

[20] V. Havel, *The Power of the Powerless*, op. cit., p. 52.

[21] David Ost, *Solidarity and the Politics of Anti-Politics: Opposition and Reform in Poland since 1968* (Philadelphia: Temple University Press, 1990), p. 2.

[22] Ibid., p. 4.

[23] See *Changing Boundaries of the Political: Essays on the Evolving Balance between the State and Society, Public and Private in Europe*, ed. Charles Maier (Cambridge: Cambridge University Press, 1987).

[24] V. Havel, *The Power of the Powerless*, op. cit., p. 43.

[25] Ibid., pp. 40, 45–6. Claude Lefort made the following insightful remark about the East European dissidents: 'As soon as the rights that they are demanding become incompatible with the totalitarian system, it is only too clear that they are involved in politics, even though they have no political aim, programme or doctrine; and it becomes equally clear that these rights turn out, in practice, to be bound up with a general conception of society – of what was once called the *polis* or city – which totalitarianism directly negates' ('Politics and Human Rights', in *The Political Forms of Modern Society: Bureaucracy, Democracy, Totalitarianism*, ed. John B. Thompson (Cambridge: Polity Press, 1986), p. 241).

civil disobedience. Thus, anti-politics was not escapism, as Stoicism or Epicureanism had once been.

Anti-politics did not mean neutrality in matters of politics. It only meant that here and now the main field of the fight against communism was not who is to wield power and what this power should be like, but rather it was how people should behave who are subjected to a bad political system which they are unable to change. In other words, 'all attempts by society to resist the pressure of the system have their essential beginnings in the pre-political area',[26] ('pre-ideological and pre-political', as he says elsewhere) – an area in which the elementary needs of 'life' and not political doctrines or ideologies have the deciding voice.

The conception of 'anti-political politics' created by the East European dissidents was truly original, and not without reason also aroused a lot of interest, even enthusiasm, far beyond the confines of the region. It has all of the makings to assume a lasting place in the history of political thought and emancipation strategies. Yet, its weak sides made it practically useless in relatively short order; it remains of immediate interest only as a warning against attaching too much importance to purely political means. Its main weakness was its programmatic aversion to designing concrete political arrangements that could be instituted after the fall of communism. As a consequence, as Claus Offe correctly emphasized, the breakthrough of 1989 turned out to be 'a revolution without a revolutionary theory'.[27]

The *language* of anti-politics, which from the start had been an obstacle to a clear understanding of its political message, also became an anachronism much sooner than expected. This was a very specific language. The dissidents' favourite literary genre was the essay, which gives the writer more licence and frees him or her from the responsibility to state things precisely and accurately. This form of expression was chosen in order to help individuals who thought and felt the same way to recognize each other in the 'lonely crowd' of citizens of a state in which there were no normal channels of social communication or established forms of public discourse other than the official one. The writings of the dissidents at the same time performed the technical function of a means for conveying opinions and the symbolic function of a means for coming to an understanding with one another. The less clearly views on specific matters were expressed, the more easily they could be accepted by anyone who wanted to come to an understanding. For the dissidents, establishing a community of moral opposition among readers was just as important as winning them over intellectually.

[26] V. Havel, *The Power of the Powerless*, op. cit., p. 85.
[27] Claus Offe, 'Capitalism by Democratic Design? Democratic Theory Facing the Triple Transition in East Central Europe', *Social Research*, vol. 58, no. 4, Winter 1991, pp. 866–7.

The peculiarities of this language were grasped perfectly by Adam Michnik, who wrote:

> I think that we know precisely what we do not want, but none of us knows precisely what we do want. There is no language which could correctly describe our aspirations – that, too, is one of the peculiarities of this time. None of the known languages grasps our experience. The language of political analyses and sociological forecasts, the language of historical reflection and religious meditation does not suffice. The values whose presence we sense intuitively – and to which we want to be faithful – are values existing at the meeting point of different spheres of our human condition, and hence the language in which they could be described cannot be internally homogeneous. Hence we are looking for another language which would pinpoint the inexpressible.[28]

It hardly needs to be shown how much the workings of this different language depended on the context and the special emotional atmosphere surrounding freedom of speech under a dictatorship.

I do not deny that things of lasting value and unquestionable analytical merits were written in this language by the authors who used it. Here, however, I am not evaluating the entire intellectual output of the democratic opposition but only the dimension that is important for the further development of political thought. In this respect, this output seems quite paltry and disproportionately small in comparison to the historical contributions of this movement to the renewal of political life. Apart from the general conception described above, which with the fall of real socialism has largely become a dead issue, more attention should be focused on the *metapolitical* context of the problem of protoliberalism.

4. *Autonomy of the individual and individualism*

According to Konrad, the democratic opposition shared the religious faith that 'the dignity of the human personality (in both oneself and the other person) is a fundamental value not requiring any further demonstration'.[29] This statement is correct in a double sense: first, because defence of the individual was all-important for the democratic opposition, whose programme referred to international treaties on human rights, and, second, because no great axiological discussions took place on this subject. At most

[28] Adam Michnik, *Polskie pytania* (Paris: Zeszyty Literackie, 1987), pp. 42–3.
[29] G. Konrad, *Antipolitics*, op. cit., p. 123.

the debate was over what to do in order to make this defence more effective. It was also incontrovertible that the cardinal sin of communism was the violation of human rights. From this point of view, the following words of Adam Michnik are typical: 'It is true that communism is foreign, not ingrained, and Soviet. But the evil present in communism is above all antihumanitarian, aimed at the destruction of the human personality, and for this reason antinational, and not the reverse.'[30]

I am inclined to believe that the literature of the dissidents implicitly contains a certain philosophy of man, a highly *individualistic* philosophy.[31] What is more, the dissident movement is probably the most serious manifestation of individualism in the political (or parapolitical, if one wishes) thought of Eastern Europe, where the individualistic tradition was meagre and confined almost exclusively to literary texts.

Individualism in this case was favoured by many things. The extremely statist or 'totalitarian' nature of communism, as the dissidents liked to call it, which was the main focus of the criticism, required a defence of the rights of the 'man in the street' paying the high costs of 'building socialism' and in fact deprived even of those rights to which he or she was formally entitled and which were limited in comparison to those enjoyed by citizens of the liberal democracies. The anti-political orientation shifted the plane of the fight against communism to the defence of human and civic rights, thereby reducing the importance of collectivist themes such as sovereignty of the people or independence of the nation in discussions on the political order. Finally, the manner of recruitment of members of the democratic opposition as individuals who make a certain moral choice independent of their group affiliation and appealing to the minds and hearts of all members of society as people, each of whom is potentially interested in changing the status quo, encouraged them to be seen as individuals and the associations created by them as a kind of contract among individuals.

This individualism was not always expressed in articles and papers, but in some cases it was put forward quite clearly. Once again I refer to Havel. The concept of 'the aims of life', so crucial to *The Power of the Powerless*, as opposed to 'the aims of the post-totalitarian system', refers to nothing less than the natural aspirations of *individuals*, each of whom has the right to dignity and to be himself despite all outside pressures. The evil of communism is that it deprives the individual of this right, makes him an object of manipulation, strips him of his identity, forces him to live in conflict with

---

[30] Adam Michnik, 'The Moral and Spiritual Origins of Solidarity', *Without Force or Lies: Voices from the Revolution of Central Europe in 1989–1990. Essays, Speeches, and Eyewitness Accounts*, ed. William M. Brinton and Alan Rinzler (San Francisco: Mercury House, 1990), pp. 148–9.

[31] See C. Lefort, 'Politics and Human Rights', op. cit.

his conscience, etc. To live within the truth is to emancipate oneself from this and to affirm freedom and diversity, which belong to the 'nature of life'.[32] It is interesting that this need for individual identity, being in harmony with oneself, was emphasized much more strongly by the dissidents than material needs. Konrad even stated outright that people need dignity more than calories.[33]

The role of the idea of the autonomy of the individual in the views of East European dissidents brings up the question of their connection with liberalism. This question is fully justified, especially when we have in mind liberalism not as a fully developed political philosophy whose starting assumptions are not clearly stated each time, but liberalism in its early phase, when on every occasion it was obvious that it was appealing to the conscience of the individual as a higher instance than the will of the ruler or positive law. I am not stating that liberalism was the direct source of inspiration for the democratic opposition in Eastern Europe, for this did not have to be so and, in most cases, was not. Just as good a case could be made for the influence of Christian personalism, existentialism, socialist humanism, etc. or, especially, for the common-sense philosophy of human rights in the form applied in international politics. The idea involved here is so general that it could come simultaneously from many different sources with no detriment to its integrity. More important than its genesis is that a closer examination of this idea will reveal its many non-liberal aspects. It is worth dwelling on this matter somewhat longer, because this will make us more aware of a few problems that are important for our argument.

5. *Collective individualism*

In comparison with the liberal tradition, the idea of the autonomy of the individual we find in the writings of the dissidents is restricted in a characteristic way: the parts of the opposition are the individual and the state, the individual and the system, but not the individual and *society*. This is quite understandable because under real socialism the individual was subjected to pressure from the omnipotent state, and in opposing these pressures expected understanding and support from the society, which he perceived as subjected to the same threats and having just as hostile an attitude towards the state.

Although the society and state opposition has often been exaggerated, in Poland it was a fact, as demonstrated by sociological studies indicating a striking discrepancy between the official system of values and the values

---

[32] V. Havel, *The Power of the Powerless*, op. cit., pp. 29--30.
[33] G. Konrad, *Antipolitics*, op. cit., p. 197.

professed by most members of the society.[34] In these specific conditions, being oneself or preserving one's individual identity postulated by the dissidents did not necessarily mean a triumph of individualism in the strict sense of the word as understood by liberalism; it could just as well have meant a victory of social conformity if it stood in opposition to the conformity required by the state. In Poland, the best example of such a possibility was the situation of a Catholic fighting for full rights to profess and practise his religion not as an individual *tout court*, but as an individual being an integral part of a religious community recognized by him as more important than the communist state. At other times, the situation was not as clear-cut. Whenever the individual rebelled against the state, it could be supposed that this was not an absolute act of non-conformity, so to speak, but was an act of non-conformity towards the state and at the same time an affirmation of solidarity with some, even imagined, non-state community.

This could be such or another traditional community, and as a rule this was the case; it could also be nascent community of 'the unsubmissive', which was described and postulated by the dissidents as the 'parallel *polis*', the 'independent society', or the 'civil society'. In any case, as a rule the manifestation of the autonomy of the individual in relation to the state turned out to be inseparable from the desire to participate in a community. Virtue was not so much to be different from what the state wanted as to be like others who refused to submit to its dictate. I am not saying that such a postulate was ever expressed explicitly. On the contrary, one can cite many encomiums of diversity. My point is that in the conditions of real socialism, this had to be the practical implications of the principle 'to live within the truth'. In this sense, one can say that we have to do with a specific kind of 'collectivist individualism'.[35]

My intention is not to praise absolute non-conformity or, even less so, to criticize the democratic opposition for the partial nature of its otherwise unquestionable individualism. Neither would make any sense at all. Absolute non-conformity seems neither possible nor desirable. Moreover, it should be remembered that the liberal fight against social conformity got under way in earnest only after tyrannies other than social tyranny had been overthrown – at least, in those countries in which the liberals were chiefly interested. My purpose was only to show that in certain conditions anti-state individualism is a *par excellence* prosocial expression.

[34] See Edmund Wnuk-Lipiński, 'Social Dimorphism and Its Implications', in *Crisis and Transition: Polish Society in the 1980s*, ed. Jadwiga Koralewicz, Ireniusz Białecki and Margaret Watson (Oxford: Berg, 1987), pp. 159–76.
[35] I borrow the term used by Richard Bellamy in his characterization of the views of John Stuart Mill (*Liberalism and Modern Society: A Historical Argument* (University Park PA: The Pennsylvania State University Press, 1991), pp. 22 ff.).

6. *The private and the public*

The special nature of the individualism discussed here appears even more clearly when we take a closer look at the opposition so important in liberal thought between what is private and what is public. It is already surprising that in the views of the democratic opposition this opposition did not play an important role, being completely overshadowed by the state and society opposition. No member of the democratic opposition stated that increasing the freedom of the individual might consist in expanding his private sphere, which, at least since the times of B. Constant, has been put forward by many liberals in the conviction that – in contrast to the freedom of the ancients – modern freedom comes to fruition precisely here.[36] To be sure, expansion of the private sphere had to and did come into consideration in so far as it was needed to limit the omnipresence of the state and to strip it of the features of a police state, but in the waning phase of real socialism this definitely was an issue of secondary importance. What is more important, the public versus private opposition looks much different in the conditions created by communism than in the conditions of liberal democracy.

Without going too far into this subject, it is worth mentioning at least three things.

First, after the victory of communism the public sphere was greatly expanded on the one hand by including the economy within it, and on the other it was nationalized and ideologically standardized, as a result of which a considerable number of potential participants lost access to it or were pushed to its margins.

Second, although the private sphere was considerably narrowed by excluding nearly all economic activities from it, reducing the freedom of assembly, the take-over by the state of some of the functions of the family, etc., the private sphere at the same time became a sanctuary, so to speak, for people pushed out of the nationalized public sphere, and took on some uncommon functions. 'Home and free time: these are the spatial and temporal dimensions of civic independence.'[37]

Third, the so-called phenomenon of 'social dimorphism' appeared on a hitherto unprecedented scale in conditions of real socialism. According to Edmund Wnuk-Lipiński, 'social dimorphism' consists in the fact that 'the public domain has its own system of values which does not operate outside

---

[36] See Benjamin Constant, 'De la liberté des Anciens comparée a celle des Modernes', in *Collection Complete des Ouvrages Publics* (Paris, 1820), vol. II, pp. 238 ff. Steven Lukes, *Individualism* (New York: Harper & Row, 1973), pp. 59–65. See Richard Mulgan, 'Liberty in Ancient Greece', in *Conceptions of Liberty in Political Philosophy*, ed. Zbigniew Pelczyński and John Gray (New York: St Martin's Press, 1984), p. 11.

[37] G. Konrad, *Antipolitics*, op. cit., p. 202.

this domain. The private domain, which refuses to submit to control, is governed by a different set of values.'[38]

During communism's 'heroic' period, which in Eastern Europe, especially in Poland and Hungary, did not last long and was not an exact copy of the Bolshevik model, the communist authorities tried to change this state of affairs in accordance with the ideological assumption that the public/private opposition was an anachronism that would fade away as the remaking of society and communist education moved forward.[39] In the decadent phase of communism, which interests us here, illusions of this kind disappeared almost without a trace:[40] no longer was it a matter of transforming or liquidating the private domain but of limiting its influence on the public domain, which was supposed to be strictly 'socialist' in nature. The communist authorities not only reconciled themselves to the permanent existence of the uncontrollable private domain but also to the fact that it would remain a sphere of values hostile to them – under the condition that these values would remain strictly private.

This meant moving away from the more or less open fight with religion to recognizing it as a private matter, and also showing increasing tolerance for 'non-socialist' life styles. What is more, it also meant that citizens were allowed to hold political views hostile to communism – obviously, under the absurd condition that they would not utter them publicly and would confine expression of them to a narrow circle of family or friends. In other words, there came a time of peculiar ideological diarchy, during which the clear separation of the public from the private domain became a principle of communist policy.[41] As Ken Jowitt wrote, 'Leninist parties made a *de facto*

[38] E. Wnuk-Lipiński, 'Social Dimorphism and Its Implications', op. cit., p. 159.

[39] See Eugene Kamenka, 'Public/Private in Marxist Theory and Marxist Practice', in *Public and Private in Social Life*, ed. S. I. Benn and G. F. Gaus (New York: St Martin's Press, 1983), pp. 267–80. Perhaps the last 'theoretical' manifestation of this orientation is Mao's brochure on liberalism of September 1937 (Mao Tse-tung, *Combat Liberalism*. Peking: Foreign Languages, nd). The ideal type of totalitarianism leaves no place for privacy. See Stanley I. Benn, 'Privacy, Freedom and Respect for Persons', in *Privacy*, ed. J. Roland Pennock and John W. Chapman, *Nomos*, vol. XII, Atherton Press, New York 1971, p. 22.

[40] Bartłomiej Kamiński gives a fine analysis of 'the syndrome of withdrawal' characteristic of the decadent phase of communism in *The Collapse of State Socialism: The Case of Poland* (Princeton NJ: Princeton University Press, 1991), Chapter 6.

[41] In the opinion of M. Vajda, 'the system's predominant contradiction lies in the fact that it can maintain its totalitarian power structure only by channeling all human activity into the private sphere; to this end, however, it is forced to introduce a mechanism which threatens the system as much as the socially oriented initiatives' (*The State and Socialism: Political Essays* (London: Allison & Busby, 1981). See Milan Simečka, *The Restoration of Order: The Normalization of Czechoslovakia, 1969–1976*, trans. A. G. Brain (London: Verso, 1984), p. 145.

trade off: active control and penetration of priority areas in return for *de facto* privatization in nonpriority areas.'[42]

Thus, for people critical of communism and striving to make a major change in the status quo, privacy, 'the peaceful enjoyment of private independence', as Constant wrote, could not be the attractive catchphrase it was and still is for Western liberals, for in the conditions of real socialism it was ambiguous: in speaking of the highly desirable limitation of the control of the state over citizens, it was agreed at the same time that the revolt would not exceed the limits set by the authorities. The problem now was no longer that the individual was not entitled to any liberties in the private sphere, since, generally speaking, there were ever more such liberties, but in the fact that the only freedoms the individual had were limited to this sphere. Thus, the postulate of autonomy and emancipation of the individual had to be directed above all to his or her participation in public life and be a declaration of rights to cross over the limits of privateness, in which nearly everything that was in conflict with the official ideology had been confined.[43] G. Konrad wrote that we are trying 'to expand the bounds of private existence',[44] which hardly meant withdrawing from the public forum. Quite the contrary.

In the conditions of real socialism, the private sphere encompassed what had always belonged to it as well as what, in other conditions, would have belonged to the public sphere; it included things which had been dislodged from the public sphere on account of its monopolization by one category of citizens and its subjection to ideological control. In other words, more than in any other conditions it included both *what is personal*, as opposed to what is social or public, and *what is social*, as opposed to what is political or belongs to the state.[45]

Thus, privateness had two dimensions, so to say: individual and social; an integral part of this sphere were values that had been suppressed in public life, but remained important enough for people not to forget them and even to cultivate them wherever possible. For instance, in this way elements of the national tradition branded as 'reactionary' and harmful survived. Consequently, questioning the values of the state-controlled public sphere and withdrawing from it if this was at all possible were not necessarily an affirmation of purely individual values; on the contrary, such behaviours might very well have meant a conscious choice of certain *social* values. This

---

[42] Ken Jowitt, 'The Leninist Legacy', in *Eastern Europe in Revolution*, ed. Ivo Banac (Ithaca NY: Cornell University Press, 1992), p. 211.

[43] See Jacek Kuroń, *Polityka i odpowiedzialność*, op. cit., p. 54.

[44] G. Konrad, *Antipolitics*, op. cit., p. 202.

[45] See Will Kymlicka, *Contemporary Political Philosophy: An Introduction* (Oxford: Clarendon Press, 1990), p. 250.

was the nature of the so-called 'internal emigration' condemned by official propaganda.

For the largely obvious reasons mentioned above, in the existing conditions, declaring oneself in favour of views in open contradiction with official state values could not lead to a fight to reform the state. Anyone who was not satisfied with withdrawal into privateness really had only two choices. One of them was to gain the right to profess his or her views within the official institutions at the cost of making certain compromises with the communist authorities, which sometimes became possible to a limited extent.[46] The second was to attempt to create independent institutions that would make up the so-called intermediate sphere, which in contrast to the private sphere would be *public* and – in contrast to the state-controlled public sphere – *social*. In this middle sphere what had been forced to become private would become public, what was public would become social.

Hence, the individualism directed against the communist state was largely a negation of the individualism which Alexis de Tocqueville described as 'a considered and calm feeling which disposes each citizen to isolate himself from the mass of his fellows, and to withdraw into the circle of his family and friends; with the result that, after his little society has been created for his use, he gladly abandons the greater society to look after himself'.[47] None the less, I stick with the term *individualism*, since no matter how strongly the need for a *greater* society was stressed, the starting points were always individuals liberated through the power of their sovereign conscience. As Vladimir Tismaneanu wrote, 'it is clear that the foundation stone of the countersociety is the individual's decision to proclaim his or her mental independence'.[48]

---

[46] The Polish social sciences in large part followed this principle. Their history after 1956 was marked by a constant effort to find a 'golden mean' between consenting to what the authorities wanted and independence. At the cost of refraining from open criticism of the official ideology and its 'theoretical' foundations, in many cases it was possible to obtain permission to make an objective description of such or other fragments of reality and even to question current policy indirectly. Obviously, this path did not lead very far.

[47] Quoted from Thomas L. Pangle, *The Ennobling of Democracy: The Challenge of the Postmodern Era* (Baltimore: Johns Hopkins University Press, 1992), p. 152.

[48] Vladimir Tismaneanu, *Reinventing Politics: Eastern Europe from Stalin to Havel* (New York: Free Press, 1992), p. 153. See Timothy Garton Ash, *The Uses of Adversity: Essays on the Fate of Central Europe* (New York: Random House, 1989), p. 203.

7. *Towards a civil society*

Today this intermediate sphere which the East European democratic opposition aimed to create is most often called *civil society*. This 'useful, if mystified, buzz-word'[49] is unquestionably of crucial importance; moreover, as some commentators have stated,[50] it implies that the views considered here are of more than local significance and are a link between the quest of East European politicians and Western political thought – both classic and contemporary.

In the context of this book this is also important, because it is situated in the very core of past and present debates on liberalism, of which it was correctly asserted that 'at the centre of this project was the goal of freeing civil society'.[51] Even though a considerable number of theorists of this trend have avoided using this disturbingly vague term, no treatment of liberalism is possible without introducing, if not the term, at least the concept of 'civil society', and no treatment of civil society is possible without referring to the liberal tradition. This is so both because 'the very idea of civil society touches on and embraces the major themes of the Western political tradition',[52] of which liberalism is an integral part, and because – as Leo Strauss averred – liberalism 'stands or falls by the distinction between state and society',[53] a distinction which is central to modern conceptions of civil society.

We should begin by recalling some facts from the most recent history of the idea of civil society in Eastern Europe. First, the term itself, which today, not without reason, is regarded as the main slogan of opposition against communism,[54] did not become popular until the 1980s. The phrase 'the rebirth of civil society' appeared in some commentaries on events in Eastern Europe towards the end of the 1970s. But – as Z. A. Pełczyński

[49] Ivo Banac, Introduction to *Eastern Europe in Revolution*, op. cit., p. 11.

[50] See Jean L. Cohen and Andrew Arato, *Civil Society and Political Theory* (Cambridge MA: Massachusetts Institute of Technology Press, 1992), pp. 15–18, 31–36; and Jeffrey C. Goldfarb, *After the Fall: The Pursuit of Democracy in Central Europe* (New York: Basic Books, 1992), pp. 7–9, 35–6.

[51] David Held, *Models of Democracy* (Stanford CA: Stanford University Press, 1987), p. 41.

[52] Adam Seligman, *The Idea of Civil Society*, op. cit., p. 3.

[53] Leo Strauss, *Liberalism, Ancient and Modern* (Chicago: The University of Chicago Press, Basic Books, 1968), p. 230.

[54] 'Indeed, one could write the history of East Central Europe over the last decade as the story of struggles for civil society' (Timothy Garton Ash, *The Uses of Adversity*, op. cit., p. 194). See also the books by Miklós Molnar, *La démocratie se léve a L'Est: Société civile et communisme en Europe de L'Est, Pologne et Hongrie* (Paris: Presses Universitaires de France, 1970), and Vladimir Tismaneanu, *Reinventing Politics*, op. cit.

observed – at that time this looked like utopianism and *wishful thinking*.[55] In any event, the term 'civil society' spread rather slowly and did not enter into the lexicon of the opponents of communism in this region right away. In all likelihood, it started to be used first in reference to Poland and Solidarity, thanks to which it was not an exaggerated formula.

Absence of the term did not mean absence of the concept, and there is hardly any doubt that 'if we wish to grasp how someone sees the world . . . what we need to know is not what words he uses but rather what concepts he possesses'.[56] The concept appeared almost simultaneously with the dissident movement under such names as 'independent culture', 'parallel structures', 'alternative society', 'independent society', parallel *polis*', 'self-governing republic', etc. In many contexts the word 'society' had a similar meaning, when, for example, some people wrote that the fight with totalitarianism must strive to 'reconstruct society, to rebuild social ties outside official institutions'.[57] From the beginning people were well aware that resistance to communism requires not only the heroism of individuals but also organization and institutionalization, which, in Havel's words, 'are the most articulated expressions of living within the truth'.[58] The first really conspicuous manifestations of this awareness were the actions of The Workers' Defence Committee (KOR) founded in 1976.[59] To be sure, the various definitions of the nascent public sphere that was supposed to be independent of the state did not have the same meaning, but we can assume that they referred to the same things, that is – as Molnar writes – to '*tous les efforts, actions et pensées mis en oeuvre contre le totalitarisme et ses vestiges*'.[60]

Second, the popularity of the term 'civil society' differed geographically; it became most widespread in Poland, somewhat less so in Hungary, and was used least often in Czechoslovakia, where the more modest term 'parallel *polis*' coined by Václav Benda was used.[61] Towards the end of the 1980s, the term 'civil society' started to make a career in the former Soviet

---

[55] See Z. A. Pełczyński, 'Solidarity and the "Rebirth of Civil Society" in Poland, 1976–81', in *Civil Society and the State*, ed. John Keane (London: Verso, 1989), p. 363.

[56] Quentin Skinner, 'Language and Political Change', in *Political Innovation and Conceptual Change*, ed. Terence Ball, James Farr, Russel L. Hanson (Cambridge: Cambridge University Press, 1989), p. 7.

[57] Adam Michnik, 'Polska wojna', *Szanse polskiej demokracji*, op. cit., p. 25.

[58] V. Havel, *The Power of the Powerless*, op. cit., p. 79.

[59] See Jan Józef Lipski, *KOR: A History of the Workers' Defense Committee in Poland, 1976–1981*, trans. Olga Amsterdamska and Gene A. Moore (Berkeley CA: University of California Press, 1985).

[60] M. Molnar, *La démocratie se léve a L'Est*, op. cit., p. 6.

[61] See Václav Benda, Milan Šimečka, Ivan Jirous, Jiří Dienstbier and Václav Havel, 'Parallel Polis or an Independent Society in Central and Eastern Europe: An Inquiry', Introduction by H. Gordon Skilling, *Social Research* 1988, vol. 55, no. 1–2, pp. 211–46.

republics. It is hard to say by what channels it spread and what its most important sources were. It may very well be that a certain role was played by an increase of the popularity of this term in the West, though Andrew Arato sees the rebirth of the idea of civil society as a gift received by the West from Eastern Europe and South America.[62] In any case, this idea, which had been forgotten for years, appeared in many different places at more or less the same time.

Third, the concept of civil society was introduced to public circulation in Eastern Europe as self-explanatory and requiring little, if any, commentary. At a certain moment, people simply started to use it as a designation either for the goal to be achieved or for the already visible results of the actions of the opposition in the form of a network of interpersonal relationships and institutions independent of the state, or, finally, for all relationships and institutions that had retained their independence from the state but had not been associated with the opposition from the start. Sometimes people spoke of the construction or reconstruction of the civil society that had been destroyed by the communists, and sometimes of freeing society from the power of a repressive state, which prevented or hindered something already existing in fact from functioning. At other times, it was stressed that as long as the communists ruled, the civil society was fated to remain in the minority; finally, there was a tendency to identify civil society with society as such, which was perceived as united and organized against the government.

This changeability of meanings was due on the one hand to different situations in individual countries (for example, the situation in Poland during the triumphs of Solidarity led some people to speak of the reconstruction of civil society as an accomplished fact), and on the other to the fact that the concept of civil society was used persuasively rather than analytically. In the latter case, the vagueness of the concept, especially the unclear boundary line between descriptive and normative aspects and between the goal and the movement leading to it, in no way made it less useful and was no reason for concern. For the historian of ideas, however, this is a source of trouble, for he must be precise about what by nature was imprecise and ambiguous; at the same time, he must take care not to go too far in his attempt to be precise by forgetting that this idea of civil society referred to common associations with the words 'society' and 'citizen' rather than to theoretical formulations of the subject-matter, which are also not characterized by exemplary precision.

---

[62] See J. L. Cohen and A. Arato, *Civil Society and Political Theory*, op. cit., p. 16; also Andrew Arato, 'Revolution, Civil Society, and Democracy', in *The Emergence of Civil Society in Eastern Europe and the Soviet Union*, ed. Zbigniew Rau (Boulder CO: Westview Press, 1991), p. 161.

8. The problem of the theoretical tradition

For this reason, little profit can be gained here from a discussion of archetypes or sources of inspiration of the various conceptions of civil society which have been created by political theorists since the times of John Locke (earlier conceptions are irrelevant in this case due to the lack of a distinction between state and society), even though this is a highly interesting and surprisingly topical subject.[63] The only thing that seems really important in this context is what is common to this entire rich tradition, namely, the formation within it of the concept of 'the space of uncoerced human association' or, to use a more complete formula, 'the picture of people freely associating and communicating with one another, forming and reforming groups of all sorts'.[64] Even if the theoretical dilemmas inherent in this tradition would surface in time in all of their sharpness, in the beginning the only thing that mattered was to open one's eyes to the fact that – as Havel, who does not use the term 'civil society', wrote – 'a different life can be lived, a life that is in harmony with its own aims and which in turn structures itself in harmony with those aims'.[65]

Of the period in which the concept of civil society started to make a big career in Eastern Europe one can say only that if there had been some references to the said theoretical tradition, which, in my opinion, is far from obvious, they would have concerned only those classic conceptions in which 'the expression "civil" gains a primarily "social" content as opposed to its original meaning and is no longer taken to be synonymous with "political"'.[66] For the issue here was not only the civil society and state distinction but also their very strong *opposition*. For this reason, a Hungarian critic of the concept of civil society in its application saw mainly Hegelian influences, manifesting themselves in the tendency of authors using it to express relationships between the civil society and the state as a zero-sum game: whatever the former gains, the latter loses, and vice versa.[67] Even though the thesis on Hegelianism seems doubtful, the observation is

---

[63] This is best expressed in the already cited works of Cohen and Arato, Seligman, Keane, and others. See also *Habermas and the Public Sphere*, ed. Craig Calhoun (Cambridge MA: MIT Press, 1992).

[64] Michael Walzer, 'The Civil Society Argument', in *Dimensions of Radical Democracy, Pluralism, Citizenship, Community*, ed. Chantal Mouffe (London: Verso, 1992), pp. 89, 97.

[65] V. Havel, *The Power of the Powerless*, op. cit., p. 79.

[66] Manfred Riedel, *Between Tradition and Revolution: The Hegelian Transformation of Political Philosophy*, trans. Walter Wright (Cambridge: Cambridge University Press, 1984), p. 139.

[67] C. M. Hann, 'Second Economy and Civil Society', *Market Economy and Civil Society in Hungary*, ed. C. M. Hann (London: Frank Cass, 1990), p. 32.

certainly correct. In fact, the idea of civil society appeared in Eastern Europe as an *anti-state idea* above all else.[68]

If it had been different, it would have been of no use, for the practical task was to create a 'public sphere of social interaction that has nothing to do with the government'[69] – a sphere in which 'the voice of the ruling power is heard only as an insignificant echo from the world that is organized in an entirely different way'.[70] If any connection at all is conceivable between these two alien worlds, it will take the form of a contract between two *parties*, each of which represents, by definition, different values and interests. The return today to the idea of civil society in the West is also unquestionably anti-statist, for there is a movement under way to oppose the impersonal structures of the state administration with relationships among citizens that are as direct as possible.[71] However, the analogy is limited, because in Eastern Europe the state was perceived not only as something that had grown to excessive, or even gargantuan, dimensions but as something that was alien and hostile by its very nature.

The tendency to oppose civil society to the state is unquestionably characteristic of all modern theories of the former. Alvin W. Gouldner aptly remarked that 'an essential aspect of civil society is that it is a sphere autonomous of the state, that it is not determined by the state of politics, but has a life of its own. The concept of civil society . . . was thus largely a residual concept, being that which was *not* the state, and what was *left over* in society after the state was "excluded". Its essential point was to establish that the state did not encompass society, that was something more of importance – but what exactly this was remained unclear.'[72] In the case that interests me here, it was precisely this feature of the idea of civil society that was radically strengthened; this society cannot be defined in any other way but through *opposition*, and the yardstick of its development is how clear and extensive this opposition becomes. 'Civil society is defined primarily as an

---

[68] Perhaps Mihály Vajda is right in putting forward the thesis that, in contradistinction to the Eastern tradition, the East-Central European tradition contains 'a fundamental conflict between state and society' ('East-Central European Perspectives', *Civil Society and the State*, op. cit., p. 345).

[69] David Ost, *Solidarity and the Politics of Anti-Politics*, op. cit., p. 21.

[70] Ivan M. Jirous, in *Parallel Polis*, ed. Benda et al., op. cit., p. 277.

[71] See Daniel Bell, '"American Exceptionalism" Revisited: The Role of Civil Society', *The Public Interest* 1989, no. 95, pp. 38–56.

[72] Alvin W. Gouldner, *The Two Marxisms: Contradictions and Anomalies in the Development of Theory* (New York: Oxford University Press, 1986), pp. 356–7. See Norberto Bobbio, *Democracy and Dictatorship: The Nature and Limits of State Power*, trans. Peter Kenealy (Minneapolis: University of Minnesota Press, 1989), p. 22.

antipode to étatism, the opposing factor in binary opposition, that everything which is not étatic society is civil society.'[73]

In the literature I even encountered the astonishing concept of the 'self-sufficiency' of civil society,[74] which almost completely deviates from the conception, let's say, of Hegel, for whom civil society was by definition incomplete and imperfect, absolutely requiring the presence of the state. Although I did not encounter the concept of 'self-sufficiency' in any of the authors whose views I am describing, it nevertheless seems to be an accurate expression of their conception, according to which the state in fact is not needed for anything. Here it should be added that, although more will be said about this later, society towers over the state in the *moral* sense or even, strictly speaking, is the only mainstay of morality in the communist state.

One can say that in this opposition of civil society to the state the matter did not concern distinguishing two different but somehow complementary spheres or dimensions of social life; rather, it concerned contrasting two opposing and mutually exclusive types or styles, whose permanent coexistence was the result of geopolitical necessity and not of the functional requirements of either of them. The role of the state is only negative. If any good state can be imagined, it would be one that would be an emanation of social self-organization, that is, it would be civil society appearing under another name and looked at from another point of view.

In a certain sense, formally speaking, the opposition of civil society to the state considered here has more in common with Spencer's opposition of industrial and military societies[75] than with Hegel's opposition of civil society and the state. Spencer also comes to mind for the reason that everything that can be said about the desired type of relationships in fact derives from what is known about the undesirable type. There are other similarities as well (especially that here and there the opposition of an organization serving people and one serving only itself comes into play); however, I will not develop this point here, because I do not want to suggest that we have to do with some kind of Spencerism, for which there are absolutely no grounds. Generally speaking, it makes no sense to try to establish a relationship between the views discussed here and such or other classic '-isms'. I have recalled the author of *First Principles of Sociology* just to demonstrate certain peculiarities of the conception discussed, as well as to call the

[73] Mykola Ryabchuk, 'Civil Society and National Emancipation: The Ukrainian Case', in *The Reemergence of Civil Society in Eastern Europe and the Soviet Union*, ed. Z. Rau (Boulder CO: Westview Press, 1991), p. 99.

[74] J. F. Brown, *Eastern Europe and Communist Rule* (Durham NC: Duke University Press, 1988), p. 197.

[75] See Jerzy Szacki, *History of Sociological Thought* (Greenwood Press, 1979), Chapter 8.

reader's attention to the fact that the traces leading back to the classic conceptions of civil society along the Locke–Hegel line are hardly any more plain than those leading in the other direction. It is also possible that, in one way or another, both are misleading.

9. What is civil society?

The positive content of the dissidents' idea of civil society cannot be described in any other way except by enumerating the opposite features of the communist state. These features were known both from direct experience and from the theory of totalitarianism, whose popularity in Eastern Europe, as mentioned before, came very late and was not necessarily deserved.[76] One critic wrote: 'If you withdrew the concept of totalitarianism from your thinking, your views would lose a lot of their assertiveness and even more of their content.'[77] The sort of Manicheism[78] manifesting itself through the opposition of civil society to the state as the opposition of good and evil was based on the conviction derived from the theory of totalitarianism that the communist state was a whole that was perfectly integrated with and penetrated all areas of collective life. With the onset of totalitarianism, civil society ceased to exist; thus, the fight for restoration of civil society is a fight against totalitarianism.

Even though people were aware that the communist state had changed in certain ways, proof of which was the existence of the democratic opposition, they continued to cling to this way of thinking. At most, the terminology was changed (for example, Havel consistently used the term 'post-totalitarianism', but nowhere did he explain how it differed from totalitarianism *per se*), or attention was focused on the practical problem of whether the totalitarian state could coexist with the democratic institutions of society and if so, how.[79] Yet, even if it were possible for such a 'hybrid

---

[76] See Jacques Rupnik, 'Totalitarianism Revisited', *Civil Society and the State*, op. cit., pp. 263–89. See also Andrzej Walicki, '*The Captive Mind* Revisited', in *Totalitarianism at the Crossroads*, ed. Ellen Frankel (New Brunswick NJ: Transactions Books, 1990); and the same author's 'From Stalinism to Post-Communist Pluralism: The Case of Poland', *The New Left*, January–February 1991, pp. 93–121. See also Paul Piccone, 'Paradoxes of Perestroika', *Telos* 1990, no. 84.

[77] Bronisław Łagowski, 'List otwarty do trzydziestolatków', *Przegląd Polityczny* 1992, no. 1–2 (14–15), p. 5.

[78] Michel Foucault spoke of 'Manicheism' connected with the concept of the civil society. See *Politics, Philosophy, Culture: Interviews and Other Writings, 1977–1984*, ed. Lawrence D. Kritzman (New York: Routledge, 1988), pp. 167–8.

[79] Thus, in 1980 Adam Michnik wondered whether 'a hybrid system is possible, a cross between a totalitarian state and institutions of a democratic society' (*Szanse polskiej demokracji*, op. cit., p. 227).

system' to emerge, this would not have changed the overall assessment of the state: the actions taken against the state were still a zero-sum game. Quite understandably, the period of martial law in Poland strengthened people in this conviction.

So what were the features of civil society conceived as an alternative to the existing political society? They can be presented in the form of the following antitheses: truth / falsity; independent thought / the official ideology; conscience / discipline; moral courage / fear; voluntary cooperation / compulsion; solidarity of equals / hierarchical dependence; spontaneity / waiting for orders; using one's mind / thoughtlessly obeying orders and prohibitions; contract / command; pluralism / uniformity; tolerance / lack of tolerance; self-organization / organization imposed from above; conscious discipline / blind obedience, etc. This list could be extended, but this is not necessary because the antithesis seems clear enough. A community of free individuals, conscious moral subjects, rises up against Leviathan, who destroys this community by stripping people of their moral independence and turning them into passive objects of its manipulations.

Within this opposition of civil society to the state, certain people in different countries have emphasized various things. Sometimes we have to do with a primarily moral, if not quasi-religious, community, in which the emphasis is on 'kindness, tolerance, respect for the opinions of others, the acceptance of different human beings with love'.[80] Elsewhere, something much more clearly political is involved, which in fact is the idea of democracy expressed in a special way. Sometimes this idea takes the form of a universal vision of the good society, while elsewhere the emphasis is on the national nature of the community.[81] In Poland, the hypothesis is justified that the idea of civil society in the form which it took there, consciously or unconsciously, turned back to the long tradition of a 'nation without a state' – a tradition in which the nation and the state were treated as two fundamentally different types of social organization, one based on voluntary cooperation and the other on compulsion.[82]

---

[80] I. M. Jirous, in *Parallel Polis*, ed. Benda et al., op. cit., p. 227.

[81] 'If this program gave unequivocal priority to something, then it was the preservation or the renewal of the national community in the widest sense of the word' (Václav Benda in *Parallel Polis*, ed. Benda et al., op. cit., p. 217).

[82] See Florian Znaniecki, 'Siły społeczne w walce o Pomorze', in his *Narody współczesne* (Warsaw: PWN, 1990), pp. 369–70.

10. *Civil society vis-à-vis the moral unity of citizens*

A detailed examination of various shades of the idea of civil society would go beyond the frame of this book, and so we confine ourselves to a general description of this concept. It was certainly an individualistic idea in the sense that, as Timothy Garton Ash correctly observed, 'the key ingredient, as it were the basic molecule, of this civil society is the individual living in truth'.[83] Yet, the system of values underpinning the joining of these molecules can hardly be called individualistic. Many observers have noted this, among them Adam Seligman, who wrote: 'In the East civil society evokes a strong communal attribute that, while apart from the State, is also equally distant from the idea of the autonomous and agentic individual upon which the idea of civil society rests in the West . . . as firmly embedded within communal, mostly primordial attributes that define the individual in his or her opposition to the State.'[84] I also remind the reader of what was said about collectivist individualism earlier in this chapter.

There are many possible explanations for this feature of the style of thinking of the democratic opposition in Eastern Europe. Here I would like to mention one in particular. Communism was perceived by its critics not only as rampant étatism, resulting in the subjugation of the individual, but also as a powerful force atomizing society by destroying traditional interpersonal ties and blocking the formation of any new ones unrelated to the 'building of socialism'. Adam Michnik wrote that the communist government 'knew how to do one thing: destroy social solidarity'.[85]

From this point of view, society under rule of the communists is not only subjugated as under any other dictatorship, for this is a special kind of subjugation, under which society loses some of the features of a society. Something takes place which Adam Michnik called 'the destruction of society or transforming a nation into a population'.[86] The society of real socialism is not only closed but also empty, deprived of fundamental social values, and thus the problem is not only to break the shackles imposed by the state but also to revive the community destroyed by the state, to renew authentic interhuman ties.

Thus when two types of social organization are set in opposition to one another, one of which typifies the civil society and the other the communist

---

[83]   T. Garton Ash, *The Uses of Adversity*, op. cit., p. 203.
[84]   A. Seligman, *The Idea of Civil Society*, op. cit, pp. 202–3.
[85]   A. Michnik, *Szanse polskiej demokracji*, op. cit., p. 27.
[86]   A. Michnik, *Takie czasy . . . Rzecz o kompromisie* (London: Aneks, 1985), p. 85.
Jacek Kuroń wrote that the main feature of totalitarianism is 'dispossessing society of organization, resulting in social atomization and the dissolution of social ties' (*Polityka i odpowiedzialność*, op. cit., p. 51, and see p. 45).

state, we have in mind not only the repressiveness of the latter, but also that it is incapable of creating a true community. Strong and many-sided relationships established at the grass-roots level voluntarily and consciously are contrasted with the organization of social life on state lines. Using the terminology of Ferdinand Tönnies, one can say that civil society is *Gesellschaft* and *Gemeinschaft* simultaneously.

This brings to mind Raymond Aron's critique of Friedrich von Hayek's *Constitution of Freedom*. Aron wrote: 'The ideal society in which everyone would choose his own gods and values may become widespread only after individuals have been educated for collective life . . . In order to leave every person a private sphere of decisions and choice, everyone or most people must first want to live together and must recognize as true the same system of ideas and acknowledge as valid the same formula of legality. Before it can be free, society must first exist.'[87]

In short, the programme for the construction or reconstruction of civil society simultaneously assumed the emancipation and *resocialization* of the individual, both autonomy and solidarity. George Kolankiewicz correctly pointed out that 'the search for civil society is an expression of the loss of genuine association, the latter being both the source and affirmation of societal values'.[88] One can admittedly argue that in the West as well the idea of civil society abounded in social and moral elements of this kind,[89] but there seems to be a qualitative difference here. First, in the West, even before Locke, the Protestant 'revolution of saints' had taken place, thanks to which 'the control has already been implanted *in men*.'[90] This fulfilled Aron's condition and greater emphasis could be put on emancipation of the individual. Second, however imperfect or incomplete civil society in the West seemed to theorists, for them it was something *given* and constituted, if one can phrase it this way, a natural social environment for the individual. Its infrastructure consisted of spontaneously developing capitalist relationships in the economy. In the East, in contrast, civil society appeared as an ideological creation. What is more, it focused on the creation of a new *moral and social* order whose economic foundations were highly unclear.

---

[87] Raymond Aron, *Études politiques* (Paris: Gallimard, 1972), p. 211.

[88] George Kolankiewicz, 'The Reconstruction of Citizenship: Reverse Incorporation in Eastern Europe', *Constructing Capitalism: The Reemergence of Civil Society and Liberal Economy in the Post-Communist World*, ed. Kazimierz Poznanski (Boulder CO: Westview Press, 1992), p. 143.

[89] See especially Seligman, *The Idea of Civil Society*, op. cit., Chapter 2.

[90] Michael Walzer, *The Revolution of the Saints: A Study in the Origins of Radical Politics* (Cambridge MA: Harvard University Press, 1965), p. 303.

11. *A society without an economy*

A member of civil society in Eastern Europe is not *homo oeconimicus* but an individual 'living within the truth', a person who in his *free time* communes with like-minded individuals, who either hold state jobs or live from who knows what. In some cases, the idea of civil society was coupled with the postulate of workers' managerial cooperation. Although much older in Eastern Europe than the idea of civil society, workers' managerial coopera- tion may be regarded as one of the more important applications of the self- organization principle underpinning civil society.[91] One can even say that workers' managerial cooperation is nothing more than extending the self- organization principle to the economy. Yet, firstly, this is by no means so simple, because workers' managerial cooperation in the state economy could not develop analogously to other institutions of the civil society – 'beside' the state and in opposition to it. Secondly, there is no evidence that workers' managerial cooperation played an important role in this conception of civil society and that it was promoted unanimously by all of its supporters.

Generally speaking, it is striking how little these supporters have to say about the organization of the economy. In fact, as Michael D. Kennedy noted, 'it is unclear where in the struggle between totalitarian political authorities and the self-organized society the economy fits in'.[92] The same author goes on to say that 'generally, civil society as emancipatory agent contains no explicit program of political economy, but rather a program of social organization'.[93] Ash also made the keen observation that economic activity independent of the state was generally viewed as an emancipatory agent alternative to the construction of a civil society and not as an integral part of its construction[94] (see Chapter V).

This matter requires serious consideration. The question arises to what extent the anti-economics accompanying anti-politics simply meant making the best of the fact that in the countries of real socialism the economy was *par excellence* politicized and an integral part of the state; and to what extent this anti-economics was a choice based on such and not another system of values, on such and not another hierarchy of more and less impor- tant matters. It seems that both of these factors played a role.

[91] See G. Konrad, *Antipolitics*, op. cit., pp. 133–40; and Witold Morawski, 'Economic Change and Civil Society in Poland', in *Democracy and Civil Society in Eastern Europe*, ed. P. G. Lewis, op. cit.

[92] Michael D. Kennedy, *Professionals, Power and Solidarity in Poland: A Critical Sociology of Soviet-Type Society* (Cambridge: Cambridge University Press, 1991), p. 164.

[93] Ibid., p. 177.

[94] T. Garton Ash, *The Uses of Adversity*, op. cit., p. 274.

On the one hand, members of the democratic opposition were aware of the great difficulties involved in the creation of enclaves of an 'independent' economy,[95] though little thought was given to this. On the other hand, they repeatedly expressed the opinion that the economy is a morally ambiguous area whose incorporation into civil society depends not only on whether it is politically and materially possible to do so. After many years, Václav Benda, author of *Parallel Polis*, admitted that he had been inclined to treat the 'parallel economy' 'in a largely negative sense, in terms of the black market, theft, bribery, and other phenomena that go along with a centrally directed economy'.[96] At best, certain analogies were perceived (and quite late, at that) between the 'second economy' and the 'second society', while at the same time emphasizing that the 'second economy' was a borderline phenomenon because, in a certain sense, it was part of the 'first society'.[97] What is most interesting, however, is not which position prevailed but how little attention was paid to economic issues in deliberations on the nascent civil society. In no case was this to be *das bürgerliche Gesellschaft*.

Therefore, it may be argued that the civil society paradigm that had been hammered out much earlier by Western political thought disintegrated in Eastern Europe. The citizen of Eastern Europe is not a *bourgeois*. Ivan Szelenyi even wrote with enthusiasm about the possibility of 'citizenship without entrepreneurship'.[98] The political scientist who comments on this region and introduces the concept of the market to the definition of civil society must immediately add that 'the market is not limited to strictly economic transactions. Voluntary exchange of political, economic, artistic, and other ideas – exchange which is considered the basis for the development of social life – is also a market process.'[99] Even though this is true to a certain extent, it hardly reduces the distance between the idea of civil society that became popular in Eastern Europe before 1989 and the classic Western tradition. There is an enormous distance between the former idea and Marx's view that 'the anatomy of civil society is to be sought in political economy'.[100]

---

[95] See Petr Uhl, 'The Alternative Community as Revolutionary Avant-Garde', in *The Power of the Powerless*, ed. V. Havel, op. cit., pp. 188–97.

[96] V. Benda, *Parallel Polis*, ed. Benda et al., op. cit., p. 215.

[97] See Elemér Hankiss, *East-European Alternatives* (Oxford: Clarendon Press, 1990), pp. 93–4.

[98] Ivan Szelenyi, 'Eastern Europe in an Epoch of Transition: Towards a Socialist Mixed Economy', in *Remaking the Economic Institutions of Socialism*, ed. Victor Nee and David Stark (Stanford CA: Stanford University Press, 1989), pp. 222–3.

[99] Zbgniew Rau, 'Introduction', in *The Reemergence of Civil Society in Eastern Europe and the Soviet Union*, op. cit., p. 4.

[100] Karl Marx, *Zur Kritik der politischen Oekonomie*, 1859.

Here we have to do with 'a civil society based neither in the state nor in the marketplace',[101] 'one that does not succumb to either the rationales of statism or the magical promises of the market'.[102] The possibility is left open for the existence of an autonomous *social* sphere of civil society, a sphere which in fact and not just analytically can be separated from both *political* society and from *economic* society. This is precisely the way in which the East European idea of civil society has been interpreted by post-Marxist Western theorists. In this idea they found a source of inspiration for political and theoretical arguments against both statism and liberalism, which, in their opinion, threatens to 'colonialize' civil society through the economy in a way similar to the enthralment of civil society by the state in other circumstances.[103]

The word 'social' used to distinguish a certain aspect of collective life from its political and economic aspects requires some additional explanation here. As previously mentioned, it has very clear *moral* connotations here. Martin Malia made the same point in these words: 'What until now has been called "civil society" has in fact been *a moral civil society* of dissidents, democrats and ecclesiastics.'[104] It is significant that the advocates of civil society tended to ignore not only the 'second economy' growing up outside the control of the state but an equally independent yet incomparably more extensive sphere of 'less-than-formal relationships', which Janina Wedel described as follows: 'Polish society has long been structured around a complex system of informational relations, in such forms as "social circles", horizontal linkage networks and patron–client connections, all carried on in one sense outside authorized institutions, such as the state economy and bureaucracy, but also pervading them and connecting them with the community.'[105] It would be beside the point to consider the matters brought up in discussions of civil society in opposition circles. These were signs of resistance of the society against the state, but – as Jacek Kuroń wrote – while

---

[101] D. Ost, *Solidarity and the Politics of Anti-Politics*, op. cit., pp. 30–1.

[102] J. Goldfarb, *After the Fall*, op. cit., p. 246.

[103] See Andrew Arato, 'Social Theory, Civil Society, and the Transformation of Authoritarian Socialism', *Crisis and Reform in Eastern Europe*, ed. Ferenc Fehér and Andrew Arato (New Brunswick NJ: Transaction Books, 1991).

[104] Martin Malia, 'Leninist Endgame', *Daedalus* 1992, vol. 121, no. 2, p. 71. See Piotr Ogrodziński, *Pięć tekstów o społeczeństwie obywatelskim* (Warsaw: Instytut Studiów Politycznych PAN, 1991), pp. 70–2.

[105] Janina Wedel, 'The Ties that Bind in Polish Society', *Polish Paradoxes*, ed. Stanisław Gomułka and Antony Polonsky (London: Routledge, 1990), p. 241. See Janusz Bugajski and Maxime Pollack, *East European Fault Lines, Dissent, Opposition, and Social Activism* (Boulder CO: Westview Press, 1989), p. 99. See Elżbieta Tarkowska and Jacek Tarkowski, 'Social Disintegration in Poland: Civil Society or Amoral Familism?', *Telos* 1991, pp. 103–9.

aimed against the state this resistance was simultaneously directed 'against all other participants of social cooperation' and assaulted the 'dignity and ethics of individuals and society'.[106]

Consequently, the inclusion of something within civil society was not a morally neutral classification based on the criterion of independence: it was simultaneously a kind of nobilitation. There is no doubt that we have to do here with a use of the term which Adam Seligman qualifies 'as pertaining to a phenomenon in the realm of values, beliefs, or symbolic action. Here civil society is identified with some more or less universalistic mode of orientation on the part of social actors, and with the definition of citizenship in terms of universalistic, highly generalized moral bonds.'[107] It is self-evident that in this approach, as Zbigniew Rau writes, 'the precondition for the existence of civil society is a normative consensus of its members. This consensus concerns the moral and social order that prevails among them. It concerns both the central moral values on which civil society is based and the rules of behaviour of its members – who are to promote rather than hinder the enforcement of those rules. It is this normative consensus that ties together the members of civil society and makes them a moral community and a distinct entity that can then act as a whole.'[108]

Few people in democratic opposition circles brought themselves to question these 'moralizing ideas of civil society as a kingdom of people liberated from totalitarianism and who by this act all become – on top of this – dynamic activists of the opposition and angels at the same time'.[109] Waldemar Kuczyński, from whose 1988 article I quoted the above passage, was perhaps the only author who raised the problem of 'the expansion of civil society to the economic sphere' in general, and asserted that until this happened, the actions of such a civil society would be only a *hobby* adding colour to life and with no real influence on the mainstream of collective life. He went on to argue that for this reason 'it is essential to support everything that leads to expansion of the area of private and group economic activity guided by the motive of profit and getting rich'.[110] But this remained a voice crying out in the wilderness, more precisely a voice drowned out by voices from a different ideological camp, which is the subject of the next chapter.

---

[106] J. Kuroń, *Polityka i odpowiedzialność*, op. cit., p. 133.

[107] A. Seligman, *The Idea of Civil Society*, op. cit., p. 204.

[108] Z. Rau, 'Introduction', in *The Reemergence of Civil Society in Eastern Europe and the Soviet Union*, op. cit., p. 6.

[109] Waldemar Kuczyński, 'Nomenklatura i bezpartyjni (dok.)', *Kultura* 1988, no. 10/493, p. 87.

[110] Ibid., p. 86.

Generally, civil society was supposed to be based on recognition of the common *cultural identity* of its members,[111] an identity that needs no economic infrastructure.

12. *Limitations of the idea of civil society*

It is not my intention here to criticize the idea of civil society, because some of its weaknesses became all too obvious and also because I completely agree with the opinion that even the fallacies it contains may be called *ingenious*.[112] None the less, it is worth dwelling on some of the limitations of this idea, which have resulted in a growing crisis of the idea observable for the past few years in all of the countries of Eastern Europe in which it has appeared – a crisis also perceived by sympathizers and enthusiastic supporters of the idea.[113] I believe that Michael Walzer expressed not only his own personal disappointment when, after rereading G. Konrad's *Antipolitics*, he wrote: 'His argument seemed right to me when I first read his book. Looking back . . . it is easy to see how much it was a product of his time – and how short that time was!'[114]

Three kinds of limitations seem involved here. The first of them is connected with the approach to the civil society and state relationship; the second with the underdevelopment of economic views, and the lack of any explanation of how it is possible to establish an independent society in conditions in which the state has almost complete control over the economy and in which most citizens are state employees who are dependent on their monopolistic employer in manifold ways; the third with the all too general vision of the good society, the social fascination with unity, and little under-standing of the existing divisions and conflicts if they are not directly linked with the basic we/they distinction.

On the basis of anti-politics these limitations could not be overcome, and it is in them that today's 'demobilization' of civil society has its main source. 'The program that was ingenious in one epoch became irrelevant the moment it succeeded.'[115]

[111] See Michael D. Kennedy, *Professionals, Power and Solidarity in Poland*, op. cit., p. 165.

[112] This word was borrowed from Ken Jowitt by David Ost, who calls attention to the effectiveness of the strategy of 'societal democratization' (*Solidarity and the Politics of Anti-Politics*, op. cit., p. 57).

[113] See Andrew Arato, 'Civil Society in Emerging Democracies: Poland and Hungary' (paper read in December 1991).

[114] M. Walzer, 'The Civil Society Argument', op. cit, p. 102.

[115] D. Ost, *Solidarity and the Politics of Anti-Politics*, op. cit., p. 57. Bruce Ackerman wrote: 'These calls for existential integrity are not nearly enough, however, to define the challenges of politics after the revolution – when the state will not wither away, but must

1. Let us begin with the radical opposition of civil society to the state. Even though before 1989 there were solid grounds for this distinction and it contained a still valid message about the superficiality of purely political changes, in the long run it was untenable for at least two reasons. First, notwithstanding spectacular successes in the symbolic sphere, the construction of civil society could not make much lasting headway in Eastern Europe 'without touching the heart of state power'.[116]

Second, it is by no means obvious whether it had ever been possible to create such a society anywhere without state power. However strongly civil society had been opposed to political society in the past, this opposition was never accompanied by the belief that the former could arise spontaneously and be self-sufficient. Quite the reverse, the latter was regarded as a complement and enhancement of the former.[117] The independence of civil society from the state does not consist in the fact that it can do without the state, but rather in the fact that it complements the state in collective life with other functions and, so to say, operates on a different principle. This does not even rule out an active role of the state in shaping civil society. Michael Kennedy made the keen observation that 'the *institutions* of civil society cannot be made without state intervention. Ultimately, a democratic polity, the rule of law based on civil liberties, and an independent judiciary can be made only with transformative gestures from above and below, by authorities and society.'[118] Western experiences seem indisputable in this respect.

It is worth noting that the author quoted touches on matters that were of minor importance in the East European idea of civil society; it was even sometimes emphasized there that the strong side of civil society is the primacy of morality in relation to the law.[119] Being primarily a moral community, civil society as such needed no legal regulations; it was rather civil society that was called upon to pass judgment on the existing legal regulations governing the activities of the state and having the aim of limiting these activities. It must be remembered, however, that with the exception of the year or so of the legal existence of Solidarity, civil society

be reorganized to support an open and just society' (*The Future of Liberal Revolution* (New Haven CT: Yale University Press, 1992), p. 32). See Jan Gross, 'Poland: From Civil Society to Political Nation', in *Eastern Europe in Revolution*, ed. Ivo Banac, op. cit., pp. 56–7.

[116] Colin Barker, *Festival of the Oppressed: Solidarity, Reform and Revolution in Poland, 1980–81* (London: Bookmarks, 1986), p. 149.

[117] See Victor M. Perez-Diaz, 'Civil Society and the State: Rise and Fall of the State as the Bearer of a Moral Project', *La Revue Tocqueville* 1992, vol. XII, no. 2, pp. 5–30.

[118] Michael D. Kennedy, *Professionals, Power and Solidarity in Poland*, op. cit., p. 353.

[119] See Václav Belohradsky, 'Trois themes libéraux pour la dissidence', *L'Autre Europe* 1988, no. 15–16, pp. 13–14.

in Eastern Europe functioned in a very limited area (which accounts for the constantly recurring *island* metaphor); and so we may well ask whether civil society in the same sense as civil societies of the West – only in embryonic form – ever existed at all or even could exist in Eastern Europe. I Ieave this question unanswered, being content to express my doubts that, in light of all that has been said thus far, this is a rhetorical question.

Admittedly, some thinkers were well aware of the limitations of the civil society idea when they emphasized that it would not be able to enter into some important areas of collective life[120] or that in the existing conditions it would be only a relatively separate entity. As Václav Havel wrote, 'even Czechoslovak or Polish citizens who express themselves most freely are (mostly) employed in state institutions where they are paid a salary by the state, with which they buy food or consumer goods (mostly) in state-owned shops; they make use (mostly) of the state health service; they live (mostly) in state-owned flats and they observe the countless laws and regulations issued by the state. In other words, they are by no means completely independent.'[121] Sometimes, quite rarely, the view was expressed that the opposition of society to the state is a necessary evil.[122] The only justification for this, it was argued, is that the communist state is not and cannot be a form of social self-organization, which a good state can and should be. Generally speaking, however, there was little thinking about the state other than in negative terms.

Attention was focused not so much on the state as an institution and its functions as on the lawful foundations of state authority and on what values it should respect in its activities. The main issue was not so much what the state was supposed to do as what constituted its legitimacy or lack of legitimacy. People seemed more concerned with subjecting the state to social control than with seriously limiting its scope.

2. Although economic matters are important in and of themselves, in the context of the emerging civil society they should be looked at from one aspect in particular, namely, whether a civil society of *free time* can possibly exist. Excluding the economy from the field of vision led to a situation in which – as Havel, who rejected such a theoretical possibility, wrote – '"lower" functions are lodged in the official structure, while "higher" ones flourish in the "parallel *polis*"'.[123] On the surface this reminds us somewhat

---

[120] Petr Uhl, 'The Alternative Community as Revolutionary Avant-Garde', op. cit., p. 195

[121] V. Havel, *Parallel Polis*, ed. Benda et al., op. cit., pp. 233–4.

[122] Jiří Dienstbier, *Parallel Polis*, ed. Benda et al., op. cit., p. 230.

[123] V. Havel, *The Power of the Powerless*, op. cit., p. 86. One observer commented upon this as follows: 'The citizen becomes a kind of social amphibian, able to live in two very different environments' (Robert Sharlet, 'Dissent and the Contra-System in Eastern Europe', *Current History* 1985, vol. 84, no. 505, p. 356).

of liberal freedom coming to fruition in the private sphere, but the analogy is false. Firstly, the 'parallel *polis*' was supposed to be a *par excellence* public sphere; and, secondly, in the conditions of real socialism this integration with the official sphere was exceptionally strong due to the fact that employees were tied to their place of employment by many bonds that had nothing to do with work *per se*. Thus, the sphere of independence was greatly reduced and for most citizens – apart from a handful of 'professional revolutionaries' and members of the free professions – was limited to cultural pursuits in time off from work for the state.

In a certain sense, this was an even greater limitation than the limitation of political interests discussed earlier. Whereas in thinking about politics the perspective of liberalism or parliamentary democracy was generally accepted, and excluded any continuation of the existing system in the future, in economics there either was no clear perspective or it was essentially socialist, assuming social participation in creating a plan and overseeing its execution.[124] Some thought was given to workers' managerial cooperation as a way in which the society could participate in the economy, but there was no concrete programme to achieve this and its implementation was unthinkable without the consent and cooperation of the state as owner of the places of work. Perhaps for this reason, some advocates of civil society ruled out in advance its entry into the economy. In any case, there was no detailed plan for reconstruction of the economy that went beyond revisionist thinking in terms of a 'socialized' economy enhanced with market mechanisms, workers' managerial cooperation and multiple sectors. Even more important, economic change was conceived as a derivative of social change rather than as an inseparable part or even condition of the latter.

Thus, the economic horizon of the democratic opposition was quite narrow. The notorious incapacity of the existing economic system was attributed not so much to its inherent features as to the fact that it was linked with a political system that smothered initiative and discouraged people from action. Looked at from this point of view, the key to the economy was in civil society, so people thought that civil society could be reconstructed without simultaneously rebuilding economic relationships, which is the reverse of the process of social and economic development in the West. Such thinking not only narrowed the programme but also excluded an area from it that in the West has displayed exceptional dynamism. For this reason, the strong side of economic liberalism (see Chapter V) is its focus on the economy.

3. Let us move on to the third question. One of the main dilemmas that theorists of civil society have always faced is the problem of how to articulate and reconcile the conflicting *interests* of a society divided along many

---

[124] J. Kuroń, *Polityka i odpowiedzialność*, op. cit., p. 56.

lines. For some of them civil society was by definition 'the place where economic, social, ideological and religious conflicts originate and occur'.[125] In fact, the civil society idea in the nineteenth century declined because people began to doubt whether it would be able to solve this problem; and if it couldn't, they asked, what would replace it? One of the responses to this challenge was Hegel's conception of the state, while other thinkers stressed interactions among autonomous individuals and opposed all forms of collective life. Marx's criticism of civil society, which was equated with bourgeois society, was based on the assumption that this society was ruled by irreconcilable self-seeking interests. Consequently, social unity would be possible only after the 'elimination' of this society.

History aside, the salient feature of the idea of civil society discussed here was that conflicts of interests would be eliminated *within* civil society itself. This conception on the one hand treated civil society as distinct and separate from economic society, thus ignoring the economic mechanisms responsible for class differentiation, and on the other opposed civil society to political society. The first matter is self-evident, but the second one requires some commentary. The opposition of society to the state went hand-in-hand with the tendency to view all conflicts appearing in the former as emanating from the fundamental conflict between them and having their source in the state.[126] Thus, contradictions of views can be traced to the assimilation by some individuals of the official ideology or to their demoralization under the influence of the conditions created by the state; and the shocking inequalities of their material status more to privileges bestowed by the state on its sycophants than to competition among individuals as members of society.

Such a viewpoint unquestionably had its reasons, which were more than psychological. It resulted from discovery of the fact that – as David Ost stated – 'by nationalizing the entire economy . . . the communist parties in Eastern Europe really did "abolish classes"'[127] and created a situation in

---

[125] See Norberto Bobbio, *Democracy and Dictatorship: The Nature and Limits of State Power* (Minneapolis: University of Minnesota Press, 1989), p. 25.

[126] As Jacek Kuroń wrote: 'The conflict between society and the power elite takes precedence over all other social divisions' (*Polityka i odpowiedzialność*, op. cit., p. 52). According to C. Lefort, 'the vulnerability of the totalitarian system in a crisis situation stems from the fact that the internal social divisions are subordinated to a general division between the sphere of power and that of civil society. Poland is certainly not a homogeneous society; as elsewhere, particular interests clash within it. But it forms a common interest, an interest of civil society in opposition to the hold of the party and the bureaucracy' (*The Political Forms of Modern Society*, op. cit, p. 310).

[127] David Ost, *Shaping a New Politics in Poland: Interests and Politics in Post-Communist East Europe*, Program on Central and Eastern Europe Working Paper Series 8 (Harvard University, March 15–17 1991), p. 7. See also the same author's 'The Crisis of Liberalism in Poland', *Telos* 1991, no. 89, pp. 91–2.

which the members of one social group or another tended to blame their deprivations not on the members of some social group or another but on the state, which acted in the role of the Great Distributor in relation to all of them.[128] Viewed from this angle, the state appears as the agent of all social injustice and the source of all possible conflicts, while at the same time society looms as an area of potential harmony, a harmony that increases in proportion to the waning of state power. According to this view, the interests of the members of society are not essentially in conflict; members of society are all interested in the same thing – in having the state meet its obligations towards them or in removing the state if it fails to meet their needs.

The most utopian feature of this view of society was not that it postulated a temporary suspension of internal conflicts in the face of a common enemy, something which is well-grounded in social psychology; rather, its utopianism lay in the assumption that these conflicts, including conflicts connected with the distribution of social wealth, and timeless ethnic, national and religious conflicts, could be eliminated permanently. It is cause for reflection how often the finger of blame here was pointed solely at communism. Even today some observers see mostly 'survivals' of communism in these conflicts. Many people firmly believed that an 'existential moral revolution' would usher in a civil society having no internal antagonisms and focusing on common values, a society in which the only form of conflict would be a discussion among friends. This explains the mistrustful attitude towards political parties both before and after 1989. The conception discussed here seems to consider only one 'front' of the conflicts that were inevitable in the passage from autocracy to democracy – the 'front' of the fight against autocracy.[129]

13. *Is this really protoliberalism?*

After this characterization of the idea of civil society, it is time to return to the question about *protoliberalism*, from which I surely strayed further than I should have had we been concerned with this problem alone. However, a sketch of the broader context of this problem seemed necessary in order to show both of what today's liberalism may be a continuation and of what it may be a negation. The attitude of liberalism towards the body of ideas

---

[128] See Edmund Mokrzycki, 'Społeczne granice wschodnioeuropejskich reform ekonomicznych', *Krytyka* 1991, no. 36, pp. 54–5. Zygmunt Bauman, 'The Polish Predicament: A Model in Search of Class Interests', *Telos* 1992, no. 92, p. 117.

[129] See Adam Przeworski, *Democracy and the Market: Political and Economic Reforms in Eastern Europe and Latin America* (Cambridge: Cambridge University Press, 1991), pp. 66–7.

discussed in this chapter cannot be other than ambivalent.

The unmistakeable sign of an opening up towards liberalism (which before 1989 was almost non-existent on the East European political scene) was the growing popularity of the two main ideas discussed here – the idea of the *autonomy of the individual* taken as the starting point of politics (anti-politics in this case); and the idea of *civil society* as a sphere of activity independent from the state and undertaken spontaneously by individual subjects, who among themselves establish new relationships and agreements and, consequently, create new forms of public life.

In my opinion, both of these ideas were an important innovation in the political thought of the region, where individualism had been rare and had been suppressed by ideologies in service of the idea of community (the nation, followed by the people and classes). It was also important that, with the rise of this new individualism, human and civic rights were raised to the status of inalienable rights lying at the foundation of liberal democracy, which became taken for granted as the form of the future social order – notwithstanding the criticisms made of it. The civil society idea was definitely less innovative on account of certain similarities between it and the Polish idea of the 'nation without a state'. What is important, however, is that this idea forged a link to the Western political tradition and signalled a focusing of attention on more universal problems in addition to strictly national ones, which was a development that was immediately noticed outside the region.

A more careful analysis of both of these ideas shows, however, that we must not be overly hasty in classifying them as *liberal* ideas *per se* or in aligning them without reservations to any Western model. While the views discussed here fit within the frame of Western liberal democracy, in many respects they are still far removed from what even the most 'social' Western liberals are wont to profess.

Referring back to the celebrated dispute of recent years among political philosophers, the proponents of these views should be classified among communitarians rather than liberals.[130] They overemphasized the fact and need of the *community* and underemphasized the relative independence of the individual from society. In Ackerman's opinion, 'the aim of liberal revolution is not collective truth but individual freedom'.[131] Even though the starting point of the protoliberals was the autonomous individual, their goal was to liberate the individual from the power of the state in order to develop

---

[130] See Stephen Mulhall and Adam Swift, *Liberals and Communitarians* (Oxford: Blackwell, 1992). According to David Ost, 'This was a kind of liberal communitarianism, with an Arendtian or Habermasian vision of a fully open society based on the universal practice of citizenship rights' (*Shaping a New Politics in Poland*, p. 18).

[131] B. Ackerman, *The Future of Liberal Revolution*, op. cit., p. 32.

his or her *social* virtues. There was much in these views about the indispens-
ability of social solidarity and moral consensus, but there was little about the
institutional safeguards of individual liberties; there was much about
morality, but there was little about the material foundations of a free society,
hence little about the economy, which occupied a prominent place in the
social thought of not only liberals. Deserving of separate study is the
tendency to identify the postulated community with the nation, a tendency
which intensified as the opposition in Poland became a mass movement. To
sum this up, my intention has been to show how many *non-liberal* (which
does not necessarily mean anti-liberal) notions there were in the thinking of
the East European opposition circles.

It is hard to determine how much conscious choice there was in this of
other than liberal solutions (for example, Social Democratic ones); how
much of an effort to best meet the challenges of the specific situation of the
countries of real socialism, in which classic liberal conceptions, not to
mention those of all other 'ideologies', might turn out to be highly inadequate; and how much, finally, of the stubborn fascination with revisionist
ways of thinking, which made it hard to accept the idea that the social good
which people longed for would be *capitalist* in one way or another – lacking
the defects of real socialism but having many of the defects of capitalism.
Such a determination is really not so important, since each of these factors
unquestionably played a role. As a consequence, the germs of liberal
thought were enfeebled and intermingled with elements of another kind. In
the context of the subject-matter of this book, the very existence of these
liberal seeds deserves emphasis. It is quite another matter whether after 1989
liberalism will spring forth from these buds or grow in an entirely different
direction.

14. *The collectivism of Solidarity*

The story that I am telling is not confined to the circle of persons who
became known as 'dissidents' or the 'democratic opposition'. Without any
question this tale culminated in Solidarity, in which all of the Polish heroes
of this story had a greater or lesser part. In Solidarity the civil society idea
reached its apogee in practical terms, thanks to the existence of a mass social
movement. It is no accident that the term 'civil society' only began to spread
in the wake of the rising fortunes of Solidarity. Had it not been for these
experiences, many of the characteristics of civil society as a counterweight
to the communist state would have been meaningless.

The links between the democratic opposition and Solidarity in both
ideology and cadres led ever more ordinary people as well as writers to

believe that Polish dissidents had conceived an idea in which, as Marx would have said, Solidarity found its material force. To put it another way (this time after Lenin), the democratic opposition 'brought in' consciousness to the workers' movement, which achieved its historical success thanks to its alliance with the 'idea-generating' intelligentsia.

The flaw in this way of thinking, which has recently been pointed out by many researchers,[132] is not necessarily that it is basically false. Although there are good reasons to doubt it, more importantly it takes a one-sided view of the rebellion against communism and diverts attention away from differences and conflicts which first surfaced dimly in disputes within Solidarity on the movement's attitude towards the Workers' Defence Committee (KOR) and towards the KOR advisers associated with the movement.[133] Without prejudging whether this popular interpretation requires general revision, even if we accept it as true and reject arguments against it, it frequently happens that when an idea becomes widely disseminated its meaning also changes along with the increase in the number of its supporters. The idea adapts itself to a changed circle of recipients and becomes more concrete. Thus, we may well ask what Solidarity *changed* in the social views discussed above; and in the case of Solidarity are we still dealing with protoliberalism?

Solidarity signified a rather fundamental change of position in respect to the two ideas discussed in this chapter. The idea of the autonomy of the individual, which underpinned the dissident movement, simply disappeared; the idea of civil society, on the other hand, was adapted to a different situation, to the mentality and tradition of a different social circle.

I contend that the elements of liberal thought distinguished earlier were reduced, but were not completely eliminated. Solidarity, which arose from the rebellion against dictatorship, clung to a persistent defence of human and civic rights and to the perspective of liberal democracy as the most desirable political order. In a certain sense, it even went further in this direction than its predecessors by advancing the postulate of free elections in the face of a reassessment of the situation and balance of forces, which led to an increase of strictly political interests. Even though its programme was limited in this respect (Jacek Kuroń's idea of the 'self-limiting revolution'), growing

[132] See especially Roman Laba, *The Roots of Solidarity: A Political Sociology of Poland's Working-Class Democratization* (Princeton NJ: Princeton University Press, 1991); and Lawrence Goodwyn, *Breaking the Barrier: The Rise of Solidarity in Poland* (New York: Oxford University Press, 1991). Goodwyn's, Laba's and Ost's books are discussed by Andrzej Tymowski in his article 'Workers vs. Intellectuals in "Solidarność"', *Telos* 1991–2, no. 90.

[133] See Jerzy Holzer, *Solidarność 1980–1981: Geneza i historia* (Warsaw: Krąg, 1983), pp. 184–5.

political consciousness was evident in the main current of the trade union's activities and even more so on its fringes.

Thus, we can fully agree with the opinion of Ash, who strongly emphasizes the syncretism of Solidarity, that it was 'predominantly liberal democratic in its political vision'.[134] Although it is somewhat exaggerated, we can also accept the view of Ken Jowitt that '"Solidarity" is the most powerful and consequential liberal democratic revolution since the French Revolution.'[135] This does not alter the fact that Solidarity was of little importance for the development of liberalism in Poland, to which it made at most an indirect contribution by introducing a 'revaluation of values' to politics and society at large. Below we will see how critically liberals, even those who had emerged from it, would evaluate Solidarity. It must be remembered that Solidarity was a very heterogeneous movement and had attracted many people simply because it offered the only opportunity for effective actions in the public domain.

Whether Solidarity was or was not *socialist* will not be taken up here, because this is largely a question of semantics. The answer to this question depends on how one defines socialism and on whether one admits the possibility of a form of socialism other than real socialism. Besides, this problem is of marginal importance to our main subject, since there are all too many views which are not liberal and have nothing to do with socialism. It is only some liberals who reduce all ideological dilemmas to the dilemma: liberalism or socialism? Yet, since socialism is one of the largest and until recently one of the most influential non-liberal ideologies, we should say a few words about the 'socialism' of Solidarity.

The opinion on the socialist nature of Solidarity, shared by both its leftist sympathizers and rightist (including liberal) critics, is sometimes based on the absurd stereotype which associates everything that has to do with workers with socialism and sometimes on an analysis of the movement's views. Especially on social issues these views rarely contained anything which, with a broad enough definition of socialism, would prevent one from asserting that Solidarity 'resembled a socialist movement in all but name'.[136] Finally, it was argued that Solidarity was socialist because it had

---

[134] Timothy Garton Ash, *The Polish Revolution: Solidarity, 1980–82* (London: Cape, 1983), p. 231.

[135] Ken Jowitt, 'The Leninist Extinction', *The Crisis of Leninism and the Decline of the Left: The Revolutions of 1989*, ed. Daniel Chirot (Seattle: University of Washington Press, 1991), p. 77.

[136] Michael D. Kennedy, *Professionals, Power and Solidarity in Poland*, op. cit., p. 84. Andrzej Walicki wrote: '"Solidarity" is a product of socialism. It might be furiously critical of socialism on the conscious level, but it is deeply socialist on the unconscious

opposed a fundamentally different model of the economy to real socialism.

The contrary viewpoint states that in its opposition to real socialism Solidarity stressed Christian and nationalist slogans and only half-heartedly espoused socialist ones. What is more, even this lukewarm attachment to socialist values weakened over time. In the face of the strong pressure by the government to keep the 'independent and autonomous' trade union within the bounds of 'socialism' by limiting criticism of the status quo to a critique of the 'distortions' of real socialism, it must be concluded that there was little enthusiasm in the trade union for calling it a socialist movement.

It is not a question of whether Solidarity openly acknowledged socialism or even whether it was in fact socialist irrespective of its various official declarations. The problem is whether it was *collectivist* in any socialist or non-socialist meaning of the word. When the question is put this way, the answer must be in the affirmative; and this answer determines my position on Solidarity and liberalism and on Solidarity and the democratic opposition which was its forerunner and which I described as a protoliberal movement.

What are the main arguments in favour of this affirmative answer? Without going into detail on a subject that fills an entire library,[137] I confine my attention to three matters which seem most germane to the subject-matter of this work.

1. In contrast to the democratic opposition of the 1970s, Solidarity from the very outset constituted itself not as a nascent community of like-minded individuals but as the representative of an *already existing community* (whether defined in class or national categories), which demanded the satisfaction of its needs. The decision to join the movement was based not so much on an individual moral choice as on whether a person regarded himself or herself as a member of this community. The main motive was consciousness of belonging and the desire to be *together*. While it is true that Solidarity was also a kind of 'moral crusade',[138] the subject of the crusade in this case was not individuals; it was the collectivity understood as

level – if by socialism we mean egalitarianism and collectivism, the primacy of politics over economics, cancelling the objective laws of the market: belief that political power can and should regulate everything in social life' ('Liberalism in Poland', *Critical Review* 1988, vol. 2, no. 1, p. 8).

[137] A good number of these works are journalistic accounts. In addition to the already cited works of Ash, Goodwyn, Kennedy, Laba, Ost and Holzer, the following most valuable, often exemplary, studies can be mentioned: Sergiusz Kowalski, *Krytyka Solidarnościowego rozumu: Studium z socjologii myślenia potocznego* (Warsaw: PEN, 1990); Jadwiga Staniszkis, *Poland's Self-Limiting Revolution* (Princeton NJ: Princeton University Press, 1984); Alain Touraine et al., *Solidarité: Analyse d'un mouvement social. Pologne 1980–1981* (Paris: Fayard, 1982).

[138] Z. A. Pełczyński, 'Solidarity and "The Rebirth of Civil Society" in Poland, 1976–81', op. cit., p. 372.

a *collective subject* striving to regain its rights, which appeared absolutely unquestionable precisely because they were vested in the collectivity. This collectivist point of view had far-reaching consequences. The postulates put forward had to be justified not so much before the tribunal of the conscience and reason of the individual person as by what the majority of the collectivity affected by these postulates thought and felt. What is more, this collectivity was greatly idealized and became completely unlike the actual collectivity, which for long years had been under the heel of dictatorship and had been more or less demoralized under this rule. Now this collectivity presented itself as purified by the *catharsis* of rebellion. Having been thus cleansed, it no longer needed internal reform, the 'moral and existential revolution' spoken of by the dissidents. It simply needed to be freed from its chains. There was a strong belief that this could happen here and now, notwithstanding the existing difficulties and limitations, because everything depended on the attitude of the majority demanding its rights.

2. By definition, this collective subject represents the social *majority*, and hence its demands require no other validation apart from stating whose aspirations these are. Politics is nothing more than a search for an adequate expression of the general will. More important than whether these aspirations are consistent with some universal principles or other is whether they are really shared by the majority, and this is determined in the course of an unceasing debate. From this point of view, *democracy* is absolutely necessary both as an ideological platform and a social engineering directive.

Starting out on the path of democratic practices was unquestionably one of Solidarity's historical contributions. At least two things should be remembered, however. First, democracy in and of itself is not the path to freedom; even if it is a necessary condition of freedom, it is not a sufficient one, as liberals have correctly pointed out.[139] Second, democracy means admitting to public life everything that occupies a prominent place in the consciousness and subconsciousness of members of the collectivity. Consequently, elements of the social heritage may come to the fore that are openly in contradiction with the vision of the good society which the initiators of the democratic changes had in mind. On the one hand, there is the threat of the expansion of nationalism and religious fundamentalism;[140] on the other,

---

[139] Perhaps the best discussion of this problem is by Norberto Bobbio in his *Liberalism and Democracy* (London: Verso, 1988).

[140] Adam Przeworski wrote: 'In spite of Havel's eloquent eulogies to the subversive power of truth, the spiritual force that provided the lasting source of opposition to communism was not a yearning for liberty . . ., but religion and nationalism; indeed, the historically specific amalgam of the two' (*Democracy and the Market*, op. cit., p. 93). See Jadwiga Staniszkis, *The Dynamics of the Breakthrough in Eastern Europe: The Polish Experience* (Berkeley: University of California Press, 1991), p. 215.

preservation of those elements of the official ideology linked with unful-filled promises of social justice, equality, and a state that cares for its citizens.[141] However we evaluate the trends coming to the surface (an assessment which does not necessarily have to be negative), they can hardly be regarded as conducive to liberalism. The role played by these trends in Solidarity made this movement a less favourable environment for liberal ideas than the circle of the dissident minority, which has no other recourse but to appeal to the conscience of the individual and to principles which may not be shared by the majority at a given moment.

3. The idea of civil society took on an entirely different meaning with the appearance of Solidarity. Above all, there was a tendency to identify civil society with society as such, which in an organized way opposed the government, with the result that the ideals of independence and self-organi-zation became a fact almost overnight.[142] While this idea remained highly normative, it now denoted not so much the limited scope of civil society as that the real society had been excessively idealized and had become a model for itself; it had not made any critical self-examination of itself, but acted, for better or worse, in accordance with its own exalted views of itself.

An ever more pressing problem became not what kind of society this was to be – for this was rather self-evident – but how its relationships with the state were to be arranged. The *real* society could not exist *beside* the state; it had to find some concrete formula of its relationships with the state: cooper-ation, confrontation, or cooperation and confrontation at the same time. In this respect, Solidarity opened a new chapter in the history of civil society in Eastern Europe. This chapter did not abolish the former opposition between society and the state (they remained *parties* that had to negotiate and come to terms with each other), but now social and political issues could no longer be considered in abstraction from the state. Moreover, the economy could no longer be ignored, and the powerful trade union had to take a stand on bread-and-butter issues. Thus, views inherited from the democratic opposi-tion evolved noticeably, but they did not go beyond the thresholds previ-ously set by the democratic opposition: in politics, the threshold of the fight for power; in economics, the threshold of the total rejection of the model of the socialist economy. People continued to cling to the illusion that social

---

[141] See Józef Tischner, *Etyka Solidarności oraz Homo Sovieticus* (Kraków: Znak, 1992), pp. 175 ff.

[142] On the anniversary of the August talks Adam Michnik wrote: 'For the first time in the history of the communist system civil society was reconstructed and a compromise was reached with the state' (*Szanse polskiej demokracji*, op. cit., p. 69). Jeffrey Goldfarb sees the watershed in the Pope's visit to Poland: 'Suddenly society saw itself set apart from the authorities' (*Beyond Glasnost: The Posttotalitarian Mind* (Chicago: University of Chicago Press, 1989), p. 22).

life as such may be an area of harmony and agreement, an illusion which even began to be regarded as one of the unquestionable achievements and the foundation of the ethos of Solidarity.

There is no room here to go into what happened with the ideas considered in this chapter during the period of the 'underground society' that existed in Poland after the imposition of martial law and the delegalization of Solidarity. Even though the term 'civil society' began to be used more widely during this period, no fundamental changes in the style of thinking described above seem to have taken place. The phraseology changed, patriotic rhetoric and symbols became more prominent, but no new idea appeared that changed the mental horizon sketched above.

15. Conclusion

As we see, the trend of thinking which can be regarded as protoliberal for some of its characteristic features did not lead to the emergence of *liberalism* in any of its 'mature' forms in Poland or in any of the other countries of Eastern Europe. This could not happen because protoliberals were either unable or unwilling to focus on the new model of the economy and because here, as a rule, elements of liberal thinking were intermingled with elements of collective thinking, which finally gained the upper hand as the goal of independence became disseminated among the masses. In this case, anti-state non-conformism did not exclude social conformism and to a certain extent even assumed it, which shut off evolution in the direction of liberalism. This was not just a question of intellectual or moral predilections, but also was dictated by the situation in which the people of this movement acted and the kinds of problems they faced. 'Real' liberalism developed in response to a different situation and attempted to solve different problems. It will also be created by entirely different people.

V   Economic Liberalism: 'A Neglected Path of Anti-communism'[1]

*But I am waiting for a rightist opposition, ideologically
glorifying capitalism, the free market, individual economic
initiative – glorifying it just to spite the communists,
but openly, without inhibitions . . .[2]*

1. 'Creative' versus 'revolutionary' anti-communism

No matter how the historian of ideas evaluates the scope and importance of the protoliberal ideas discussed in the previous chapter, these remained unnoticeable for the wider circles of society and perhaps even for many of their creators and advocates, who never thought of having recourse to the liberal tradition. Only after the fact do some of them discover that from the beginning they have been speaking liberal prose.

The liberal tradition in Eastern Europe was not vigorous enough to provide a frame of reference for discussions conducted during the period of real socialism; furthermore, before 1989 hardly anyone except for the Last Mohicans of communism were keen on precisely stating their political or ideological affiliations. The opposition was generally content to take the side of values reviled by the communists and the idealized society as a counter force to the state. What mattered to the mass audience (in those few countries in which there was such an audience) was, on the one hand, criticism of the status quo that went beyond the sphere of private complaints, and, on the other, reclaiming social independence and 'agenticness' contained in catchwords of self-organization and reform, which did not have to have much in common with liberalism and, as a rule, did not.

Thus, protoliberalism in itself did not lead to any liberalism, especially

---

[1] The part of the title in quotation marks was borrowed from Bronisław Łagowski (see 'Dzielski i zaniedbana droga antykommunizm', in *Wiedzieć mądrość w wolności. Księga pamięci Mirosława Dzielskiego*, ed. Bogusław Chrobota (Kraków, 1991), pp. 41–5).

[2] Stefan Kisielewski, *Wszystko inaczej* (Warsaw: Oficyna Wydawnicza, 1986), p. 185.

not to economic liberalism as a 'system of ideas describing and propagating free-market capitalism';[3] people yearned for Western political institutions, a Western standard of living, Western freedom, etc. but not for capitalism, which, it should be remembered, until recently had also been rejected by many circles whose official programmes were anti-communist.

Even many people who admitted to some form of liberalism took pains to make sure they were not identified with 'liberalism of the capitalist economy'.[4] This protoliberalism coexisted comfortably with economic views which tended to be called 'socialist' by liberals who showed as little capacity for discrimination in respect to socialism as the communists showed in respect to 'bourgeois' views. What is more important, the economy, as we have seen, was not a top priority: the centre of attention was *civil* society, later followed by *political* society, but not *economic* society. There was a lot of truth in the statement of a Polish pamphleteer that people wanted to introduce Western democracy to Poland 'in a miraculously luxurious and easy way: skimming it off like cream from the Western economic system and placing it delicately on top of the socialist economic system'.[5]

Consequently, economic liberalism could come into existence on a wider scale only after the intellectual tradition created by the democratic opposition and then by Polish Solidarity had been overcome. This is not negated by the fact that many later liberals in one way or another had passed through Solidarity. It is one thing to join a great social movement in which the 'entire society' seems to be participating and to use the opportunities for public action created by this movement to 'take away a piece of power from the communists';[6] the logic of the development of ideas is quite another thing, however, and here this interests me more than the biographies of individuals, which in Poland so often dovetail with the history of Solidarity.

The first attempts to create a liberal political platform were closely linked with the 'revaluation of Solidarity as a crowd in action'[7] and with the

---

[3] Mirosław Dzielski, 'Wolni wobec wyboru (14 maja 1983)', *Duch nadchodzącego czasu* (Warsaw: 'Wektory', 1989), p. 101.

[4] See Tadeusz Kotarbiński, 'Odpowiedź, *Wybór pism* (Warsaw: PWN, 1958), vol. II, p. 208.

[5] Piotr Wierzbicki, *Myśli staroświeckiego Polaka* (London: Puls, 1985), p. 48.

[6] See Teresa Torańska's interview with Jan Krzysztof Bielecki in *Kultura* 1992, no. 9 (540), p. 106.

[7] See 'Liberalizm stosowany', a conversation among Jan Krzysztof Bielecki, Dariusz Filar, Jacek Kozłowski, Janusz Lewandowski and Donald Tusk in *Przegląd Polityczny* 1991, no. 1 (13), p. 9. One of the participants of the First Gdańsk Congress of Liberals stated: 'Only after the crushing of Solidarity was the intellectual and programmatic weakness of the Polish left laid bare. It lost its ideological impetus and turned out to be politically helpless, making room for other groupings' (*Przegląd Polityczny* 1989, no. 12, p. 60).

questioning of its methods of combating communism. The decisive date in this respect seems to be 13 December 1981. Some liberals, to be sure, had pronounced their separateness earlier, but others remained in Solidarity until 1989 or longer.[8] In any case, there is no doubt that – as Janusz Lewandowski said – liberalism 'was a separate, economically positivist opposition trend. Averse to empty gestures, oriented towards concrete changes, local and tangible . . ., this was an opposition overcoming the attitude of denial and boycott.'[9]

A condition for the appearance of economic liberalism, which Mirosław Dzielski called 'creative' anti-communism to distinguish it from 'revolutionary' anti-communism,[10] was rejection of both communism, which in Poland at the beginning of the 1980s was neither a novelty nor unusual, and popular 'revolutionary anti-communism'. The same author, who is commonly regarded as the main creator of contemporary Polish liberalism, wrote that, notwithstanding its unquestionable contributions, 'revolutionary anti-communism' contributed to the appearance 'of a political wasteland, on which one can only hear moralistic whining and patriotic barking'.[11]

In that situation, the rejection of communism was nothing exceptional (it had even become unattractive as an ideology for many leaders of the ruling party), but the change in motivation deserves careful attention. For liberals, the critique of communism became primarily *economic* and lost its connection with the political critique of totalitarianism. Liberals were inclined to believe that the worst thing about communism is not that it is authoritarian or totalitarian (the latter feature of East European, especially Polish, communism had been questioned along with other dogmas of 'revolutionary anti-communism'), but that its economic programme is completely ineffective and has disastrous consequences for society. This change in the main line of criticism of communism meant a change in the strategy of combating it and

---

[8] Without going into the details of the history of events, it should be mentioned that before 1981 (apart from Stefan Kisielewski, who 'always' had appeared in this role) Mirosław Dzielski and Janusz Korwin-Mikke had professed themselves as liberals. Today the most influential circle of liberals, the Gdańsk ones, from which the Liberal-Democratic Congress emerged, constituted itself after martial law. Complications resulting from the attitude of liberals towards Solidarity are best exemplified in the biography of Dzielski, who admitted that the origination of Solidarity bowled him over and forced him to revise his earlier views, to which he subsequently returned, however. (See 'Robota w "bazie",' *Duch nadchodzącego czasu*, op. cit., p. 65.)

[9] Janusz Lewandowski, 'Jaki liberalizm jest Polsce potrzebny?', *Kongres Liberalno-Demokratyczny. Biuletyn Informacjny*, March-April 1992, no. 3 (11), p. 12.

[10] See M. Dzielski, 'Potrzeba twórczego antykomunizmu (21 listopada 1983)', *Duch nadchodzącego czasu*, op. cit., pp. 127–44.

[11] M. Dzielski, 'Jak zachować władze w PRL?', *Duch nadchodzącego czasu*, op. cit., p. 8.

in the way of evaluating its opponents: what would matter was not so much the radicalism of political postulates as determination in fighting against the economic system imposed by communism. Mirosław Dzielski wrote: 'It is recognized that the person who is against communists automatically gives the best guarantee that he is not a communist. This was an adequate criterion fifteen years ago, but not today!'[12]

On the one hand, the rejection of anti-communism in its hitherto dominant form was based on the ascertainment of its ineffectiveness and lack of realism and, on the other, on the recognition that it is basically inconsistent or even make-believe. Hiding behind the facade of the political radicalism of anti-communism was a conception of the economy similar to the communist one, so anti-communism belongs to the same leftist ideological camp as communism.[13] For this reason, liberals believed, they had switched the dispute with communism to 'a parochial dilemma within socialism' on who would wield power and what this power would be like,[14] while – as Dzielski wrote – 'the important problem is not who will rule and how he will rule, but whether the government will be limited'[15] and whether it will permit the 'social cosmos' whose centre must be the economy to function freely. This debate with the democratic opposition obviously was conducted only with its Solidarity wing; the dissident movement that preceded Solidarity was either ignored completely or mentioned only curtly: for the liberals this was no longer a political problem.

The liberals perceived the 'revolutionary' anti-communists as people who, in the words of Stefan Kisielewski, 'had been imprisoned by the myth of the left and, instead of calling for a revolution, limited themselves to the claptrap of slogans postulating liberty and democracy, without touching the core of dictatorship. They flattered the West, extolling its political and cultural liberties, but did not venture to praise the free market and free production.'[16]

This meant not only moving away from really 'substantive' matters but also choosing a battlefield against communism in which victory was impossible. Communism not only had sufficient means to defend itself, but its defeat would simply have substituted one socialism with another. While this would have been a step forward at a given moment, it would not have

---

[12] 'Credo. Z Mirosławem Dzielskim rozmawia Wiesław Walendziak', *Widzieć mądrość w wolności*, op. cit., p. 20.

[13] M. Dzielski, 'Wolni wobec wyboru', op. cit., pp. 98–9.

[14] Ibid., p. 107.

[15] 'Okrakiem na barykadzie i co dalej (marzec 1983)', *Duch nadchodzącego czasu*, op. cit., p. 83.

[16] S. Kisielewski, *Wszystko inaczej*, op. cit., p. 334.

contributed much to the necessity for a radical change of the system. One of the liberal journalists wrote that 'Poles must . . . decide what they want. Whether to fumble blindly with the detonator of revolution and to believe that once the masses go out in the streets, all problems will be over . . . or to concentrate potential energy, reason and political strength on making more room for free enterprise, private business, and freedom.'[17]

The position of these 'new anti-politicians'[18] now sketched here only roughly constituted a very radical reorientation of the dispute with communism. Amending the economic programme of Solidarity in one way or another was no longer the issue. In the liberals' opinion, this programme in fact still posited control over the way the system functioned, and its foundations would have remained intact. Neither was it a matter of adding a new chapter on reconstruction of the economy to this programme, for this chapter would have been in conflict with the general, 'collectivist' (in the liberals' opinion), assumptions of the programme. Thus, the 'new anti-politicians' searched for an *entirely different programme*. Acceptance of this programme required a complete change in the way of thinking and the system of values, such as rejection of the belief in the self-contained value of democracy, freedom and equality, and recognition of the fundamental importance of individual freedom primarily manifesting itself in economic activity. To the liberals, the most radical postulates of Solidarity on economic arrangements seemed too moderate and clearly anachronistic. Liberals accorded them only relative value, and only in so far as these views could reduce central control over the economy.[19]

This different programme obviously also rested on a different diagnosis of the situation from the one which had fired the collective mind in Poland after the imposition of martial law and the delegalization of Solidarity. It was impossible to remain a liberal without rejecting the social vision

---

[17] Piotr Wierzbicki, 'Czas wyboru', *Głos* 1986, no. 3 (49), p. 10. After the fall of communism, this author seems to have changed his views. Now he seems to believe that revolutionary political changes are the most important. At one time, however, he was one of the most prominent advocates of the liberal economy.

[18] The phrase coined by Alexander Smolar in 'The Polish Opposition', in *Crisis and Reform in Eastern Europe*, ed. Ferenc Fehér and Andrew Arato (New Brunswick NJ: Transaction Publishers, 1991), p. 213.

[19] This applies in particular to workers' managerial cooperation, which some liberals initially strongly supported. See *Samorząd w dobie 'Solidarności'*, compiled by J. Lewandowski with the cooperation of Jan Szomberg (London: Odnowa, 1985). In an interview with Teresa Torańska, J. K. Bielecki summed up the matter pithily as follows: 'We wanted to take away a piece of power from the communists. Today, however, workers' managerial cooperation is a mortal danger to efficient management' (op. cit., p. 106). See Leszek Balcerowicz, *800 dni. Szok kontrolowany* (Warsaw: BGW, 1992), p. 12. For similar reasons, Dzielski reverted back to the idea of cooperatives.

reducing itself to a war between organized society and the communist state, a war whose outcome would have to be some division of power and thus institution of greater or lesser (for now) political democracy as an initial condition of any kind of progress at all.

Thus, liberals swam *against the stream of majority opinion* and ran the risk of finding themselves in the morally ambiguous position of 'straddling the barricade'.[20] And probably for this reason they did not enjoy wider popularity and did not have a noticeable influence on the course of events. None the less, in the second half of the 1980s their position began to be regarded as a serious political proposal at least in some circles of Polish society. Towards the end of 1987, Andrzej Walicki could write that 'they have already been successful in changing the intellectual climate of Poland'.[21]

As may be surmised, increasing doubts as to the prospects of 'revolutionary' anti-communism – understandable in light of the course of events – were mainly responsible for this volte-face. Solidarity's survival and later success are no evidence that it remained a political force after its dissolution; on the contrary, its power inhered in the fact that it symbolized the continuity of resistance against communism, which was rapidly losing the remnants of its social support, but not in universal support for Solidarity's programme. One may even doubt whether this programme was accepted by the vast majority of Solidarity sympathizers, who were more united by what they opposed than by what they supported.

It is also possible that the liberal orientation became more influential because ever more people in Poland were willing to cast their lot with private enterprise. After 1981 these ranks were swelled by ever larger numbers of politically active people, who precisely for their political activity had been deprived of 'normal' career chances in the state sector. The biographies of many 'Gdańsk' liberals are typical in this respect.

One of the conditions of a turn in this direction was that during this time the communist authorities cast off one ideological taboo after another, loosening the straitjacket of prohibitions and restrictions and even encouraging private economic initiative. Even members of the party took up private economic activity, which until recently had been regarded as something shameful.[22] There were all the indications that the authorities

---

[20] M. Dzielski, 'Okrakiem ma barykadzie', op. cit., pp. 80–6.

[21] Andrzej Walicki, 'Liberalism in Poland', *Critical Review* 1988, vol. 2, no. 1, p. 33.

[22] At the beginning of the ninth decade, Jan Tomasz Gross wrote about the appearance in Poland of 'an ethos of *enrichessez-vous* without a *laissez-faire*, liberal ideology – a spirit of petit-bourgeois capitalism without the Protestant ethic' ('Poland: Society and the State', in *East Central Europe: Yesterday – Today – Tomorrow*, ed. Milorad Drachkovitch (Stanford CA: Hoover Institution Press, 1982), p. 318).

would abandon the remnants of communist ideology and 'let go' of the economy, but would be reluctant to make any real political concessions. Yet, these changes should not be exaggerated. They were great enough to attract the attention of part of public opinion and inspire ideologists, but they were not far-reaching enough to lay a solid social foundation for economic liberalism. The 'new entrepreneurship' was still very limited in scope; even more important, it was necessarily entangled with the existing economic system and served to overcome its bottlenecks rather than competed with it directly.

Like the dissident movement, economic liberalism started from meetings of like-minded individuals, who then looked for social support and were aware that their only resource was the force of their arguments derived mainly from the economic theory and practice of the West. As we will see below, the problem of the social base will plague Polish liberalism for a long time. From the beginning it was clear that the social base must first be created and that this must be done in highly unfavourable conditions. Polish liberalism started out as an *elitist* movement, and for this reason was fated to be a marginal phenomenon as long as the political scene was shaped by the conflict of basic forces of that time.

Before 1989 there was no place for liberals on the main battle front, and they were not strong enough to shift this front in the direction of their own strategic plans. Thus, they worked on their conception, tried to popularize it as much as possible, and applied it on a limited scale. This was the *preparatory* period of contemporary Polish liberalism, only a harbinger of its real history. Even with its limitations, this liberalism was more visible in Poland than in the other countries of the region, in which it found almost no public expression. Paradoxically, liberalism in Poland owed its public expression to the 'revolutionary anti-communism', which first opened up the field of public discussion.

2. *Direction of the reorientation*

The conception that emerged at this time can be summed up in a few main points. It was best expressed in Mirosław Dzielski's underground publication *Duch nadchodzącego czasu* (*Spirit of the Time to Come*),[23] which does

---

[23] The bulk of this book consisted of articles written by Dzielski for the underground journal published by him in 1983–5 under the subtitle *Pismo chrześcijańsko-liberalne*, whose original title was *13 grudnia* and then (from March 1984) simply *13*. Mirosław Dzielski's role as the pioneer of contemporary Polish liberalism is virtually unquestioned, as is attested to by the commemorative book cited earlier and numerous other sources. Janusz Lewandowski, one of the leading Gdańsk liberals, wrote: 'At that time in Poland only one person was building the liberal political platform; this person was

not mean that it can be regarded as the conception of a single author. Although there is no question of Dzielski's leading role, there are reasons to believe that this conception emerged from group discussions and also that many people who did not participate in these Kraków discussions reached similar conclusions at more or less the same time.[24] The individual authorship of one idea or another is not the most important thing here. For the time being I am more interested in ideas which were hanging 'in the air' at that time. These ideas were not original intellectual discoveries, but were a carrying over to real socialism of the rudiments of liberal doctrine. While emphasizing the 'collective' nature of the most important liberal ideas, it should be remembered that we are dealing with a highly diverse community, a fact which would become fully evident only after 1989 when the 'hazy prospect of changing the political order turned into real reform'.[25]

1. The main intention of economic liberalism was to reverse the hierarchy of problems characteristic until then of both communism and its various opponents, by *pushing politics into the background*. Before this time, politics, in a certain sense, had been the main interest of even the ideologists of 'anti-politics'. In 1983 Stefan Kisielewski wrote that 'the new opposition should start by exerting social and economic pressure, not by hurrying to institute forms of Western political democracy, which was one of the mistakes of Solidarity, and in our conditions . . . had to take on a grotesque form. One first has to democratize the "base" by empowering society, and only after this start working on the "superstructure".'[26]

From this point of view, politics appeared as make-believe activity in a certain sense. Like moralizing, it did not lead to a change of the *economic* system, which – irrespective of a more or less democratic political form – determines the essence of communism. Replacing dictatorship by democracy and directors by workers' councils would not constitute a change of the system, for it would remain 'socialist'.[27] The concern was sometimes even expressed that democracy might strengthen undesirable tendencies in society on account of its 'objective economic interest', which is defended

---

Dzielski' ('Liberalizm stosowany', op. cit., p. 5). For more information on the beginnings of Polish liberalism see the articles of Andrzej Walicki, 'Liberalism in Poland', op. cit., and 'Notes on Jaruzelski's Poland', in *Crisis and Reform in Eastern Europe*, op. cit., pp. 335–91. I largely base my characterization of liberalism before 1989 on these articles.

[24] See 'I Gdański Kongres Liberałów – materiały', *Przegląd Polityczny* 1989, no. 12.

[25] Janusz Lewandowski, 'Pięć mitów prywatyzacji', *Gazeta Wyborcza*, 30 April 1992.

[26] S. Kisielewski, 'Wstęp do programu opozycji', *Bez cenzury* . . . (Paris: Editions Spotkania, 1987), pp. 265–6.

[27] M. Dzielski, 'Wolni wobec wyboru', op. cit., p. 99.

by liberals, and hence forcing through democracy is 'not only nonsensical but even harmful'.[28]

According to the 'revolutionary' anti-communists, communism is above all *totalitarianism* – a system based on political repression, an all-powerful police, censorship, etc.[29] From this point of view, 'socialization' of the means of production was not the greatest evil. There were even stern judges of communism who in their verdicts were inclined to regard state-control of the economy as one of communism's few saving graces.[30] These critics were not fully aware that the premise and foundation of communist 'totalitarianism' was replacement of the market by the state, which thanks to this not only extended control over society but completely absorbed it. Liberals on the other hand contended that communism was first and foremost an insane ideology of 'socialization' of the means of production, which on no account could be forgiven. One could put up temporarily with the repressive nature of communism (diminishing over time), but not with what it had done to the economy by driving the spirit of private initiative from it. In such a case, the institution of political democracy is not a sufficient or even a necessary condition of emerging from communism. Communism will cease to be dangerous only after extirpation of the remnants of its ideology hostile to the economy. If this is done, one can resign oneself to communism for a certain time. One can allow it to remain an autocratic system, for autocracy as such does not rule out economic freedom, as the example of Pinochet's Chile shows. What is more, autocracy is not a greater threat to economic freedom than democracy, but democracy is not the *sine qua non* for economic freedom. Autocracy may even facilitate the achievement of economic freedom.

Liberals tended to believe that communism was evolving in the direction of authoritarianism without an ideology and recommended adjusting the anti-communist strategy to this fact. In their opinion, there were two additional arguments in favour of this. First, in the countries of real socialism people are the least intent on democracy and are completely unprepared for it[31]; second, as a rule economic freedom paves the way for all other liberties, including political ones, and thus it is not a question of giving up political liberties but of choosing the right sequence of events.[32]

---

[28] Florian Krakowski [Wojciech Büchner], 'Czy potrzebna nam jest demokracja?', *Konkakt* 1986, no. 9, p. 7.

[29] Adam Michnik, 'Nietotalitarny komunizm u władzy istnieć nie może. Albo staje się totalitarny, albo przestaje być komunizmem', *Szanse polskiej demokracji* (London: Aneks, 1985), p. 97.

[30] See Milan Šimečka, *The Restoration of Order* (London: Verso, 1984), p. 148.

[31] M. Dzielski, 'Jak zachować władzę w PRL?', op. cit., pp. 11, 21.

[32] Ibid., pp. 19–20.

Insisting on political freedom as the first and main goal would be – as expressed in Leopold Staff's poem – like starting to build a house from the smoke coming out of the chimney. A positive example of the overcoming of communism is China and not Poland. As Dzielski wrote, in China we see a 'restoration of mercantile civilization', whereas in Poland a useless political debate is going on that contributes nothing to solving the basic problem and may even make it harder to solve by strengthening democratic and egalitarian illusions.[33]

2. Thus, economic liberalism *shifted anti-communist radicalism* from political to economic views. Moderate or even conciliatory in its political views,[34] it professed the need for a real revolution in the 'base', a revolution aimed at instituting a market economy or capitalism *tout court*. The liberals were the first to state this position straightforwardly, thereby going beyond the frame of earlier discussions on introducing market mechanisms which, despite the sharp criticisms of the socialist economy, did not reach such a conclusion.[35]

This does not mean that the liberal assessment of the political system existing in Poland was positive. Quite the contrary, even though it was unquestionably less unequivocally negative than the assessment prevailing in other anti-communist circles. Liberals saw the possibility (even a great one) of a gradual change of this system for the better and assumed that, since it was currently impossible to replace it by another one, without waiting for some Big Bang the proper thing to do was to take advantage of the existing opportunities to prepare the way for more far-reaching changes in the future. It cannot be said that all liberals were averse to and disrespectful of political democracy. In any case, such an attitude cannot be attributed to the Gdańsk circle. None the less – as Donald Tusk said – they shared the opinion that 'more important than combating a certain existing system, than striking at and breaking up the power structure, is attempting positive actions to fill in gaps, to limit this power, its omnipotent and ubiquitous rapacity'.[36]

This is why the dispute on totalitarianism taken up by Dzielski, among others, was so important.[37] The use of this term in analyses of the situation

[33] See M. Dzielski, 'Podróż do Chin (11 marca 1985 roku)', *Duch nadchodzącego czasu*, pp. 267ff.

[34] At the First Gdańsk Congress of Liberals Janusz Korwin-Mikke said: 'It is entirely indifferent to us who introduces liberal principles, Mr Wałęsa or Mr Rakowski. What matters is that they be introduced' ('Zapis dyskusji', *Przegląd Polityczny* 1989, no. 12, p. 71).

[35] See *Reform and Transformation in Eastern Europe: Soviet-type Economics on the Threshold of Change*, ed. Jano Mátyás Kovác and Marton Tardos (London: Routledge, 1992).

[36] Donald Tusk, 'Prawo do polityki', *Przegląd Polityczny* 1989, no. 12, p. 8. The monthly *Niepodległość*, which had appeared since 1982 and from November 1984 was

of that time obscured the unquestionable signs of evolution (theories of totalitarianism tended to treat it as a *par excellence* static system) on the one hand, and on the other reduced all possible relations of citizens with the authorities to obedience or rebellion, to 'collaboration' or struggle. The path sought by liberals did not fit into any conception of totalitarianism because it was supposed to be the path of compromise, as a consequence of which political power would completely change its nature. According to Dzielski, the compromise would consist in abandonment of communism by the ruling elite in exchange for respecting its political privileges and prerogatives. Communism would thereby be transformed into an 'ordinary' authoritarian government, a regime allowing the unrestricted development of economic activity and in time autonomous activity of other kinds,[38] which would become ever more natural as economic freedom expanded.

There was no sense in discussing matters with representatives of a system regarded as totalitarian. Yet, paradoxically, it was not the liberals who sat down at the Round Table but the 'revolutionaries' criticized by them. Dzielski's proposal appeared completely unrealistic and, in fact, was at the time; none the less, its starting point was the correct observation that what had really become important for the communist elites was staying in power rather than, as in the past, carrying out a certain ideological social design. It should also be remembered that Dzielski's idea originated when hardly anyone was expecting the imminent collapse of communism and the post-Yalta balance of forces. Thus, this was a strategy with a long time-horizon and, as such, perhaps quite sound. To be sure, its acceptance required immediate rejection of the vision of the communist state as a sinister force by definition in opposition to society. Dzielski made a distinction between the 'regime' and the 'system' (or the 'ruling elite' and the 'political order'); one could and should negotiate with the former if this in time can result in destruction of the latter.[39]

3. Consequently, there had to be a fundamental change in the *diagnosis of the situation* both in respect to the state and in respect to society. The stereotypes of the opposition were questioned in both cases. The state not only

the mouthpiece of the Liberal-Democratic Party 'Niepodległość', took an entirely different position. The authors writing in this journal came out strongly for liberalism and for this reason, among others, were critical of the legacy of the democratic opposition and Solidarity; none the less, they took a very radical position on political changes. However, this group did not play a major role and is generally not considered as part of the liberal orientation.

[37] M. Dzielski, 'Duch nadchodzącego czasu', in *Duch nadchodzącego czasu*, op. cit., pp. 173–97.

[38] M. Dzielski, 'Jak zachować władzę w PRL?', op. cit.

[39] See M. Dzielski, 'Credo', op. cit., p. 16; 'Budowa historycznego kompromisu', *Duch nadchodzącego czasu*, op. cit., p. 34.

ceased to be the embodiment of evil, but also was given a positive role to play in maintaining a balance of social forces and the tranquillity indispensable for fruitful economic activity. Only on the surface – said a participant of the First Gdańsk Congress of Liberals – is our thinking similar to the thinking of the advocates of social self-organization and an independent society. 'The main difference lies in the approach to politics. . . . The experiences of recent years have shown that politics cannot be rejected and neither can the state. The system cannot be transformed without the participation of state institutions – the state cannot be rejected or ignored, but must be changed.'[40]

Society ceased to be an idealized collective subject which, as soon as it is liberated from political compulsion, will immediately let loose its unlimited creative powers. The state lost its demonic features; society, on the other hand, its angelic ones. In light of the liberal diagnosis, Polish society was atomized, demoralized and permeated with socialist ideology. The decline of customs and habits would take generations to repair. There is no civil society as a fact; the term itself only denotes the desired direction of changes.[41] The term may be used only if one remembers that it means something different here than for the advocates of civil society spoken of in the previous chapter. Only on the surface did economic liberalism seem to be a logical fulfilment of that idea, which in reality proposed an entirely different path by which society could gain independence from the state.[42] Liberals did not attach much importance etc. to all of those forms of activity which attracted attention at home and abroad as the 'rediscovery of civil society'.[43] For them, these forms of activity were not harbingers of better times.

If seeds of an almost ideal future can be observed anywhere right now, it is only in the domain of non-state *economic* activity, within the reviled 'second economy'. Of this 'parallel Poland', 'places of remarkable intensification of freedom', Dzielski wrote with enthusiasm that it is not 'a militarized organization run by bureaucrats, but a civilized mercantile society in which money (not necessarily the złoty) functions and in which not force but freedom rules. The parallel Poles are smiling, friendly and cheerful – in contrast to the normal Poles, who are stiff, serious, sulky.'[44] The tone of

[40] The statement of Piotr Kapczyński, 'Zapis dyskusji', *Przegląd Polityczny* 1989, no. 12, p. 59.

[41] D. Tusk, 'Prawo do polityki', op. cit., p. 9.

[42] Timothy Garton Ash, *Pomimo i wbrew. Eseje o Europie Środkowej* (London: Polonia, 1990), p. 255.

[43] Under this title the American Helsinki Committee in 1986 published a large set of information about the various forms of non-state activity that had developed in Poland in the 1980s.

[44] M. Dzielski, 'Polska równoległa (15 kwietnia 1983 roku)', *Duch nadchodzącego czasu*, op. cit., p. 95.

this quotation is a bit waggish, but Dzielski's catchphrase – *we are building a parallel Poland from the Baltic to the Tatras* – expressed a very serious idea: the decisive battle with communism, opening the way to a reconstruction of 'civilization' and revival of society, would be fought on the field of economic activity.

An essential part of this revision of stereotypes had to be and was a change in views on the working class. Liberals not only ceased to view this class as the driving force of the desired social changes (a picture which Solidarity had made expressive and credible, thereby prolonging the life of the 'myth of the worker' derived from the official ideology). They also started to regard it as a potentially dangerous and conservative force, because it was an integral part of the economy instituted and perpetuated by communism. It is interesting that the notion of the opinion-creating intelligentsia disappears from liberal journalism along with the 'myth of the worker'.

With liberals the 'myth of the worker' and the allied intelligentsia are replaced by the myth of the entrepreneur and the *middle class*. Of course, this is not a middle class understood in one way or another as a part of the existing social structure; rather, it is presented as a great social need and a fundamental part of the future social structure. Liberals bestow a special civilizational mission on the middle class – after the fashion of similar ideological creations of the nineteenth century. As Dzielski wrote, 'the person who trades is the pillar of civilization, and in conditions of socialism also its heroic champion'.[45] It is hard to say to what extent statements of this kind were intended as theses about the emerging reality and to what extent they were attempts to create an ideological counterweight to the ideological biases prevalent in society.

4. Another slogan of economic liberals was *realism*,[46] with whose lack they charged the 'revolutionaries', thereby renewing in changed form the old Polish debate on the attitude towards organic work and insurrection. The 'constructive' opposition – like the positivists of the nineteenth century – was supposed to be distinguished by the view that 'even in such conditions as those in People's Poland today there exists a certain reality, one poorly identified theoretically from which one cannot abstract, but on which the future should be built, taking various limitations into consideration'.[47]

Expressions of this realism were Dzielski's programme for a 'historical compromise' with the communist authorities, the altered and rather critical evaluation of Polish society, and, finally, recognition that 'civilization'

---

[45] M. Dzielski, 'Szewczyk Dratewka ma pomysł', *Duch nadchodzącego czasu*, op. cit., p. 206.

[46] M. Dzielski, 'Jak zachować władzę w PRL?', op. cit., p. 19.

[47] M. Dzielski, 'Po śmierci księdza', *Duch nadchodzącego czasu*, op. cit., p. 223.

would not be rebuilt on the ruins of communism in a revolutionary act of creation but would probably take many years. Even more important was the rehabilitation of the concept of *interest* in politics – not the national or societal interest to which everyone was wont to refer, but private interest, which in Poland commonly was regarded as something shameful. 'Every society', Dzielski wrote, 'consists of groups and circles whose interests are largely in conflict',[48] and the task of politics is to somehow reconcile these interests, because 'a durable system cannot be based on enthusiasm alone'.[49] It is natural that liberals were the first to criticize 'revolutionary' anti-communism for relying solely on the 'ethics of convictions' and comprehending society as 'groups of spirits' instead of 'real people joined together by certain interests'.[50]

Dzielski's conception of the way out of communism rested on these somewhat timeworn truths on the role of interest. For this was a conception 'which took into consideration the forces that mattered in People's Poland'[51] and appealed to the interests of well-defined groups in the power apparatus. The author of *Duch nadchodzącego czasu* wrote that 'the opposition must understand the existential interests of the opposite side and even look after them'.[52] When he pondered on the need for gradual narrowing of the gulf between the authorities and society, he asked how to create 'areas of common interests between certain people of the power elite and certain social groups'.[53]

In short, the category of *interest* was an important feature of this style of thinking – in contrast to the style of thinking of the 'revolutionary' circles, which placed emphasis on imponderables, inflexible principles and emotions and remembered private interest only when they wanted to 'demask' an opponent by accusing him of neglecting the social interest out of egoism. The explanation of liberals' aversion to 'moralistic moans and patriotic barking' should be sought here. Another probable reason for taking the interests of the ruling group into consideration was the awareness that it represented a certain economic potential, which the supporters of liberal ideology still lacked.

It should be emphasized, however, that Dzielski, to whom I constantly refer here, was not an advocate of vulgar *Realpolitik*. On the contrary, he placed surprisingly strong emphasis on the relationship between politics and

[48] M. Dzielski, 'Budowa historycznego kompromize', *Duch nadchodzącego czasu*, p. 30.
[49] M. Dzielski, 'Szewczyk Dratewka', op. cit., p. 206.
[50] F. Krakowski [W. Büchner], 'Czy potrzebna nam jest demokracja?', op. cit., p. 8.
[51] M. Dzielski, 'Jak zachować władzę w PRL?', op. cit., p. 8.
[52] M. Dzielski, 'Po śmierci księdza', op. cit., p. 230.
[53] M. Dzielski, 'Robota w "bazie"', *Duch nadchodzącego czasu*, p. 67.

morality; and in rehabilitating the principle of compromise he clearly defined its limits and made its very possibility dependent on recognition of a minimum set of common values by both sides.[54] This unquestionably was linked with the Christian orientation of Dzielski's liberalism and was not necessarily characteristic of all liberals.[55] It seems important here to bear in mind that this programme appealed not to altruistic feelings but to egoistic interests, which was one of its characteristic features.

5. Finally, another innovation worth mentioning is that the circle discussed began to use *self-determination of liberalism* consistently in a rather strict sense, which until recently had been quite uncommon. While not too much importance should be attached to labels, it is hard to gainsay that they play a considerable role in politics. They force people to take into consideration a wider frame of reference and to state their views plainly enough, so that it is clear with what these views agree and disagree in the set of views to which a given label is usually applied. One can say that a name binds; its acceptance has more than classificatory import. It means ascription to such and not another tradition, which was of particular importance in Eastern Europe, where liberalism was relatively new and where the average recipient of political ideas did not readily associate it with particular trends of Western thought. There is no doubt that in this particular case the name matched the thing almost exactly and appeared more or less at the same time as the thing.

Dzielski not only formulated a number of opinions earlier and more clearly than others, but he also called them *liberal* and attempted to put them into a broader ideological and theoretical context.[56] Although quite modest against the background of contemporary liberal literature and containing many obscure passages, his small work of 1980 entitled 'Who Are the Liberals?' may be regarded as the symbolic starting point of contemporary Polish liberalism and perhaps even of East European liberalism as a whole.

I do not contend that this work is fully representative either of Dzielski himself, whose views later evolved,[57] or of all Polish liberalism. The point is that this work introduced basic categories of liberal thought into the contemporary Polish political language and created a new platform of discussion. Besides, it did this in a way acceptable to liberals of different orientations. This cannot be said of the writings of Janusz Korwin-Mikke, for example, even though he also played an important role in shaping the

[54] See M. Dzielski, 'Budowa historycznego kompromize', *Duch nadchodzącego czasu*, pp. 42–9.

[55] For a discussion of this question see the next chapter.

[56] M. Dzielski, 'Kim są liberałowie?', *Duch nadchodzącego czasu*, pp. 42–9.

[57] The initial emphasis on cooperatives was replaced by praise for private initiative alone.

liberal consciousness in Poland. Korwin-Mikke himself yields the palm to Dzielski, calling him a Moses in a posthumous eulogy.[58] Translations, a considerable number of which started to appear from the end of the 1970s, also played an important role in informing the reader of the specific features of the liberal attitude. The bulk of these publications, which were illegal at the time, were the first editions in Eastern Europe of the twentieth century classics of liberal thought.

For Polish liberals, the 1980s were primarily a time of study and discussions as well as practical activity on a rather small scale. This activity first took the form of publications and clubs 'shaping the way of thinking of the young intelligentsia and enabling them to understand the traditions and institutions of the West'.[59] This activity peaked in the second half of the decade with the formation of regional economic associations, which often grouped as many intellectuals as businessmen. Liberals made rather good use of this period; and when their first national meeting was held in Gdańsk at the end of 1988, they made up a rather sizeable group.[60] This was the start of an entirely new period, however – one which would require them to face problems they had only read about.

3. Various dimensions of the liberal reorientation

These first manifestations of economic liberalism had a few aspects worth clearly distinguishing.

First, they can be seen as an attempt to work out a new strategy of fighting for a change in the political order in the conditions of political stagnation existing from the time of imposition of martial law, an alternative strategy to the 'revolutionary' one, which – though still attractive for a large part of Polish society – gradually revealed its weaknesses. This new strategy shifted the emphasis from politics to the economy; it not only came out clearly in favour of capitalism, but also allowed for the possibility of a 'historical compromise' with communism as a political system as a means for reaching this goal. Second, they can be regarded as a quest for a new conception of abolishing communism as a system – a conception independent of whether the 'historical compromise' idea was sound. This conception was based on the assumption that communism would continue to exist for as long as the economy was not put on the capitalist path of development, since communism in essence was a way of organizing economic life.

[58] J. Korwin-Mikke, 'Mojżesz', in *Widzieć mądrość w wolności*, op. cit., p. 12.

[59] J. Lewandowski, 'Jaki liberalizm jest Polsce potrzebny?', op. cit., p. 12.

[60] See Maria Dunin-Wąsowicz, 'Kaganek liberalizmu', *Przegląd Tygodniowy*, no. 28 (380), p. 5. See *Przegląd Polityczny* 1989, no. 12.

Despite the multiplicity of political forms in the world today, only two economic systems are conceivable, hence rejecting communism means choosing capitalism; there is no other alternative. Third, in these early manifestations of liberalism one can detect the striving for a radical change in the way of thinking supposedly dominant in Polish society, reshaping its mentality by developing the spirit of entrepreneurship and removing the residues of collectivism.

In other words, this liberalism, which by mutual agreement can be called Dzielski's liberalism, was at the same time an idea for creating capitalism within the frame of a communist state; a collection of opinions on what communism is and the conditions for liquidating it; and, finally, a social philosophy attempting to establish a system of views and values in opposition to both communist values and to the one which became popular under the influence of 'revolutionary' anti-communism. In this last matter, the goal was to develop bourgeois virtues and liquidate the 'nobleman's-Marxist abhorrence for free trade' on the one hand, and on the other to exorcize the spirit of leftist tendencies, which in any of its manifestations was the greatest possible evil for many liberals.

Although these three themes were closely intertwined in Dzielski, each of them could stand on its own – including outside the boundaries of liberal thought. One can say that the author of *Spirit of the Time to Come* answered various political and psychological needs which neither the official ideology nor the opposition counterproposal was able to satisfy.

4. *Capitalism in a communist state*

On the surface, the idea of building capitalism within a communist state and with the gradually increasing acquiescence of this state – which was doubtful from the start – became completely obsolete in 1989, when it turned out that this state was far less durable than anyone could have imagined. Before the liberal experiment of buying over the *nomenklatura* and converting it to capitalism could be carried out, the communist state simply ceased to exist, and thus the question of the possibility of a 'historical compromise' remained unanswered for ever.

No matter how interesting the approach was in itself, any further discussion of it became pointless. From the practical point of view, there is really nothing to talk about. Yet, it may be that Dzielski's recipe will be proven correct in China, to which he so often alluded. However, this is not the subject-matter of this book; and even if events take such a course in China, this does not mean that Dzielski's idea would have worked at that time in Poland or Hungary. It is very likely that in those countries the political crisis was so grave that no compromise that left the *political* power of the communist party intact was possible. As long as there was not at least a limited political change, no one would have taken any concessions of this party seriously. The fate of the Mieczysław Rakowski administration shows this clearly, since he acted as though he had accepted Dzielski's proposal in its entirety.

Theoretically, one may ask whether Dzielski correctly gauged the evolutionary tendencies of real socialism in its decadent period, which were especially evident in Poland and Hungary. Both the changing policy in the 1980s in respect to the traditional private sector and the expansion of what Jadwiga Staniszkis described as 'political capitalism', which in common political language became known as 'making owners of the *nomen-klatura*',[61] seem to indicate that Dzielski was referring to realities to which future historians will have to pay careful attention. In any case, there is no doubt that they will describe the ninth decade in a much less romantic way than is done today and will pay more heed to the psychological, social and economic changes taking place at that time, changes which to some extent paved the way for further development, even though they had little to do with the struggles of Solidarity with 'totalitarianism'.

It is worth adding that the problem of a 'historical compromise' is indirectly linked with the later question of decommunization, towards which liberals took the following stance: we want the liquidation of communism as a system, not settling scores with people who were once communists; we want the reconstruction of institutions, not political gestures. After 1989 liberals emphasized that the main problems were 'closing the wide civilizational gap' and 'overcoming the hidden evil of communism in the form of habits and ways of thinking'[62] – a position completely in accord with the anti-political attitude demonstrated in the debate with 'revolutionary' anti-communism. This is a marginal issue which would not be worth mentioning except for the fact that it reveals a permanent feature of the liberal way of thinking.

5. How can communism be liquidated?

After 1989 the second thread of 'pre-political' liberalism distinguished above became all-important: what to do to achieve a real and not a sham

[61] Jadwiga Staniszkis, *The Dynamics of the Breakthrough in Eastern Europe: The Polish Experience*, trans. Chester A. Kisiel (Berkeley: University of California Press, 1991), Part I.

[62] Janusz Lewandowski, 'Wolność i odpowiedzialność', *Przegląd Polityczny* 1992, no. 3 (16), p. 43.

victory over communism and to pave the way for the birth of a free society? The role of liberals consisted largely in the fact that they were unequivocally in favour of *capitalism*, 'in a market economy without adjectives',[63] which unquestionably was a novelty. In one of his last interviews Dzielski stated: 'From the very beginning we thought about how to introduce capitalism in Poland. This was our theoretical idea – how to pass from real socialism to modern capitalism.'[64] Liberals never doubted for a moment that the pivotal matter was replacing the plan with the free market, state ownership with private ownership. When real socialism collapsed, this was not self-evident, because it was overshadowed by the question of political liberties and social demands. In the opinion of liberals, everything depended and depends on changing the economic system. That is why this chapter treats of *economic* liberalism and not liberalism *tout court*.

This obviously does not mean that the supporters of economic liberalism confined their interests to economic problems. In fact, it would even be impossible to do so, because – as has been correctly pointed out – 'a market economy can exist only in a market society'.[65] Peter L. Berger wrote: 'Economic institutions do not exist in a vacuum but rather in a context (or, if one prefers, a matrix) of social and political structures, cultural patterns, and, indeed, structures of consciousness (values, ideas, belief systems). An economic culture then contains a number of elements linked together in an empirical totality.'[66] Economic liberals were well aware of this – Dzielski, perhaps more than others, devoted a lot of attention to the question of 'moral rearmament' and was inclined to put his conception of capitalism in the broader context of a theory of civilization.

When I speak of *economic* liberalism, I have in mind mainly three things: first, according absolute primacy to the economic system; second, accepting liberal or neoliberal views on the economy in their orthodox form,[67] hence

---

[63] Václav Klaus, quoted from 'Poisoning of the Soul: New leaders of Russia and Central Europe Talk about the Evil Empire', compiled by Kevin Acker, *Policy Review*, Winter 1991, p. 63.

[64] M. Dzielski, 'Credo', op. cit., p. 12.

[65] Karl Polanyi, *The Great Transformation: The Political and Economic Origins of Our Time* (Boston: Beacon Press, 1962), p. 71.

[66] Peter L. Berger, *The Capitalist Revolution: Fifty Propositions about Prosperity, Equality and Liberty* (New York: Basic Books, 1991/1986), p. 24.

[67] I am aware that the concept 'orthodoxy' is not entirely clear in this case both because neoliberals are not of one mind and because their Polish pupils, who expressed themselves in rather general categories, did not clearly spell out their economic views. In speaking of 'orthodoxy', I have in mind above all their good intentions, as expressed in declarations of agreement with neoliberalism and justifying all conscious departures from it by appealing to exceptional and temporary circumstances, which, they believed, would not have made sense in 'normal' conditions.

favouring capitalism in its 'purest' possible form and rejecting the possibility of its hybridization, usually under the influence of some non-economic reasons or other; third, recognizing these views not only as a necessary but also as a sufficient condition of being a liberal and thus admitting their linkage with any views on non-economic matters as long as they are not in contradiction with the postulate of economic freedom.

Thus, an economic liberal does not have to be an advocate of political liberties or, even less so, of loose morals. There is no reason why in many respects he cannot be a conservative and an implacable enemy of 'leftist liberalism',[68] which was wont to defend all possible liberties, but readily consented to limitations of market freedom. Obviously, this does not imply that economic liberalism must always be rightist or conservative. This is a logical *non sequitur*, but, in fact, such is often the case. Rightist economic liberalism is most attractive in the post-communist world on account of the repulsion felt there – especially just after the fall of real socialism – for all leftist tendencies.

The thesis on economic liberals as the first and, initially, the only supporters of replacing real socialism with capitalism perhaps should be delimited somewhat. Their 'exclusive right to trade in capitalism in Poland' was questioned even before the breakthrough of 1989.[69] Soon after this, it turned out that nearly everyone was in favour of capitalism, and the dispute was over what kind of capitalism this would be and when it would be introduced.

It is hard to pinpoint the moment when the long growing awareness of the need for a *market* was transformed into the conviction that – to use Marx's terminology – the project of the socialist economy was based on false premises and that it was high time to trumpet a retreat on the entire front.

Theoretically, the difference between *supplementing* the plan with some market mechanisms and *replacing* the plan with the market is fundamental, but this difference was not always stressed. It should be remembered that economic discussions before 1989 were conducted in conditions of limited freedom of expression. It is quite possible that some of their participants, those who had no illusions about 'market socialism', did not express their views with full candour, believing that these views were too 'utopian' or too premature.

Leszek Balcerowicz recalls that these people may have believed that 'it is necessary to stay within the confines of real socialism, and this excludes the restitution of capitalism'.[70] The ideological and political taboos in existence

---

[68] I introduce this term in the meaning given to it by Wojciech Sadurski ('Etos lewicy, etos liberalny', *Po prostu*, 28 June 1990, no. 20).

[69] See Waldemar Kuczyński, 'Kłopoty z socjalizmem', *Kultura* 1988, no. 6, p. 28.

[70] L. Balcerowicz, *800 dni*, op. cit., p. 12.

at that time caused people to use euphemisms (they spoke of the superiority of a market economy over a command economy, but not of the superiority of capitalism over socialism) and ersatz formulas. It should also be remembered that for a long time not only communists and socialists but also people of other orientations otherwise hostile to the left were revolted by the word 'capitalism'.[71] Be that as it may, there is much evidence that for a considerable number of people interested in a radical transformation of the economy the restoration of capitalism as such did not seem either probable or desirable for a long time. There was perhaps only a glimmer of awareness that the introduction of market mechanisms depended greatly on a fundamental change of ownership relations, namely, on mass privatization. People tended to believe that the market was a neutral mechanism that could also be introduced successfully in conditions in which state ownership was absolutely dominant, providing the proper organizational changes were made.

To put it briefly, the long discussion on the defects of the command economy and the urgent need to reform it did not result in a clear proposal of an *alternative* system.[72] It is of little importance whether this happened on account of the attachment of economists to socialism, lack of imagination, or the rather realistic view that as long as the country remained within the sphere of influence of the USSR, any thoughts of a return to capitalism were an illusion. In any case, only the general *direction* of reform 'from Marx to the market' was laid out. It was unquestionably the liberals who put an equals sign between the market economy and capitalism and also stated that the biggest hurdle to be jumped over was the hurdle of *privatization*. Perhaps this is their biggest success so far, for they set the framework for discussions after 1989 on reconstruction of the social and political order. One can even speak of an exceptional success, because in a relatively short period of time their point of view became the dominant one, notwithstanding the continued popularity of euphemisms[73] and the fact that economic liberalism had a considerable number of opponents.

The point is that right after the breakthrough of 1989 the plane of

---

[71] See Michael Novak, *The Catholic Ethic and the Spirit of Capitalism* (New York: The Free Press, 1992), chapter 2.

[72] See J. M. Kovács, 'Epilogue', *Reform and Transformation in Eastern Europe*, op. cit., pp. 203ff.

[73] 'Clearly, when discussing the market economy most political forces in Eastern Europe are talking about capitalism. Nonetheless, for political reasons they consider it prudent not to mention the word': Misha Glenny, *The Rebirth of History* (Penguin Books, 1990), p. 191. A good example of this language was the speech given by Leszek Balcerowicz before the Polish Diet on 17 December 1990 on the economic reform programme which was later called the 'Balcerowicz Plan'. He spoke of a 'tried and tested model', 'market mechanisms', 'ownership structure of the developed countries', etc., but not about capitalism, whose reconstruction was just beginning.

discussion changed *de facto* into a discussion on how to introduce capitalism or, at most, what eventual changes should be made in the liberalism model of capitalism[74] and/or at what pace it should be introduced. In other words, the problem became how to find the most beneficent variety of capitalism but not something fundamentally different from capitalism. Almost no one any longer spoke of the 'third way'.[75] It is significant that this change took place earliest and most perceptibly in those countries in which liberals had most strongly marked their presence. In this sense, liberals played a considerable role in the most recent history of Eastern Europe, quite apart from whether their ideological success will be translated into a political one.

6. *A different civil society*

Economic liberals succeeded not only in radicalizing views on the indispensable reconstruction of the economy and in calling a spade a spade. Moving from the dilemma *totalitarianism or democracy?*, which dominated the thinking of opposition circles before the breakthrough of 1989, to the dilemma *socialism or capitalism?* had consequences that went far beyond the problem of choosing this or another path of economic development. Since they regarded themselves as economic experts and pragmatists and not ideologists, liberals did not speak out on this subject often, but the consequences are plainly visible – especially against the background of the views discussed in the previous chapter.

A radical change can be noticed in the notion of the emancipated individual on the one hand, and in the vision of civil society on the other. The gauge of the emancipation of the individual here is not so much participation in public life and the capacity to articulate the social interest as

[74] If one can regard as a discussion such statements as those of Adam Michnik: 'We agree that a market is necessary, but what kind of market? A ruthless market according to Milton Friedman and the Chicago Boys, or, perhaps a "market with a human face", a market that will not, in its ideological consequences, be an apology for egotism, brutality, and the Roman maxim *Homo homini lupus*. A market in which mercy rather than ruthlessness will pay, because only this kind of a market will allow the redistribution of goods, needed to save our country from upheavals of social discontent' ('The Moral and Spiritual Origins of Solidarity', in *Without Force or Lies: Voices from the Revolution of Central Europe in 1989–1990*, ed. William Brinton and Alan Rinzler (San Francisco: Mercury House, 1990), p. 248).

[75] I only found this formula in the programme of the Polish Social Democratic Party, but even there it was bracketed in quotation marks. See *Polska postępu, prawa i demokracji. Program społeczno-gospodarczy Socjaldemokracji Rzeczpospolitej Polskiej* (Warsaw, March 1991), p. 5. The leitmotif of this programme is construction of a 'social market economy' without 'painful social sacrifices'.

relying on his or her own powers and initiative as well as the factual limitation of state authority – even that of a democratic state.[76] Civil society is not
so much a moral community standing in opposition to the state as a network
of relationships among individuals, who pursue their own private interests
but have to come to an understanding and cooperate with one another. The
foundation of civil society is *economic*. This is worth emphasizing not only
because every society must have a 'base', but also because, according to
liberals, the economy must be separated from politics, thanks to which
protest against the state may be replaced by real independence. Liberals in
this way called attention to a dimension of civil society that is very important in its classic conceptions, but was almost completely ignored by the
East European democratic opposition, for which the most important thing
was civic spirit not economic growth, public opinion not the self-regulating
economy.[77]

The Marxian reduction of civil society to economic society certainly does
not merit imitation, and many authors have pointed out the flaws in this
conception.[78] The separation of civil society from the economy not only
loses an important element of classic conceptions, but also makes the
concept of little use for analysing the present situation in the post-communist countries. In these countries, the main business no longer is the fight
with 'totalitarian' subjugation but the construction of a new order. Even
earlier it had been pointed out that 'as soon as bread appears in the independent world in addition to freedom, this signifies a qualitative leap in
strengthening its foundations'.[79]

It is hard to disagree with Piotr Ogrodziński that 'at this stage the most
important question is the introduction of market mechanisms not only

[76] 'Freedom in Poland', said Donald Tusk, who seems to have been alluding to B.
Constant, 'is understood primarily as the freedom to participate in power as widely as
possible and not as the separation of power from private life. Poles understand freedom
more as the equal right of their shout to be heard than as freedom from state authority,
from moral compulsion.' Stated in an interview with Damian Kalbarczyk in
'Zdecentralizowane, neutralne, liberalne', *Res Publica Nowa* 1993, no. 2 (53), p. 22.

[77] I refer to the alternatives expressed by Ernest Gellner ('Civil Society in Historical
Context', *International Social Science Journal* 1991, 43 (129), p. 500), and Charles
Taylor ('Modes of Civil Society', *Public Culture* 1990, vol. 3, no. 1, p. 109).

[78] See Edward Shils, 'The Virtue of Civil Society', *Government and Opposition* 1991,
vol. 26, no. 2, pp. 9–10.

[79] Waldemar Kuczyński, 'Nomenklatura i bezpartyjni', *Kultura* 1988, no. 10 (493), p.
86. Antoni Z. Kaminski in 1988 wrote: 'A necessary guarantee of public life is the
existence of resources outside the direct control of the state. The institution of private
ownership ensures this.' See Antoni Z. Kamiński, 'Res Publica – Res Privata', in
Załamanie porządku etatystycznego, ed. Witold Morawski and Wiesława Kozek
(Warsaw: Instytut Socjologii UW, 1988), p. 104. See also E. Gellner, 'Civil Society in
Historical Context', op. cit., p. 498.

because this process lays the foundations for the independence of civil society, but also because it teaches a different form of co-operation – no longer a negative attitude characteristic of a crippled civil society, but the creation of social space in accordance with formal rules of the game'.[80]

The problem is that in the post-communist world an economy independent of the state has not yet been formed. Thus, at the present time it cannot be expected to play the society-creating role assigned to it by liberals. Besides, liberals themselves hardly believe that everything depends on economics. One cannot say that they ignore problems of morality, for instance, to which Mirosław Dzielski ascribed a key role. He had in mind not 'public virtue', which makes the individual a citizen, but traditional religious morality, which makes him or her a decent person regardless or whether he or she takes any part in public life.[81] Be that as it may, here we have two entirely different styles of thinking about the individual and society, though in both cases the starting point is individualistic. From this aspect, the contrast between liberalism and the collectivism which manifested itself in Solidarity is all the greater. To be sure, another matter of primary importance was rehabilitation of the state, which the civil society of liberals by no means could do without. What is interesting is that in the post-communist countries it is liberals who are so often advocates of the state, and a strong state at that. While their aim is to limit the presence of the state in social life, at the same time they are emphatically in favour of a strong state. The reason for this is that they attach greater importance to *the law*, which is indispensable for conducting normal economic activities. Thus, liberals have their own specific interpretation of the concept of civil society.

7. *Liberalism as a whip against the left*

The supporters of economic liberalism were and are perfectly well aware that what they propose differs fundamentally from what exists and from what people, even those most dissatisfied with things as they are, have

---

[80] Piotr Ogrodziński, *Pięć tekstów o społeczeństwie obywatelskim* (Warsaw: Instytut Studiów Politycznych PAN, 1991), p. 79. For more on the 'crippled' civil society see ibid., pp. 68–70.

[81] M. Dzielski, 'Kilka wstępnych uwag do dyskusji na temat przyczyn upadku obyczajów w PRL', *Duch nadchodzącego czasu*, p. 170. See Kazimierz Z. Sowa, 'Czy Mirosław Dzielski był liberałem?', *Socjologia – Społeczeństwo – Polityka* (Rzeszów: WSP, 1992), p. 158. Ethical problems occupy a prominent place in liberal thought, though not necessarily in religious colouring as in Dzielski. See 'Zdecentralizowane, neutralne, liberalne', Damian Kalbarczyk's interview with Donald Tusk. Also Jan Krzysztof Bielecki's speech at the National Electoral Convention of the Liberal-Democratic Congress of 19 July 1993.

become accustomed to. The several decades of real socialism which Eastern Europe has behind it and the fact that no real 'capitalist revolution' ever took place in this part of the continent have left their mark.

Therefore, not only laws and institutions need to be changed but also *morals*. Dzielski would even say that the enemy of freedom is not the police but 'morals based on the socialist social consciousness'.[82] He emphasized repeatedly that 'a reform cannot be . . . a good reform unless it is accompanied by a change in the social consciousness. All great advances of economic civilization were connected with social movements and affected the moral and economic sphere, the sphere of economic imagination, the sphere of psychology, praxeology, and in general were programmes for the individual.'[83] This had to be so, because for a liberal it was obvious that capitalism – unlike socialism – is not a system imposed by superior authority, but originates from an infinite number of spontaneous individual actions. For this reason, the development of capitalism is inconceivable without a change in people's ways of thinking and morals.

Carrying out such a change in a post-communist country of Eastern Europe is a doubly difficult task. On the one hand, there is the Weberian problem of overcoming economic traditionalism, which is deeply rooted in the region's past and cannot be reduced to the simple explanation of 'Sovietization' by any thinking person; on the other hand, there is the problem of socialist 'residues' in the minds of people, who spontaneously reject communism but in many cases cannot imagine life in conditions entirely different from those in which communism placed them. In addition, communism's failure to keep many of its ideological promises did not discredit all elements of its ideology in equal measure. Some of them immediately started to live a second life, freed from the suspicion that they do not make sense outside of the context in which they originated and are absolutely incompatible with the new order which their advocates supposedly favour.

Thus, the educational programme of liberalism had to consist of two parts. The first was nothing really new and may be regarded as a repetition of what had been done a hundred years ago by the Polish positivists. The latter taught their countrymen middle-class virtues and tried to convince them that making money is really a noble civic duty and that accelerated economic growth would be the greatest blessing for the country.[84] The

---

[82] M. Dzielski, 'Wolni wobec wyboru', op. cit., p. 104.

[83] M. Dzielski, 'Robota w "bazie"', op. cit., p. 70.

[84] See Jerzy Jedlicki, *Jakiej cywilizacji Polacy potrzebują. Studia z dziejów idei i wyobra ni XIX wieku* (Warsaw: PWN, 1988); and Andrzej Jaszczuk, *Spór pozytywistów z konserwatystami o przyszłość Polski, 1870–1903* (Warsaw: PWN, 1986).

arguments here really have not changed for centuries[85] and belong to the rudiments of economic liberalism, which hardly means that in certain situations they may not have the fascination of something new. To some extent, these are simply arguments in favour of *modernization*. When the communists came to power, they used the same arguments in praising the positivist tradition and attacking the romantic one.

Much more interesting is the second part of the educational programme. It is directed not against economic traditionalism but against *socialism* – irrespective of whether socialism strengthens traditionalism (Dzielski wrote of the 'nobleman's-Marxist abhorrence for free trade') or comes out against traditionalism. To an economic liberal the threat from socialism appears so grave that he tends to see it as the main enemy, against whom all social forces should be mobilized – including those which as a rule were anti-liberal in the past and, in the broader understanding of liberalism, still are.

This explains the tendency to define liberalism as a *rightist* orientation *par excellence* and to prune from it anything that might bring it close to even the moderate left, namely, the idea of the welfare state and democracy as a political value in itself. It also accounts for the clear preference in Eastern Europe for those currents of the liberal tradition which are most consistently anti-socialist in principle and for the avoidance of those whose 'progressivism' now and then had a leftist colouring. To be sure, it is hard to determine what is the cause and what is the effect here: hostility to all leftist tendencies may just as well be regarded as resulting from acceptance of the neoliberal interpretation of liberalism.

Be that as it may, in Eastern Europe economic liberalism (in the beginning at least) turned out to be a *whip against the left*. Sometimes this theme was stronger than anything else, and now and then only enthusiastic approbation of the free market betokened that we have to do with liberalism.[86] 'Liberal-conservative' rightist tendencies of this kind are not an East European invention, of course, because they have their Western counterparts.[87] Yet, it seems that the situation of the post-communist world was more conducive than any other to mixing various ideological ingredients and for using them simultaneously as an ideological weapon against

---

[85] See Albert O. Hirshman, *The Passions and the Interests: Arguments for Capitalism before Its Triumph* (Princeton NJ: Princeton University Press, 1976).

[86] *Stańczyk. Pismo Konserwatystów i Liberałów*, a journal appearing since 1986, may serve as an example.

[87] Ernest Gellner wrote of two kinds of rightist ideologies which 'logically . . . should be bitterly opposed to each other, and sometimes they were. In the contemporary West, they are most often blended in an illogical, incoherent cocktail, combining all those who resent central interference' ('Civil Society in Historical Context', op. cit., p. 497).

communism. Attempts to 'baptize' liberalism and fuse it with Christianity are an example of such a mixture. This question requires separate treatment, however, because something more is involved here than seeking allies on the right (see Chapter VI).

8. Liberalism after 1989: the perspective of the big leap

In broad outlines this was the ideological horizon of Polish liberalism before 1989 – in the period which I have called preparatory. In East European conditions, the ideas contained in this period were unquestionably quite innovative, but it cannot be said that any of them was a local invention. The originality lay more in the exceptional circumstances in which they were applied than in discovery in the strict sense of the word. What we are dealing with here is primarily an attempt to transplant one of the traditional Western ideologies to soil that was still under communist rule. The arguments in favour of such a transplantation were that this ideology seemed to provide answers to questions about real issues in the East and that it was experiencing its second youth in the West. East European liberals did not claim to be original. On the contrary, as an additional point in their favour they argued (and still argue) that they were professing views which had been successfully tried out elsewhere and were not advocating any risky experiment. The main argument in support of capitalism, in their opinion, is that it is a *tested* system. After the period of the socialist aberration, they simply wanted to live once again within the bounds of *normality*, to return to a *natural* socio-economic order, so to speak.[88]

They were aware that contemporary capitalism does not work in keeping with the classic rules of economic liberalism persistently recalled by neoliberal theoreticians,[89] but they thought that this was a temporary inconsistency whose end was forecast in the great 'turn to the right' symbolized until recently by Ronald Reagan and Margaret Thatcher. Besides, living as they did in the world of real socialism, they did not have to worry much about the real possibility of 'pure' capitalism. The most important thing was to choose the direction. In their opinion, every step in the right direction could be regarded as a success. In the world of real socialism the *feasibility* of the free market ideal did not present any special practical or

---

[88] Here it is worth quoting a characteristic statement of Dušan Třižka (Klaus's adviser): 'The market economy and democracy are natural conditions of mankind, and it should be possible to return to such a natural state.' In *The Velvet Revolution: Czechoslovakia, 1988–1991* (Boulder CO: Westview Press, 1992), p. 162.

[89] See M. Dzielski, 'Powrót cywilizacji (19 lutego 1985)', *Duch nadchodzącego czasu*, op. cit., pp. 256–66.

theoretical difficulties. As is only natural, the goal was to be realized gradually on the scale possible, which at that time was quite limited.

In a certain sense, the East European liberals of the 1980s found themselves in the situation of the earlier pioneers of capitalism, who, wrestling with all sorts of difficulties, tried to promote their point of view and created smaller or larger enclaves of the new civilization in a social environment hostile to them. The situation of the former was exceptional and more difficult only in that their social environment was not pre-capitalist but socialist and resisted capitalism more deliberately, doggedly and totally.

There is no evidence that at that time they saw themselves in the role of politicians and reformers on a national scale. Before he became a minister and then prime minister in Prague, Václav Klaus even wrote that 'true liberalism has as its main task the promoting of ideas, not the organizing of social reform'; he criticized 'reform romanticism' and in a Popperian spirit warned against reformatory radicalism, which 'can easily lead to another unproductive discontinuity which can be very harmful to the whole of society'.[90] Thus, liberalism simultaneously extolled capitalism and the evolutionary path to arriving at it, for any other way still had to seem highly unrealistic.

The strategy of the liberals before 1989 was necessarily a strategy of small steps taken either in opposition to the authorities or with their at most partial consent. Dzielski's 'historic compromise' could speed up evolution in the direction they desired, but any such compromise would not change the goal. A completely new situation came into being only after the fall of communist rule. Now, almost overnight, the possibility of *quickly introducing capitalism* in the most deliberate manner became a live issue. Given the additional circumstances (the degree to which the system of real socialism had lost its legitimacy, opening up to the capitalist West and the almost universal tendency to see it through rose-coloured glasses, the economic crisis, which could no longer be overcome by statist methods, etc.), such a possibility no longer looked like pure theory. Not only had the previous political obstacles suddenly disappeared, but the psychological climate was friendly to capitalism.

In other words, an opportunity came up to develop economic liberalism as *applied* liberalism, and, into the bargain, applied on a macro-social scale, which until now had been impossible for the supporters of capitalism in Eastern Europe. In Poland or Hungary it looked as though the programme for the 'restoration of capitalism' chosen by the non-communist authorities

---

[90] V. Klaus and T. Ježek, *Social Criticism*, op. cit., p. 37.

would have clear sailing.[91] The very fact that it was an openly non-communist programme greatly favoured this course at the very outset: the experience of real socialism legitimized capitalism as its obvious antithesis.

Moreover, people were under the strong illusion that this radical change of direction would improve the living standard of every household immediately. People were clearly unaware of the social costs of such an operation; they expected that it would bring only gains and no losses. They could not imagine what a shock it would be for many people to lose the security of guaranteed state employment and suddenly to be forced to rely on themselves. In any case, economic liberalism was presented with a great opportunity, which, not without reason, one of its representatives called 'an unbelievable stroke of good luck'[92] – very clearly aware of the fact that its adherents lacked everything except an idea; they had no tradition, no social base, no experience, no detailed programme of action, etc.

Seizing this opportunity carried a great risk. It meant setting out on the road of utopian social engineering, which in the past had not been part of the liberal programme. To remain faithful to their conception of the good society, they had to take up the unparalleled challenge of *building* a social order which they valued because people would do things by themselves, without the help of the government and a preconceived plan. Klaus himself, who shortly before the 'velvet revolution' had warned against discontinuity, now had to say: 'We need an unconstrained, unrestricted, full-fledged, unspoiled market economy, and we need it now.'[93]

9. Capitalism as an ideological project

It is obviously untrue that capitalism originated and developed in a completely spontaneous manner. Even if this happened here and there, this was the exception rather than the rule. Although Karl Polanyi certainly exaggerated when he said that 'the road to the free market was opened and

---

[91] As early as 1984, public opinion surveys in Poland showed more than eighty per cent of the society in favour of a free market. It is quite another matter what this support really meant in a society whose members had only a foggy notion of how a free market works. See Lena Kolarska-Bobińska, 'The Myth of the Market and the Reality of Reform', in *Polish Paradoxes*, ed. Stanisław Gomułka and Antony Polonsky (London: Routledge, 1990), pp. 160–79.

[92] Jan Krzysztof Bielecki in an interview entitled 'Liberalizm stosowany', *Przegląd Polityczny* 1991, no. 1 (13), p. 7. Klaus and Ježek wrote that 'history gave us an exceptional opportunity to try out what two months ago was pure liberal theory' (*Social Criticism*, op. cit., p. 39).

[93] Václav Klaus, *Dismantling Socialism: A Preliminary Report*. The 1991 John Bonython Lecture (Sydney: The Centre for Independent Studies, 1991), p. 4.

kept open by an enormous increase in continuous, centrally organized and controlled interventionism',[94] it can hardly be denied that its cradle was rocked not only by the 'Invisible Hand'. In many instances, the development of capitalism was spurred from above by governments or stimulated and accelerated by administrative measures.

It goes without saying that even the actions of a completely free market are dependent in many ways on conditions which only the state is capable of creating and maintaining, one of them being a proper system of legal safeguards. One can say that the independence of the economic system from the political system is completely attainable only on the micro-economic level, but remains utopian on the macro-economic level. Irrespective of the extent of intervention to promote capitalism in the past, such intervention had always undertaken to accelerate an ongoing process and to assist already active social forces. After the fall of communism in Eastern Europe, something more was involved, however. Whatever the scope of private enterprise, it did not represent a significant social force, even less so a political one. Since private ownership had been almost completely abolished here, it had to be re-created virtually *ex nihilo*. What is more, it had to be done quickly, whereas the formation of the capitalist economy, which occurred in more favourable historical conditions, usually lasted decades if not centuries.

Claus Offe summed up this situation well when he said:

> In contrast to its Western pendant, the market economy that is emerging in Eastern Europe will be, if in fact it emerges, 'political capitalism'. It is a capitalism designed, organized, and set into motion by reform elites. Its driving motive is not the prepolitical datum of the owner's (Lockean) natural right to his property and its free enjoyment. Rather, the driving motive is what in the case of Western countries was only discovered subsequently as a welcome functional side effect of an economic order based on the freedom to property, namely, the fact that an efficient economic mechanism serves at least arguably and in the long run the overall interest of society. Thus the reform elites, by taking responsibility for and helping to start a capitalist economic mechanism, represent the interests of society, without, however, being able in the process to rely upon and comply with the demands of an already existing class of capitalist owners and their interests, power, and ideological propositions.[95]

[94] Karl Polanyi, *The Great Transformation*, op. cit., p. 140.

[95] Claus Offe, 'Capitalism by Democratic Design? Democratic Theory Facing the Triple Transition in East Central Europe', *Social Research*, vol. 58, no. 4 (winter 1991), p. 877. See E. Gellner, 'Civil Society in Historical Context', op. cit., p. 497.

Thus, in a certain sense liberals in the post-communist countries found themselves in a position similar to the decades-earlier one of the communists who took up the task of building socialism: they (the communists) had an ideological *blueprint* of the future which they firmly believed in, but not much else. Favouring this social design were only theoretical arguments. According to these arguments, the practical implementation of this scheme was beneficial to society or its majority in the long run, but was not consistent with the current interests of members of society initiated under real socialism. The liberals had incomparably greater social consent for their project, but they could not expect this social support to last or deceive themselves that it was support given to liberalism as such. On the surface of things, liberals had a powerful argument. After all, they were proposing a 'tested' system, but they must have been aware that – as Peter Murrell wrote – the practical knowledge accumulated for centuries about how it works 'loses much of its value when applied far from the framework of activities in which it was acquired. It is hardly likely to be productive in deliberating the consequences of implementing some radical blueprint for a new society.'[96]

What is more, the liberal project had weaknesses inherent in the very nature of the system it advocated. Although capitalism really is a 'tested' system, there is no model of capitalism that has been conceived and tested as a model to be imitated. Kenneth Minogue convincingly argued

> that the whole idea of Capitalism rests upon a muddle, which confuses its logical grammar with that of the term 'Communism'. Communism is, in the fullest sense, a system: under Communist rule, the guiding party will determine a social plan of life for all members of the community. Now, in free liberal-democratic societies there is no single way of life or overriding set of values: rather, there is to be found an immense variety of ways of life sustained by individuals making their own decisions, individuals ordered only in terms of the abstractions of law. The central point is that societies of this kind are *not* 'systems' in the same sense as Communism is a system.[97]

In this respect, there is no symmetry between capitalism and communism.

In a certain sense, capitalism cannot be planned. When an attempt is made to do so, capitalism loses its main advantage, which is that it is not a contrived system, but is the by-product of countless individual actions taken irrespective of ideological motives. Capitalism owes its efficiency to the

---

[96] Peter Murrell, 'Conservative Political Philosophy and the Strategy of Economic Transition', *East European Politics and Societies* 1992, vol. 6, no. 1, p. 6.

[97] Kenneth Minogue, 'Societies Collapse, Faiths Linger: On Christians and Communists in Confusion', *Encounter* 1990, vol. 54, no. 2, p. 10.

empirical knowledge of individuals, which is *par excellence* practical knowledge.[98] Planned capitalism inevitably becomes like other rationalistic utopias whose starting points are abstract *principles* and not *practice*.[99] It may be contended that in this case these principles are just conclusions drawn from centuries of experience. Even if this is so, it does not really alter the situation: a good system first must be introduced; and a liberal is in danger of committing the sin of *constructivism*, which in the eyes of the classics of liberal thought was one of the cardinal sins.[100]

10. *The sin of constructivism*

I am aware that liberals in the post-communist countries could not avoid this 'sin' except at the price of capitulation, whose necessity, despite everything, was not obvious; and so this argument is not meant as a criticism of them. In their favour is the fact that those post-communist countries which did not apply the 'neoliberal shock therapy' and opted for gradual changes did not gain any tangible advantages. My sole concern here is to describe a situation in which economic liberalism had to start by accepting the *utopia* of capitalism and then search for ways to adapt this utopia to recalcitrant reality. On the other hand, economic liberals could make little use of elements of the liberal tradition that concern *methods* of action. The latter – best summarized in Popper's praise of social engineering – spoke against solutions which liberals regarded as salutary on account of their content. For a liberal in a post-communist country it would have been ideological suicide to accept Popper's view that 'it is not reasonable to assume that a complete reconstruction of our social system would lead at once to a workable system'.[101]

[98] See John Gray, *Hayek on Liberty* (Oxford: Blackwell, 1984), pp. 13–15; Peter Murrell, 'Conservative Political Philosophy', op. cit., pp. 3–11.

[99] 'Misled by the obviously superior efficiency and performance of capitalist institutions, such proposals mistakenly draw the conclusion that these institutions can be replicated according to instructions, whereas the deeper and more pertinent comparative lesson is that the failure of socialism rested precisely in the attempt to organize all economic processes according to a grand design. The notion that the more rational institutions can be implemented by conscious design thus duplicates the rationalist fallacy evidenced during the introduction of socialism with, for example, the Leninist notion that property relations could be changed overnight by administrative decree.' (David Stark, 'Path Dependence and Privatization Strategies in East Central Europe', *East European Politics and Societies* 1992, vol. 6, no. 1, pp. 17–18.)

[100] See John Gray, *Hayek on Liberty*, op. cit., pp. 27–30. Friedrich von Hayek, *New Studies in Philosophy, Politics, Economics and the History of Ideas* (London: Routledge and Kegan Paul, 1978).

[101] Karl R. Popper, *The Open Society and Its Enemies*, vol. I (Princeton NJ: Princeton University Press, 1971), pp. 167–8.

This had serious consequences for the features of liberalism in the post-communist world. The necessity of starting from a grand design of a new order which had no real base encouraged radical economic views and turning to those authorities of political economy who favoured 'pure' capitalism and condemned all moderate positions as 'socialism' in disguise. In effect, only in this way could capitalism be presented as a *system*, an approach which was indispensable in order to change macro-economic relationships. Only in this way could doubts resulting from the existence of *many* capitalisms be dispelled. From this point of view, the partiality of East European liberals for neoliberalism, astonishing to many Western observers, was not merely a close imitation of a fashionable world trend, which, despite everything, outside Eastern Europe remained limited. The leaning towards neoliberalism also resulted from the correct belief that its spokesmen articulated the most coherent model of capitalism as a system opposed to socialism in every respect and for this reason best suited to serve as the theoretical inspiration for reconstructing an economy based on socialist principles. A Polish journalist wrote: 'Liberalism offers the most radical form of escape from the totalitarian system, for it is its exact opposite.'[102] This accounts for the allure of neoliberalism and deafness to John Kenneth Galbraith's argument that it has little in common with East European reality,[103] or with any other reality for that matter. For East European liberals, all conceptions making use of models of a 'mixed' economy, whatever their merits in the eyes of Western economists, were simply inconsistent, lacked boldness, and yielded to socialist ways of thinking. Besides, there was a plethora of such conceptions, and no unequivocal arguments in favour of any of them.

Moreover, liberals (and some non-liberals as well) believed that arrangements inconsistent with orthodox liberalism had a logical basis for existence only in countries that had already achieved prosperity thanks to having had a free market for a long time. Here I omit many incidental factors such as the position of Western financial institutions, on which the post-communist countries became dependent in one way or another, or the viewpoint of most Western experts, for whom it was easier to think in simple neoliberal categories than to delve into the details of the local situation, as the taking of any other standpoint would have required.

Time and again this penchant of East European liberals for 'pure' capitalism evoked astonishment and criticism. Kazimierz Poznański wrote:

[102] Janusz Węgiełek, 'Pułapki liberalizmu', *Przegląd Polityczny* 1991, no. 1 (13), p. 11.
[103] John Kenneth Galbraith, 'The Rush to Capitalism', *New York Review of Books*, 15 October 1990, pp. 51–2.

'There is already growing evidence that liberalism has often been reduced in the region by many of its most devoted "disciples" to a few principles totally unrelated to the mainstream of liberal doctrine. It is largely deprived of its traditional concern for universal well-being and instead praises the "jungle" struggle for survival (or "private warfare").'[104]

Although otherwise I would be inclined to side with such criticisms, economic liberalism in its extreme form has its inner logic. Economic liberalism could abandon this inner logic only at the cost of losing its ideological identity; in coming out in favour of capitalism, it had to highlight those features of capitalism which distinguish it clearly from socialism. In any case, economic liberalism had to do this at the outset, when its supporters still had no political experience and were not fully aware of the social resistance they would encounter. Moving from theory to practice would show that a considerable number of liberals were quite flexible in their thinking. This flexibility was reflected in taking account of realities and making temporary concessions, but there was little inclination to revise principles previously recognized as absolutely true. Liberals were few and far between who came to the opinion that the flaw might be in the theory.[105]

11. *The allure of authoritarianism*

How East European liberals imagined capitalism does not seem to be the most important thing. One could also find persons who advocated not 'pure' neoliberal models but the German 'social market economy' model (to be sure, they did not use the term 'liberalism', but were in favour of building capitalism as rapidly as possible). This model allowed for a considerable degree of state welfare, which was a kind of 'socialism'. From the very beginning, the positive attitude towards the 'restoration of capitalism' in the post-communist world had many shades. This is quite understandable, not so much on account of the differentiation of interests as because there were so many ideological models and traditions to choose from. The main problem seems to lie not so much in the concept of capitalism as in the concept of its *formation*. No matter how we imagine the best form of this system, its rapid *construction* on ideological order is as difficult as it is

---

[104] Kazimierz Z. Poznański, 'Property Rights Perspective on Evolution of Communist-Type Economies', *Constructing Capitalism: The Reemergence of Civil Society and Liberal Economy in the Post-Communist World*, ed. Kazimierz Z. Poznański (Boulder CO: Westview Press, 1992), p. 91.

[105] One of these exceptions is the article of Jarosław Gowin, 'Nędza liberalizmu, czyli o perspekywach ładu liberalnego w Polsce', *Przegląd Polityczny* 1992, no. 4 (17), pp. 49–55.

unprecedented. It is by no means certain that the road from real socialism to a 'social market economy' is shorter and smoother than the road to pure capitalism.

In any case, some *act of creation* seems necessary to bring into being a system whose very essence supposedly consists in its spontaneous origination and development. This system is subsequently improved in one way or another – in contrast to socialism in the Marxist-Leninist version, which, conceived in a slap-dash manner by ideologists, is then imposed upon society. The liberal ideology does warn against the danger of revolutionary changes, but its advocates also believe that the special situation of the post-communist world calls for revolutionary measures, that is, for a shock therapy.[106] The following paradoxical statement of Kisiel touches the core of the problem which liberals must solve in the post-communist world: 'Grab people by the throat and introduce liberalism!'[107] In other words, the development of capitalism in the post-communist countries requires not only abolishing the prohibitions and restrictions derived from the communist doctrine, which until recently was gospel in these countries; also required are creative actions on the part of the state to *introduce* capitalist economic relationships, not merely to permit them or, at most, support them in some way. 'It is complete mumbo jumbo to say that liberalism can be introduced in a way that will not require intervention by the state', said Donald Tusk.[108]

The non-communist governments in Eastern Europe not only have an extraordinarily wide range of duties; they must also be aware that a change in the state of affairs, for example in the economy, cannot be made by just standing aside, but also requires intensive creative actions. This is best illustrated by the ups and downs of the privatization process, which requires not only willingness on the part of the state to hand over property under its control to other economic entities, but also finding such entities and even creating them if they do not exist. Offe wrote: 'This "capitalism by design" (or capitalism without capitalists as active promoters of their class interests) depends in every detail on highly visible *decisions* which hence require justification, and its development cannot rely on blind evolutionary emergences, which has largely been a pattern in the history of Western capitalisms. The new class of entrepreneurs . . . is created according to a blueprint designed by political elites.'[109]

An irony of fate is not only that in this situation a liberal is forced to

---

[106] See 'Demokracji nie uważam za wartość samą w sobie', an interview with Tadeusz Syryjczyk in *Życie Warszawy*, 2 January 1992.

[107] Quoted after Janusz Korwin-Mikke, statement for *Życie Warszawy*, reprinted in *Nowy Dziennik*, 1 December 1992.

[108] 'Zdecentralizowane, neutralne, liberalne', op. cit., p. 20.

[109] Claus Offe, 'Capitalism by Democratic Design?', op. cit., p. 879.

become a *constructivist* against his nature, so to say, but also that his very liberalism greatly depends on whether he becomes one, because his liberalism is defined by the *goal* he wishes to achieve and not by the method he uses to reach it. This strange phenomenon of 'liberalism as constructivism' was described by Radzisława Gortat, who argued convincingly that in Poland we have to do with 'the birth of liberalism in a way that contradicts its nature'.[110] One can argue for a long time about the 'nature' of liberalism, but in this case we have to do with the violation of a principle shared by most varieties of liberalism – a violation which prompted Jeffrey Goldfarb to use the following astonishing expression: 'a new totalitarian temptation of the *laissez-faire* kind'.[111] Although this expression is highly exaggerated, it accurately conveys the atmosphere of impatience noticeable in liberal circles.

Gortat gives a political interpretation of this phenomenon. She describes how the programme for the construction of capitalism came to be accepted, and the characteristics of the new political class standing behind it. This class very soon became so sure of itself that it did not think it was necessary to keep the election promises of Solidarity[112] or pay heed to the easily predictable reactions of society. This interpretation is correct as far as it goes, but it ignores the important fact that such a sweeping change in the social order may have stalled if the reformers – as the author recommends – had been content to 'open up the space for a self-reforming society and the uninhibited articulation of its diverse interests within democratic institutions' instead of 'introducing ready-made solutions regarded as natural by the new political forces'.[113]

One can surmise that the structural transformation would have slowed down or even halted, so it is not surprising that 'liberals' (the author uses this term in the broad sense for all supporters of the so-called Balcerowicz

[110] Radzisława Gortat, 'Liberalizm jako konstruktywizm', *Przegląd Społeczny* 1992, no. 6, p. 19.

[111] Jeffrey C. Goldfarb, *After the Fall: The Pursuit of Democracy in Central Europe* (New York: Basic Books, 1992), p. 48. Ryszard Bugaj spoke of the 'Bolshevik arguments' of the liberals ('Rynek bez dogmatu', an interview with Ryszard Bugaj, leader of 'Solidarność Pracy' in *Życie Warszawy*, 7 October 1991).

[112] The political platform of the Citizens' Committees for the June 1989 elections did not announce such an economic policy; it just used the ambiguous word 'reform'. Neither was Deputy Prime Minister Balcerowicz explicit on this point when he presented his programme in a speech before the Diet (see note 73). David Ost called attention to the paradox in Eastern Europe of carrying out a collectivist revolution to build an individualistic system. According to him, the market revolution today is being implemented thanks to the victory of those oppositionists who not long ago supported collectivist values ('Interesy i polityka', *Konfrontacje* 1991, no. 10 (45).

[113] R. Gortat, 'Liberalizm jako konstruktywizm', op. cit., p. 19.

Plan) chose another path; the more so as, formally speaking, democratic procedures were hardly violated. The belief in the need for reform was so strong and society's notion of it so hazy that the liberal project did not meet any serious resistance. It was not someone's manipulation that was to blame for this but the lack of imagination on the part of both political representatives and those whom they represented. Having the promised land before their eyes, liberals had no reason not to seize a historic opportunity. This argument is oversimplified, however, because it assumes that some 'liberal revolution' had already taken place in Poland, which is very debatable. Yet, even if we make allowance for the limitations of this revolution, this does not change the heart of the matter. In one way or another, what was at issue here was the relationship of the liberal utopia to *democracy*.

No matter what the situation was at the time the Balcerowicz Plan was accepted or later, this issue is of cardinal importance for our subject, and so is the general question of what should a politician do who is convinced of the correctness of his or her project but at the same time is aware that it will be resisted and cannot be carried out with the use of fully democratic procedures. Accustomed to the notional hodge-podge 'liberal democracy', and even to the interchangeability in certain cases of the words 'liberal' and 'democratic', we tend to forget that – logically and historically – two entirely different things are involved here which many a time were in conflict.[114] One could be (and can be) a liberal without paying much heed to the political and social rights of the citizen that determine his status in a democratic state; for the *sine qua non* of liberalism are *civil* rights, hence 'the rights necessary for individual freedom – liberty of person, freedom of speech, thought and faith, the right to own property and to conclude valid contracts, and the right to justice'.[115]

If these rights, or at least some of them, are guaranteed, many a liberal unhesitatingly would agree (at one time this was almost the rule) to reduce greatly the participation of citizens in political power and, even more so, their social welfare benefits. Such a liberal may even be pleased by these limitations if they lead to the achievement of goals he or she regards as all-important. Such an attitude was very clearly manifested in what some liberal

---

[114] Norberto Bobbio in perhaps the best discussion of the problem of 'liberalism vis-á-vis democracy' leans towards the view that over time the distance between them has narrowed and that in the contemporary world liberalism without democracy and democracy without liberalism are inconceivable (*Liberalism and Democracy* (London: Verso, 1990), p. 38). On liberalism and democracy see Giovanni Sartori, *Theory of Democracy Revisited* (Chatham NY: Chatham House Publishers, 1987), chapter 13.

[115] T. H. Marshall, 'Citizenship and Social Class', in *States and Societies*, ed. David Held et al. (New York: New York University Press, 1983), p. 249.

circles thought about Pinochet. Friedrich von Hayek wrote as follows of the dictator's activities: 'It is possible for a dictator to govern in a liberal way. And it is possible that a democracy governs with a total lack of liberalism. My personal preference is for a liberal dictator, and not for a democratic government lacking in liberalism.'[116]

The East European liberals faced a similar dilemma after 1989 (in their case more theoretical than practical). This dilemma had manifested itself even earlier,[117] but before the fall of real socialism it appeared in a less intense form, namely, whether economic freedom was possible without political freedom – not whether a limitation of political freedom could advance economic freedom. At that time, the lack of political democracy appeared more as a necessary evil than as an opportunity for carrying out a radical economic reform when society still tended to think in leftist categories. After the fall of real socialism, the question had to be asked whether democracy, no matter how desirable for many reasons, would not be detrimental to the 'objective' interest of society and whether in certain conditions it would not be necessary to limit it. And one possible answer – shocking for many – was that 'capitalism can succeed only in a dictatorship'.[118] This was unquestionably a sensible answer considering the fact that in the politically divided contemporary society the institution of any 'pure' form of capitalism would have been impossible without a considerable amount of compulsion.[119]

It would be wrong to say that East European liberals succumbed to the allure of authoritarianism. There were only the faintest signs of such a tendency in their complaints about political obstacles on the road to building capitalism or in their view that the trade-union movement posed a threat to capitalism, but they took no real political measures to limit democracy. The idea of a pro-capitalist dictatorship was confined to rhetoric. In the main, such a view was voiced by persons of little political importance; or, in the worst case, there were calls to grant special powers to the governments carrying out the reforms. Nowhere (except perhaps in Yeltsin's Russia) has the dilemma of anti-liberal democracy and liberal dictatorship yet become a practical dilemma. It could easily become such if the hasty reconstruction of the economy does not improve the living

[116] F. Hayek in an interview for *El Mercurio*, 12 April 1981. Quoted after Samuel Bowles and Herbert Gintis, *Democracy and Capitalism: Property, Community, and the Contradiction of Modern Social Thought* (New York: Basic Books, 1986), pp. 11–12.

[117] See Florian Krakowski [W. Büchner], 'Czy potrzebna nam jest demokracja?', op. cit.

[118] Aleksander Popiel in a discussion at the First Gdańsk Congress of Liberals. Minutes of the discussion in *Przegląd Polityczny* 1989, no. 12, p. 64.

[119] See John Dunn, 'The Economic Limits to Modern Politics', in a collective work of the same title edited by the same author (Cambridge: Cambridge University Press, 1990), p. 36.

standard of the population or if this improvement is confined to narrow segments of the population. Unfortunately, such a development is not unlikely.

Be that as it may, this is a matter of no little importance, and East European liberals must have been aware that in this region of Europe the connection of liberalism with democracy is less evident than in contemporary Western countries. As Ellen Comisso wrote:

> While the introduction of democracy to Eastern Europe and the Soviet Union is highly desirable for many reasons, it is unfortunately unclear if enacting a major economic transformation is one of them. On the contrary, it would seem that the basic preconditions required for the creation of self-regulating markets in the economy are not so much 'democratic' as they are 'liberal'. That is, the political requirements of economic reform lie less in the introduction of institutions for popular control of the state than in the establishment of mechanisms that would limit the use of political authority in the economy regardless of who exercises it.[120]

12. *'Pragmatism' or étatism*

The main problem, however, is not whether the introduction of liberal reforms requires abandoning democratic procedures and resorting to autocratic measures. Even following the path of democracy does not guarantee avoidance of the 'constructivist' trap mentioned above. The occasional analogies with Chile are completely misleading in this case. In the post-communist countries, the matter concerned a radical transformation of the entire economic system, and this is impossible without significant involvement on the part of the state – whether this state is democratic or authoritarian. In Chile, on the other hand, it was just a question of letting the economy work unimpeded, with the authoritarian state seeing to it that economic freedoms are respected. Despite similarities of one kind or another, these are really two entirely different situations. East European liberals who became involved in the practice of politics soon became convinced of this. They discovered to their dismay that a considerable number of the economic entities with which they had to deal after the collapse of real socialism were behaving in a shockingly irrational manner but consistently with the practices of the previous system.

[120] Ellen Comisso, 'Property Rights, Liberalism and the Transition from "Actually Existing" Socialism', *East European Politics and Societies*, winter 1991, vol. 5, no. 1, p. 162.

The tragedy of East European liberals was not that they had to resort to authoritarian measures, for there was no need to do so in the face of almost universal approval of the direction of the changes. Rather, it was that, in order to achieve their liberal objective, time and again, even when they did not encounter political resistance, they had to be untrue to their liberal principles. In striving for economic freedom, they had to rely more and more on the state to create the indispensable conditions for such freedom. This is the origin of the liberalism which in Poland is called *pragmatic* or *practical*, which, as Janusz Lewandowski said, 'must bend to realities',[121] and which consists in the fact that at every step intervention of the state is required – no matter what the political form of this state. A Western observer wrote: 'The list of activities which governments must undertake in countries attempting the transition to a market economy is truly staggering.'[122]

In Lewandowski's opinion, 'a liberal knows that the social order taking shape in Poland cannot be planned in detail, but he also knows that a market cannot be built on state-owned property. A mature market economy requires less state intervention than during the critical period in which we find ourselves. That is why today the state, as the creator of many institutions, cannot avoid participation in shortening the way to the market.'[123] An excellent illustration of this viewpoint is Lewandowski's activity as Minister of Ownership Changes, thanks to which the privatization of the economy became *par excellence* a state matter; and not without reasons its critics associated it with the nationalization of decades earlier whose effects it was supposed to remove.[124] Balcerowicz said that 'in our conditions the state is responsible for introducing the new economic order'.[125]

The ideology of 'pragmatic liberalism' is perhaps best summarized in the following statement of former prime minister Jan Krzysztof Bielecki: 'Liberalism means that one believes that someday there will be liberalism in Poland. Today, since the reaction of economic entities to market signals is limited or weak, certain state instruments of influence must be sought, and this is no longer liberal behaviour. To go further, one can say that my motto today is that the state must participate in building the conditions of a market

[121] 'Liberalizm praktyczny'. Danuta Zagrodzka interviews Janusz Lewandowski, Chairman of the Liberal-Democratic Congress and Minister of Ownership Changes, in *Gazeta Wyborcza*, 13 April 1991.

[122] Christopher Clague, 'The Journey to a Market Economy', *The Emergence of a Market Economy in Eastern Europe*, ed. C. Clague and Gordon C. Rausser (Oxford: Blackwell, 1992), p. 5.

[123] 'Gra o własność', an interview with Janusz Lewandowski in *Przegląd Polityczny* 1992, no. 1–2 (14–15), p. 70.

[124] R. Gortat, quoted earlier, wrote of 'étatist constructivism' ('Liberalizm jako konstruktywizm', op. cit., p. 23).

[125] Leszek Balcerowicz, 'Szybciej w tym samym kierunku', *Gazeta Wyborcza*, 10 January 1991.

economy. . . . This is not a liberal motto at all, but that is how things really are.'[126] 'The "Invisible Hand" Disappears' was the title of an article in the Polish press about the actions of the Bielecki administration. It contained the opinion that 'it seems like a paradox that a government headed by liberals is taking actions so far removed from orthodox liberalism'.[127] In effect, today it is the Social Democrats who are evolutionists and advocates of piecemeal social engineering.

This is not the place for a detailed analysis of the views or, even less so, of the actions of liberal politicians directly involved in carrying out the reforms. The above statements suffice to point out the change that took place in 'purely' liberal views under the burden of ruling a post-communist country. Even people who were quite conscious of what liberalism is none the less decided to modify it or even reverse it. They ever more often stated that 'the period of true liberalism is still before us'[128] – but at the present time we find ourselves in a protracted transition period, in which, unfortunately, different rules of the game are in effect; before the role of the state in the economy withers away, it must be strengthened. The proviso was voiced that the 'active structural policy of the state' should be limited to ownership changes.[129] However, this is not little and, besides, the limitation concerns what is desirable. The situation changes when politicians come to power and find themselves under the pressure of their political allies.

This position may be criticized from two sides – both for its alleged liberal 'doctrinairism' and for departing from it. Some critics castigate 'pragmatic' liberals for the purpose to which they would employ the state, others for assigning a prominent role to the state in transforming the economy, thereby violating the sacred principle of non-intervention. In one way or another, the state is at the centre of the dispute. In learning from Western liberals, East European liberals either did not accept the postulate of least government or transformed it into an ideological slogan that would be realized in the indefinite future. On the contrary, while reiterating that the state should be limited, they of necessity turned it into the main instrument for creating the liberal order. Many of them did this quite deliberately. They did not hesitate to state plainly that in the process of building capitalism in a post-communist country 'the major role would be played by the state, which not only creates the institutional conditions for the play of market forces, but also accelerates and extends its protection to the process in which entities

[126] 'Nie mam konfliktów sumienia'. Marek Rudziński interviews Jan Krzysztof Bielecki, Prime Minister of Poland, *Sztandar Młodych*, 24–26 May 1991.

[127] Ryszard Holzer, 'Znika "niewidzialna ręka"', *Życie Warszawy*, 7 October 1991.

[128] Janusz Lewandowski, 'Strach przed kapitalizmem', *Nowa Europa*, 2 April 1992.

[129] See 'Logika reformy prokapitalistycznyej'. Theses to the KLD programme presented by J. Lewandowski and J. Szomberg at the National KLD Congress, in *Biuletyn Informacyjny KLD*, 1–16 November 1992, no. 6 (14) p. 5.

that can participate in this give-and-take come into being. In post-communist conditions a liberal order often must be created with non-liberal methods.'[130]

The reasons for this 'étatization' of liberalism are rather self-evident. The most important of them is unquestionably that – as Offe phrased it – the idea had to replace interests.[131] Thus, the accelerated development of capitalism in the post-communist countries started from an ideological blueprint; it was not an economic process in which major social forces conscious of their interests and capable of defending them on a nationwide scale were involved here and now. The ideology of economic liberalism does contain the thesis that capitalism, as a 'natural' way of conducting economic activities, never fails to develop when nothing stands in its way. In the post-communist countries, however, this thesis was confirmed mainly on the micro-level in pavement trade, but the economy as a whole proved surprisingly hard to budge, reacting very weakly to market signals. From the very outset it was evident that the development of capitalism required creation of a proper infrastructure, and in the existing conditions this task had to be assumed by the state.

In short, as Jacek Kurczewski keenly observed, liberals faced the paradoxical and sad necessity of 'restoring capitalism with the hands of state officials'.[132] As a result, as Lech Mażewski wrote, 'the Polish reforms still have the character of a programme imposed by the ruling elites and carried out by the state bureaucracy, a programme which the citizen does not understand and in which for this reason he does not participate as an individual'.[133]

The point is not only that the state takes upon itself the task of promoting capitalism and postpones its withdrawal from the economy until the new system becomes self-regulating. However non-liberal the methods used to achieve this end, this need not trouble the conscience of economic liberals, because – as János Mátyás Kovács wrote – 'the distance to be covered between the point of departure and even the least liberal and most social

---

[130] Lech Mażewski, 'Od teoretycznego do realnego kapitalizmu', *Życie Warszawy*, 16 October 1991.

[131] Piotr Marciniak, 'Po neoliberalnym szoku', *Przegląd Społeczny* 1993, no. 9, p. 19. See Lech Mażewski: 'In Poland the transformation of the post-communist system was undertaken in the name of the "theoretical interest" of building democratic capitalism. On the other hand, the entities whose real economic interest would be linked with a continuation of the process of changes were supposed to appear only after these changes were well-advanced' (op. cit.).

[132] 'Wolne społeczeństwo upaństwowione', an interview with Professor Jacek Kurczewski in *Spotkania*, 9 October 1991, p. 18.

[133] Lech Mażewski, 'Thatcheryzm po polsku', *Przegląd Polityczny* 1992, no. 3 (16), p. 11.

stage in the process of transition is so great, the real-socialist inheritance is so pressing, and the tasks of transformation so divergent that the need for some engineering of the process is difficult to dispute'.[134] In effect, the most orthodox neoliberals advised that privatization be carried out as soon as possible, even though they were aware that this would have to be an administrative operation and not a result of the 'normal' interplay of interests.

13. *The legacy of socialist étatism*

Perhaps an even more vexatious crucible for the liberal utopia is that the state not only undertakes to make this utopia a reality ('shortening the way to the market'), but that, in practice, it also retains a number of functions inherited from real socialism which are incompatible with this utopia and clearly hinder its realization. After the fall of real socialism, there was a perceptible reduction of the interests and obligations of the state authority, but they still remained excessively wide. The state did not cease to be the biggest employer and did not transfer responsibility to anyone else for all of those areas which in a non-communist state do not belong to the state at all or even primarily. No matter what different opinions Western liberals have on the proper scope of state activities, in the post-communist countries it is incomparably greater than dreamed of by even the most 'socially minded' liberals. The consequences are all the more serious because the core of the state bureaucracy was shaped under real socialism, and for this reason the average civil servant in questionable cases tends to choose an étatist solution rather than trying to find some other one. Even more important, a majority of the society has become accustomed to étatist solutions.

Time and again liberal publications call for folding up the 'social umbrella', that is, for a radical reduction in the welfare functions of the state, using both the doctrinal argument of the liberal social philosophy and pointing out that poor countries cannot afford a welfare state. In practice, however, the matter is much more complicated. On the one hand, there is the concern that, at least for the time being, certain important areas of social life cannot stand on their own without assistance from the state; on the other hand, it is quite obvious that a large segment of the population expects assistance from the state in one form or another (for example, a clear majority thinks that the state should provide them with a job in line with their qualifi-

---

[134] János Mátyás Kovács, 'From Reformation to Transformation: Limits to Liberalism in Hungarian Economic Thought', *East European Politics and Societies* 1991, vol. 5, no. 1, p. 67.

cations). Consequently, it would be a big political risk to withdraw such assistance. Step-by-step the state is being forced to reduce such assistance under the influence of a budget deficit, but this is done pusillanimously out of fear of going too far. Thus, as a rule, what matters most is not the most rational solution in the present situation but how far one can go without causing a political crisis or a social 'upheaval'.

As a consequence, politicians and journalists blame society for its supposed still unchanged 'communist mentality', but they cannot afford to ignore this mentality. A liberal theoretician can say that 'the state should be built first and foremost with the state of nature in mind, and only after this think about the state of the social consciousness',[135] whereas a practitioner – to a greater or lesser degree – is forced to follow 'the line of collective illusions', even if he regards them as dangerous and absurd. It is highly debatable whether the origin of these 'illusions' is necessarily socialist. In any case, what sometimes is regarded as a residue of the communist mentality cannot be distinguished from timeless reactions of citizens to the deprivation of their formerly acquired rights.

That is why a 'practical' liberal would say the following about doctrinally 'pure' liberalism: 'It's a good thing that it existed, for it prepared the ground, pricked public opinion poisoned by communism', but at the same time he would say that if it were applied in practice 'it would blow up the Polish road to capitalism within a month'.[136] The situation in Poland is exceptionally complicated. The fall of communism was preceded by a collectivist revolution whose participants, not without cause, saw themselves as victors and expected their hopes to be fulfilled. Meanwhile, these hopes turned out to be not only excessive but also completely incompatible with the course of development on which the country embarked after the victory over communism. In one of his interviews Janusz Lewandowski said: 'Eighty percent of the society consists of frustrated working men and women who believe that they deserve a reward for overthrowing communism. To save the reform, something has to be done for these people.'[137]

In connection with this, some supporters of economic liberalism have not hesitated to state outright that – in contrast to Hungary and Czechoslovakia – 'Poland, unfortunately, is burdened with the legacy of ten years of opposition. . . . Now it seems, unfortunately, that liberal thinking is clearly losing – or at least is on the sidelines – while anarchistic tendencies from the time

[135] Bronisław Łagowski, 'List otwarty do trzydiestolatków', *Przegląd Polityczny* 1992, no. 1–2 (14–15), p. 10.
[136] 'Liberalizm praktyczny'. Danuta Zagrodzka interviews Dr J. Lewandowski in *Gazeta Wyborcza*, 13 April 1991.
[137] Ibid.

of the former opposition are rising to the ascendancy.'[138] The unfortunate use of the word 'anarchistic' in this context is of less importance. The observation itself is 'correct', though one might question the appropriateness of the word 'unfortunately', since it was to Solidarity that liberals owed the opportunity to start their reforms sooner than expected and, into the bargain, for some time were under Solidarity's umbrella, without which they would have had an ever harder time.

To their vexation, the advocates of a rapid introduction of capitalist relations in Poland encountered both a popular collectivist ideology (which was not simply a legacy of communism, but for an entire decade served effectively as the battle standard against it) and a powerful trade-union movement which was primarily made up of employees of large state enterprises and was pledged to defend their interests, not to create a new middle class.

Thus, the problem faced by 'pragmatic' liberals was not only that they had to resort to 'non-liberal methods' to build capitalism, but also that they had to come to some accommodation with social forces whose interests were obviously incompatible with the liberal programme. Their social philosophy notwithstanding, liberals had to maintain the *status quo* in social welfare programmes and subsidies and privileges for state-owned heavy industry. Yet, any compromise otherwise indispensable for creating the *political* conditions for a sweeping economic reform would inexorably reduce the scope of this reform or delay it. By no means am I contending that, as a result, reform would be impossible or a sham. I am only calling attention to the objective difficulty of holding to a 'purely' liberal course.

The practical result of tactical concessions may be the same as the result of actions deliberately taken in contravention of the principles of economic liberalism. Hence, it was easy for so-called liberal 'columnists' to reproach liberals who entered the political game with cardinal errors, especially those liberals who assumed government positions and somehow tried to square faithfulness to liberal principles with political effectiveness, which necessarily meant distancing themselves from the liberal utopia from which they

---

[138] 'Dokąd zmierza Polska?', a discussion in the journal *Kapitalista Powszechny* (supplement to *Przegląd Tygodniowy*) of 1 March 1992, no. 4 (10). The opinion quoted was uttered by M. Miszerak, then adviser to the minister of finance. One cannot say that the attitude of liberals towards the legacy of the opposition and Solidarity was completely negative – if only because a considerable number of liberals had belonged to the Solidarity camp for a long time. The dominant opinion was that the 'Solidarity mass movement created opportunities but dangers as well', with the latter intensifying as time went on. Of decisive importance was the argument that both the democratic opposition and Solidarity were dominated by socialist views on the economy. In the opinion of some liberals, both of these political groupings essentially belonged to the left.

had started. A liberal faithful to this utopia assesses the result as follows: 'The present political system is only a masked form of socialism.' If he is consistent and aware of social tensions, he will not hesitate to mention dictatorship as perhaps the only solution which can save the building of capitalism.[139]

I have no intention of reflecting on whether the prospect of a pro-capitalist dictatorship is a realistic possibility today in Poland or in any other post-communist country, even though deliberations on this subject can be found not only in journalists who like to speculate.[140] The point is that the idea of dictatorship irresistibly suggests itself as a theoretical possibility when we consider the fact that there are only two courses of action open to applied liberalism in a post-communist country. One of them is to force through the programme for building capitalism at all cost and with all available means; the other is to modify this programme in such a way as to make it acceptable to the major political forces in the existing conditions of political democracy, while bearing in mind that most of them are not personally interested in its realization. Acceptance of the second option necessarily means reducing the scope of the reform and prolonging its realization.

As it becomes ever more involved in practical affairs, 'pure' liberalism starts to flirt with authoritarianism. 'Pragmatic' liberalism is immune to this temptation, but it thereby jeopardizes the integrity of its liberal principles by being forced to defend its arguments in the give-and-take of democratic procedures, in which other participants often have entirely different ideas of what is good for society. As a result, we have a situation in which part of society complains about liberalism being everywhere, while another part doubts whether we yet have any liberalism at all.[141]

To be sure, I am using two 'ideal types' here and am not trying to draw precise lines between organizations and people. Such lines could be drawn, but my intention was not to describe the political situation in one country or

[139] Interview with J. Korwin-Mikke for *Życie Warszawy*, printed in *Nowy Dziennik*, 1 December 1992.

[140] See John Gray, 'Totalitarianism, Reform and Civil Society', in *Totalitarianism at the Crossroads*, ed. Ellen Frankel Paul (New Brunswick NJ: Transactions Books, 1990), p. 34; Peter Bihari, 'From Where to Where? Reflections on Hungary's Social Revolution', in *Socialist Register*, ed. R. Miliband and Leo Pantich (London: Merlin Press, 1991). The latter author wrote: 'Democracy is threatened by capitalism itself . . . It may well be that at the end of the twentieth century, in Eastern Europe, capitalism can only be created through dictatorial means. Irrespective of whether or not the leading politicians of the present government have an affinity to dictatorship, they may be forced into a dictatorial regime' (p. 287). See Janusz Reykowski, 'Czy dyktatura to bajka o żelaznym wilku?', *Res Publica Nowa* 1993, no. 5 (56), pp. 12–14.

[141] See Wacław Wilczyński, 'Czy w Polsce liberalizm ekonomiczny?', *Wprost*, 15 August 1993, no. 33 (560), p. 68.

another, but to show the political dilemmas faced by liberals in the post-communist world. These dilemmas seem all the more remarkable in that, in one sense or another, they can be dilemmas of the very same people.

14. *The political crossroads of applied liberalism*

Relying on democratic methods of reaching capitalism confronts liberals with the dilemma of where they should look for allies. Since there is no real middle class which liberal groupings could represent *de facto* and not just *in potentia*, they have to think of other ways to gain support for their ideas. For a certain time after 1989 this was not really a problem, for the following reasons. First, the very prospect of changing the economic system appealed to most of society because it promised the liquidation of real socialism, and only liberals had available a relatively comprehensive programme for such change; second, the social majority really had no inkling of the costs of carrying out such a programme; they just expected the economic crisis to end or even that all of their heretofore unsatisfied expectations would be fulfilled – including those which had been promised (but not kept) by real socialism.

As a result, coming out in favour of *reform*, whose exigency became incontestable when a real possibility appeared of carrying it out, was tantamount to advocating a *liberal economy*, which encountered no serious competition capable of mobilizing social opinion. Thanks to this, liberals surprisingly became a political force to be reckoned with. Sometimes they even gained support for their measures from unexpected quarters, for example from the trade union movement. In Poland, even the first signs of social dissatisfaction time and again turned out to their advantage. For instance, the election of Lech Wałęsa as President of the Polish Republic not only did not change the economic policy of the state, but even consolidated it and for a certain time strengthened the position of liberals. For a rather long time, people continued to believe that there was no alternative and that only liberals really knew what should be done to fix the economy. Here I do not go into whether the reforms as actually carried out were liberal in the full sense of the word or whether the initial confidence in them was warranted; that is, whether they were in the 'theoretical interest' of society as a whole, as their enthusiastic supporters claimed. Now these are purely academic questions, and only completely irresponsible politicians would call for a roll-back of the reforms.

Be that as it may, we had to do with a situation in which anti-socialist resentments and nebulous hopes for a better future provided advocates of more or less liberal solutions with a social base of support. Quite irrespective of its catchphrases, promises and sources, the democratic revolution of 1989 gave the first push to the economic revolution in the direction wished for by liberals. Conflicts over how this revolution should be carried out were still brewing, but liberals were more aware of them than those who supported the liberal programme non-consciously or semi-consciously. In the years that followed, the situation changed completely. A crisis of faith in the reforms arose and confidence waned in its supporters and realizers, who – quite often for no reason at all – started to be blamed for all sorts of things. The general conclusion reached ever more often was that liberalism as such was a mistake. In some circles, the very word 'liberalism' took on a very negative colouring; it became associated mainly with the social pathologies cropping up in the wake of the introduction of free market economies in the post-communist countries.[142]

I do not intend to describe these processes in detail here. It should only be emphasized that one of them was the disintegration of the recent political unity of all (or nearly all) persons who had placed their hopes in the fall of communism, a process that was fed not only by disillusionments over how the reforms to build the economy on new foundations were going (for the very surfacing of the liberal orientation was both the symptom and harbinger of that process). In any case, the chequeredness of the political arena and real participation in it, what was happening there, compelled liberals to be more precise about their position on many issues and on their attitude towards the emerging new political forces.

The role in which many economic liberals saw themselves became unten-able, namely, the role of self-styled economic experts acting in an area in which a consensus is attainable of the entire anti-communist camp, opposed at most by the heirs of the *ancien régime*. For a long time these liberals kept up the pretence that such a role was possible. To implement economic liber-alism in the new situation at least in a curtailed version (and without resorting to otherwise unavailable autocratic measures), it was necessary to have a political programme and to be able to find political allies. This confronted liberals with new dilemmas: since they are too weak to achieve victory on their own, on which side of the political spectrum should they seek agreement and on which political forces should they rely? These dilemmas have divided the liberal community and are one of the reasons for the various party affiliations of persons who profess liberalism. Today, it is unclear what political road in the post-communist countries leads to full-blown economic liberalism.

---

[142] Leszek Balcerowicz wrote: 'I fear that in the course of the political struggle in the last few years in Poland the words "liberal" and "liberalism" have suffered great damage and have taken on a negative connotation' ('Zaproszenie do myślenia', *Wprost*, 18 July 1993, no. 29).

One of the possible roads is to form an alliance with the political right. At the cost of renouncing all traditional liberal values except private ownership and a free market economy, liberals would gain support for those few values which seem most important in economic liberalism. As mentioned earlier, from the very beginning Polish economic liberalism has leaned in this direction and has been tied with the right *par excellence*. Some of its critics reproach liberalism for its remarkable tendency to compromise with traditionalism.[143] This is the formula of 'Thatcherism in the Polish style' (Czech, Hungarian style, etc.), liberalism as *conservatism*, in which admiration for neoliberal principles in political economy may go hand-in-hand with strong aversion to everything that smacks of liberalism in any other sense. There seem to be many arguments in favour of this formula, especially the intensity of the resentments directed against the left, and the alleged attachment of East European societies to traditional religious and moral values; the only argument against it is that the economic views popular on the right were not (and are not) necessarily liberal, though the cult of private ownership has never completely faded there. Recently, there have been many signs that tendencies are resurfacing on the right to push through an economic policy which an orthodox liberal would associate with socialism.

The second possible road is to situate liberalism in the centre of the political spectrum. This would be attended by greater flexibility of economic views (for example, on the maximum size of the welfare state), greater submissiveness to the anti-traditionalism of the left, and the tendency to go beyond economic liberalism. This road is also attended by the acceptance of a wider gamut of liberal values, which 'liberalism as conservatism' firmly rejects in concert with its rightist friends. Here one can also observe the relatively strongest effort to set the liberal orientation apart by targeting its own political clientele (the new middle class, young people, educated people) and presenting a vision of a new civilization. From this point of view, the chief merit of liberalism is not its rather obvious anti-leftist tendencies combined with the sacralization of private property and the free market, but its capacity to promote something really *new*, something which although it turns against socialism is, at the same time, incompatible with the ideas of the traditional Christian-nationalist right. Liberalism in this sense seems consistent with numerous varieties of past liberalism – in Poland especially, Enlightenment and positivist ones – as an ideology of the modernization and Europeanization of Eastern Europe, for which it is often criticized from the right. This liberalism is closest to the mainstream of the European liberal tradition and addresses a wide range of non-economic problems in the conviction that in Eastern Europe backwardness in many

---

[143] P. Marciniak, 'Po neoliberalnym szoku', op. cit., p. 22.

areas besides economics preceded real socialism and combined with its legacy. Hence, the striving to restore the status quo ante means something entirely different here than for contemporary American conservatism, which wants to go back to capitalism before Keynes. Another main characteristic of centrist liberalism seems to be its democratism (as expressed in the most desirable model of capitalism) and its conception of the state. Liberalism here is not placed in opposition to democracy; on the contrary, the fullest possible participation of citizens at all levels of government as well as the widest scale of private ownership are basic conditions for the success of the state.

There is no leftist liberalism, of course, though rightist demagogy sometimes uses the epithet 'soc-demoliberalism'[144] and associates liberalism as such with all manifestations of criticism of the Christian-national tradition which the left in the past and today has been wont to express. This is either manipulation of a very ambiguous term or a direct consequence of the fact that no person in his right mind can construct his philosophy of life in such a way that it is not like some other philosophy of life in some point, for no philosophy of life consists solely of nonsense statements. In respect to liberals, this means that when they appear as advocates of a 'new civilization', they cannot avoid being similar in some respects to other advocates of modernization, even if the conception of the latter was wrong and unsuccessful in practice. What seems important is that in present conditions East European liberals do not appear inclined to seek allies on the left. This is all the more noteworthy because during the crisis period of communism the left attracted at least some elements of economic liberalism, and in some post-communist parties of Eastern Europe one can sometimes find real enthusiastic supporters of the economic liberalism. It is remarkable how many former communist administrators have found their calling in the field of private enterprise, as if they had taken to heart Dzielski's generous offer. So it is conceivable that in time some liberals will try to reach an understanding with an ideologically unbiased Social Democratic Party.

In any case, contemporary economic liberalism in Eastern Europe is fated to search constantly for support outside the circle of liberals themselves, which, despite everything, is rather narrow and has a very small social base. It may find such support because its main ideas have been received positively in the post-communist societies. Despite visible signs of disillusionment, people have not turned their backs on these ideas completely, but are somehow trying to correct them or develop them. The final outcome of these operations may be a turn away from these ideas, but for the time being all signs indicate that the question has not yet been settled. There is still a

[144]   See Jan Maria Jackowski, *Bitwa o Polskę* (Warsaw: Ad Astra, 1993), pp. 75–126.

rather wide area of possible agreement of the so-called pro-reform forces, who are willing to accept some part of liberal ideas for their own. This is unquestionably an opportunity for economic liberalism, but it also carries a danger. In searching for wide-scale support, economic liberalism runs the risk of losing the clear identity which it had as long as it was only an ideological project.

15. *Conclusion*

Economic liberalism unquestionably played an important role in shaping today's political scene in Eastern Europe, especially in Poland, Hungary and the Czech Republic. Whatever the links of its individual representatives with the earlier (and before 1989 more influential) democratic opposition, it was no doubt a separate ideological movement that prepared the ground for the total rejection of communism in the economy, which was the weak side of communism's earlier and, in many respects, more radical critics. The distinguishing features of this orientation were and have remained strong support for capitalism and rejection of the idea of a 'third road', and a concentration on transforming the economic system.

This was not and is not a homogeneous orientation. Apart from obvious differences resulting from a dissimilar political situation before and after the fall of communism, there are conspicuous differences resulting from the fact that its supporters had to act in special and unprecedented conditions. They were confronted with the necessity of conducting social engineering on a vast scale to create a new order. While they borrowed the general *principles* of this order from the Western liberal tradition, East European liberals could not imitate its accepted *methods*, which favoured changing the world step-by-step – with no shocks and upheavals. In any case, they could not put this idea into practice without moderating their ultimate goal; on the other hand, an uncompromising pursuit of this goal required the use of non-liberal methods. Liberalism owed its biggest successes in overcoming communism to its criticism of any preconceived social order imposed on society. However, in the post-communist countries liberalism was confronted with the same temptation as communism: having mainly a theory and little other means than political ones to implement it. The situation of liberals turned out to be more difficult because of their very narrow social base, which forces liberals to seek allies and compromises on both the goal and methods of reaching it. This creates dilemmas, which inevitably lead to disputes and divisions, and each success is paid for with some capitulation. Even worse, the field of manoeuvre of liberals has not increased much as time has passed. On the contrary, everything seems to indicate that criticism of them is increasing and time and again is also being expressed by persons who only a few years ago accepted the liberal vision without question. Perhaps the situation was correctly summed up by Jarosław Gowin, who said that 'liberalism proved itself as a technique of departing from communism, but failed completely as a theory of passing from communism to capitalism'.[145]

[145] J. Gowin, 'Nędza liberalizmu', op. cit.; see Zygmunt Bauman, 'The Polish Predicament: A Model in Search of Class Interests', *Telos* 1992, no. 92, pp. 115–30.

VI Does Political Liberalism Exist in Poland?

The question arises, is economic liberalism the whole of liberalism? Can liberalism be confined to economic categories alone?[1]

1. How far does liberalism reach?

The protoliberal and liberal ideas discussed in the last two chapters owe their relative popularity primarily to the hatred of real socialism – a feeling that gradually intensified in the wake of the economic crisis, laying bare the irremediable flaws of the socialist economy, and as ever wider social groups became aware that the existing system blocked nearly all individual and collective aspirations. This feeling that a roadblock existed was common to both of the anti-communist movements discussed earlier. The differences between them can be reduced to the fact that for one of them morality, social relationships and – sometimes – politics were the top priority, while the other stressed the need for a radical change of the *economic* system. One of them strove to develop democracy, the other private ownership and a free market.

We may now well ask whether such a formulation of the problem is not oversimplified. Economic liberals themselves contributed to this by putting exaggerated emphasis on economics and criticizing the 'revolutionary' point of view. Yet, they were unable to cleave consistently to the role of reformers of the economy alone – both because they remembered, as Janusz Korwin-Mikke admonished, that their goal is 'freedom and not a full stomach',[2] and they did not regard reconstruction of the economy as a goal in itself and were aware that the new economic system (if not immediately, then in time) would require certain political conditions to be met and a revolution in morality and customs.

[1] Pawel Śpiewak, 'Skazany na życie umysłowe', *Teczki liberałów*, compiled by Janina Paradowska and Jerzy Baczyński (Poznań: Obserwator, 1993), p. 189.

[2] J. Korwin-Mikke, 'Mojżesz', in *Widzieć mądrość w wolności. Księga Pamięci Mirosława Dzielskiego*, ed. Bogusław Chrabota (Kraków, 1991), p. 162.

Most liberals were aware that 'equally important is the psychological and cultural foundation, and there is also a lot of work to be done in this area'.[3] Had it been otherwise they would not have differed much from the communist 'liberals' of the Mieczysław Rakowski team, who, while they appreciated the potential benefits of a liberalization of the economy, until the very end attempted to hold changes in the 'superstructure' to a minimum. Since liberalism was not just a proposal of a *new economic policy* in the socialist style, it must be acknowledged that the picture of it sketched so far is incomplete, even though occasional references have been made to the views of liberals on non-economic questions.

The question is to what extent economic liberalism was and is at the same time liberalism in the broad sense of the word, which includes a programme for the reconstruction of *society* and not just its economic 'base'. Here it is worth asking to what extent the non-economic postulates of economic liberals, whose views were discussed earlier (for example, on the state of morals), concerned and/or concern only additional conditions for economic efficiency (every programme for reconstruction of the economy must include some non-economic conditions), and to what extent they made and/or make up an autonomous reform programme comparable with classic liberalism and also capable of attracting people who are either not interested in political economy or are not enthusiastic supporters of the free market.

We must now give some thought to whether a liberalism also appeared whose liberal identity would be determined not so much by economic views as by views of another kind: political, philosophic or any other ones – a liberalism championed not by Friedrich von Hayek or Milton Friedman but by John Stuart Mill or John Rawls. Earlier (see Chapter II), I tried to show that such liberalism, not necessarily economic, was not only nothing exceptional in the West, but constituted the mainstream of liberal thought. It preceded economic liberalism and was incomparably more influential than the latter.[4]

The opinion has been expressed that Polish liberalism, which originated primarily out of resistance to communism regarded as the main or only evil, lacked – as Ireneusz Białecki contends – 'mainstays' in the form of a positive *political* programme, one which would revert back to what was most important in the liberal doctrine, hence to 'the idea of individual rights, personal liberties, and freedom of choice, which society should guarantee to the individual'.[5]

---

[3] Janusz Lewandowski, 'Jaki liberalizm jest Polsce potrzebny?', *Biuletyn Informacyjny KLD*, March–April 1992, no. 3 (11), p. 13.

[4] See Giovanni Sartori, *Theory of Democracy Revisited* (Chatham NJ: Chatham House Publishers, 1987), chapter 13.

[5] Ireneusz Białecki, 'Obywatel we mgle', *Res Publica Nowa* 1992, no. 3 (51), pp. 19–20.

It obviously cannot be stated that Polish liberals had nothing to say about the political order, the reconstruction of society or culture as such, but their programme in these areas was rather poorly articulated in comparison with their economic programme, and quite often was indistinguishable from any other anti-communist programme. In any case, the contours of their political identity (even more so, of their world-view) were hazy and emerged slowly. This was reflected in the dispersion of liberals among different political parties and in the lack of an opinion or a firm stand on most non-economic issues. Many a politician who regarded himself as a liberal and was regarded as one by others for his or her views on economic reform shied away from the liberal label on non-economic matters and preferred to speak of his or her conservatism, central-rightist views, or *liberal-conservative* stance. Now we must ask ourselves whether any kind of liberalism other than economic liberalism exists in Poland; and if it does, what constitutes this liberalism and who represents it?

The answer to this question is by no means obvious, even though quite a lot is said about liberalism as such, which is sometimes regarded as a very strong tendency in all areas of life. Perhaps the expression 'political liberalism' – which I have borrowed from Białecki – is not the most appropriate one here. It refers not so much to politics in the common and modern sense of the word as to politics in the expanded, Aristotelian, sense, which embraced all matters vital for the society-state to work well. Perhaps a better expression would be integral liberalism or liberalism *tout court*, having in mind attitudes and views that go back to classic liberalism in all its aspects. In its expanded meaning, the aim of this liberalism is to find a comprehensive formula for a good organization of society that differs fundamentally not only from real socialism but also from most of what had existed in Eastern Europe before real socialism.

It really does not matter what term we use, because the questions seem clear enough. Do the non-economic postulates of today's Polish liberals refer only to the necessity of rooting out the remnants of real socialism from all areas of life, or do they also call for transcending the traditional forms of Polish thinking and Polish life? The old ways survived the period of real socialism relatively intact. After the fall of real socialism, a strong tendency arose to sanctify these ways, including ones which long since had become anachronisms. People who act in this manner believe that had it not been for communism, everything would be fine. For them the only really important problem is the fullest possible *restoration* of what had existed combined with a defence against foreign influences, which although they no longer threaten private ownership are no less dangerous to the moral order than communism had been.

In short, does the programme for the modernization of Eastern Europe put forward by liberals advocate only *decommunization* of the economy, or – counter to the neo-traditionalists – does it have a wider aim: creation of an *open society* such as has never existed before in this region, a society patterned after the liberal democracies of the West? I place strong emphasis on this point, because what is really important for today's political discussions is whether and to what extent their participants are willing to accept the fact that 'Poland found itself on the peripheries of Europe not 45 years ago but three centuries ago',[6] or even to doubt whether Poland ever belonged to Europe.

It is very difficult to answer this question both because it requires reconstructing the views of liberals on an enormous number of issues and because these views are so variegated in their case – incomparably more so than their views on the economy. In respect to the latter, liberals differ not so much on which system is the best in the abstract, but on which one is possible in a given country, in given conditions and at a given moment. Disputes arise not from disagreement over definition of the goal, but from differences of opinion on whether and when it will be fully achieved.

As soon as we go beyond the confines of economic problems, everything becomes inordinately complicated, however. Now differences of views also concern the *goal* to be achieved. It is not even certain whether some specifically liberal goal is involved in all cases associated with liberalism for whatever reason some goal that can be defined similarly to the economic goal as the practical application of tested Western models. In other words, the existence of an other than economic liberalism is by no means obvious; more precisely, it is less obvious than the existence of pure economic liberalism. In any case, one cannot state explicitly just what non-economic liberalism is. The greatest difficulty stems from the unprecedented expansion of the concept of liberalism in Eastern Europe.

First and foremost, we find a tendency to treat as liberal all views which extol liberty (or even greater liberty), irrespective of how they understand liberty and what use of liberty they are inclined to advocate for the future. These views contain few guidelines for the future use of liberty, because before 1989 the prospect of emerging from real socialism had been regarded as uncertain or even doubtful. In the main, ideas regarded as liberal under communist rule were not a conscious continuation of a distinct liberal tradition, but had their source in the negation of real socialism, in whose fall everyone except the ruling elite was more or less interested.

The advocacy of such views was not so much an affirmation of liberalism as of certain general principles that every person who favours modern

---

[6] Witold Morawski, 'Polska: wyzwanie cywilizacyjne', *Życie Warszawy*, 23 June 1992.

democracy in the Western style can endorse – irrespective of whether he or she is a liberal or a Christian Democrat, a conservative or a social democrat, or a communist converted to 'democratic socialism'. The slow and difficult assimilation of principles which owe their origin in no small measure to liberalism belongs to another history and does not have to be recalled here. One should be aware, however, that when the main enemy was communism, there was a tendency not to question the common 'liberal minimum' in any way and to show great restraint in accenting eventual differences of opinions and values. In the face of a common enemy, there was no place for a normal discussion and politics as usual: everything that combated communism was taken under the protection of its opponents; everything that communism could be expected to support was thus rendered suspect and politically awkward.

This situation helped to popularize the liberal minimum, but it also had a paralysing effect on liberalism as a separate orientation capable of opposing not only communism but also other ideologies that liberalism had been against in the past. As a result, the concept of liberalism was greatly expanded, giving the illusion of like-mindedness and the 'triumph of liberalism' as a natural consequence of the fall of real socialism. In reality, only *economic* liberalism scored a victory and not even a complete one at that.

The collapse of this illusion did not mark the end of disagreements over the understanding of liberalism. Liberalism did start to define itself as a separate anti-communist movement, but this process took place mainly in reflections about the economy which often completely ignored other areas of social thought. Moreover, this process was accompanied by mystifications that, instead of defining the concept of liberalism more precisely, expanded it beyond reason. Liberals themselves, who lacked the energy to formulate a clear programme for the reconstruction of society in areas other than the economy, were not solely to blame for such an expansion. Even more responsible were their opponents, who feared that not only real socialism would lose out from such a reconstruction.

One can say that right after the collapse of the *ancien régime*, an inevitable conflict appeared between two different but not yet fully articulated tendencies within the heretofore relatively united anti-communist camp. The goal of one of these tendencies was the fullest possible restoration of the world of values that had existed before real socialism; the goal of the other was modernization, which in some ways might call these values into question.

The opponents of communism united in a common front were really influenced by different motives. For some of them the evil of the system they opposed inhered in the fact that it was a negation of the Truth embodied in the religious and national tradition; for others, the system was evil because it eliminated pluralism from social life and ruled out tolerance.[7] For some the main problem was how to enthrone this Truth, while for others it was how to create an open society in which pluralism and tolerance would be inviolate. In other words, for some, communism's cardinal sin was that it chose the wrong goal; for others, the main flaw of communism was that it was a *teleocracy*, that is, it attempted to subordinate everything absolutely to the goal it had set.[8] No matter how moderate the utterances of the latter, they were often received by the former as an attack on the truth which they were defending and as approval of complete relativism, which gave equal rights to truth and falsity.

A new plane of the debate on the future of society thus appeared – a plane on which the attitude towards real socialism became ever less important because none of the sides considered the possibility of its return. What troubled them, however, were the supposed dangers which appeared right after its fall. For the defenders of traditional values, liberalism, understood as transcending the boundaries set in the past and loosening traditional moral and social values, was perceived as such a threat. In this context, a second expanded conception of liberalism originated – this time taken to mean all views in conflict with the tradition of putting the 'mono-idea'[9] above every-thing else as the *sine qua non* of a good society. As soon as real socialism disappeared from the scene, the 'mono-idea' did not seem so bad to everyone. What seemed bad was pluralism, which challenged not only the monopolistic claims of communism but also any monopoly of ideas as such. The word 'liberalism' started to appear ever more often as a collective name for all sorts of manifestations of a retreat from traditional values – irrespec-tive of whether this retreat was in any way inspired by liberalism. 'Liberalism' was often equated with social *anomie*, implying that the spread of normlessness could be ascribed to the expansion of false doctrines. Thus, *anomie* was not seen as an inevitable outcome of participation in contempo-rary civilization, whose invasion after the fall of real socialism loomed on the horizon. Such an understanding of liberalism accented its negative features: liberalism was defined in terms of whom it was directed against and whom it threatened, but not in terms of what it proposed. In this sense, critics lumped together various attitudes and views, including non-liberal ones.

[7] See Paweł Kłoczowski's apt comments on the conflict between the 'formal' and 'substantive' conceptions of communism. In 'Zniewolony umysł po latach', *Nowe Książki* 1993, no. 10.

[8] For comments on teleocracy see Friedrich von Hayek, *New Studies in Philosophy, Politics, Economics and the History of Ideas* (Chicago: University of Chicago Press, 1978), p. 89.

[9] This term comes from Adam Doboszyński's book *Ustrój narodowy*. See Bogumił Grott, *Religia, Kościół, etyka w ideach i koncepcjach prawicy polskiej* (Kraków: Nomos, 1993), pp. 146–7.

2. *Liberalism versus Christian values*

The problem of the attitude towards Christian values occupied a prominent place in the discussions around liberalism that materialized in Poland after 1989. If liberalism started to be perceived as a threat in certain circles, it was because liberalism was regarded as an orientation very unfriendly towards these values – especially in their Catholic and institutionalized form. This is probably why one of the letters of Polish bishops in 1991 contained the following passage: 'Yesterday it was the East, but today the West will insist that Poland fully accept social, political and also whole-hearted religious liberalism. So we are confronted with a new form of totalitarianism, that is, intolerance of the good, of God's laws, so that with impunity we may propagate evil and in effect once again wrong the weakest.'[10]

People started to write about liberalism in such a tone ever more often, thereby reviving the old dispute that had been put into cold storage under the rule of real socialism. This is not the place to give the details of the course of this dispute,[11] whose historical and doctrinal sources have deep roots. In the past, the dispute was a heated one, with both sides to blame. In many cases, both of them had good reasons for accusing one another of attacking each other's most important values. The history of this dispute can be written, but my sole concern here is what shape it took right after the fall of real socialism.

The question that really needs to be answered is whether this criticism of liberalism from Catholic or Catholic-nationalist positions is part of the tendency visible today, especially in rightist circles, to interpret everything from the standpoint of categories that were in vogue before the fall of real socialism, or whether it is an answer to the liberal ideas that appeared in recent years.

There is much evidence that the 'liberalism' being criticized today does not have much in common with the liberalism professed in Poland by a large number of people who regard themselves as liberals. On the contrary, it is a stereotype of liberalism that spread in conservative circles a long time ago and ignores the changes that have taken place both in Catholicism and liberalism. There is a striking disproportion between the vehemence of the attacks on liberalism by the defenders of traditional values and the restraint

[10] Quoted from Jarosław Gowin, 'Chrześcijaństwo – liberalizm: zapełnianie pustki', *Tygodnik Powszechny*, 7 July 1991. See Jan Maria Jackowski, *Bitwa o Polskę* (Warsaw: Astra, 1993).

[11] See Gene Burns, 'The Politics of Ideology: The Papal Struggle with Liberalism', *American Journal of Sociology* 1990, vol. 95, no. 5, pp. 1123–52; see also Jakub Karpiński, 'Wartości i argumentacje w liberalizmie i chrześcijaństwie', *Przegląd Polityczny* 1993, no. 19/20, pp. 73–9.

shown in the sporadic criticisms of these values by liberals. What is more, a sizeable group of the liberals discussed in this book display a strong attachment to these values and openly express hostility to the anti-religious varieties of liberalism with which we had to do in the past.

Understandably, in light of the Catholic criticisms of capitalism – contained both in social encyclicals and in many Christian Democratic publications[12] – these liberals asked at most whether prejudices against the economic arrangements proposed by liberals can be overcome without challenging traditional values. Such a question was posed by Janusz Lewandowski in 1991 when he asked: 'In Poland is a reinterpretation possible of Christianity in the style of Michael Novak, in which proper rank is given to individualism and economic resourcefulness? I don't know. Perhaps the encounter of Catholicism with the attempt to build capitalism will create an unsolvable dilemma.'[13] Hardly any liberal was eager to start a dispute on basic philosophical issues or, even less so, to question the value of religion as such. Quite the reverse: there were efforts to give liberalism a Christian character or at least one free from any hostility towards Christianity. It is worth looking at the liberalisms of recent years from this angle.

Among the economic liberals, there were three basic positions on Christian values. The first one, after Mirosław Dzielski, should be called *Christian liberalism*, the second the *conservative liberal* position, while the third one may simply be called *liberal*.

The most original approach unquestionably was Dzielski's attempt to invalidate the dispute between liberalism and Christianity by creating a Christian-based liberalism whose programme contained all of the essential elements of the liberal tradition (including its characteristic individualism) without severing ties with the dominant religious tradition. Whether this was an entirely consistent conception that was convincing to both of the sides at odds with each other will not be discussed here. Although no direct criticism was levelled against Dzielski, one can surmise that both sides could have found some fault with his views. Such criticism would have been voiced in other historical circumstances. Probably both sides would have agreed with the criticism that Revd Jan Piwowarczyk aimed many years ago against Stefan Kisielewski, who made such a great contribution to the liberal renaissance of recent years: 'What Kisiel calls liberalism is not liberalism. One can call it the politics of emancipation, the postulate of human rights, free trade, the principle of private initiative, but this is still not liberalism. Liberalism is not only human rights, not only free trade and

---

[12] See Revd Jan Piwowarczyk's 'Spór o liberalizm' in his *Wobec nowego czasu* (Kraków: Znak, 1985), pp. 269–86.
[13] 'Liberalizm stosowany', *Przegląd Polityczny*, June 1991, no. 1/13, p. 10.

private initiative. It is something more and something different.'[14]

The point is that, in suggesting a way to reach an accord, Dzielski skimmed over the most sensitive issues, and sometimes he even posed them as if they needed no discussion at all. It should be remembered that he formulated a new political conception and not a comprehensive social philosophy. Characteristically, his 1980 article entitled 'Who Are the Liberals?', and especially his second point on the attitudes of liberals towards religion, is both an impassioned declaration of the genetic and substantive ties of liberalism with Christianity and an expression of no confidence in institutionalized religion combined with praise for religious pluralism and the independent search for God.[15] In other words, Dzielski did not precisely define the problems that would have to be resolved for a reconciliation of liberalism and institutionalized religion in the form of Catholicism to take place. He really did not go into the philosophical and social roots of the conflict. Rather, he focused on certain somewhat obvious points of contact that had appeared in the face of communism. This diminishes the worth of his theoretical contribution but not the value of his *political* conception, which is more important for the subject-matter of this book.

In fact, there are good reasons to believe that Dzielski achieved all that is possible under the slogan of Christian liberalism. He was convinced that this does not have to be a marriage of convenience. In his case, religious faith was really perhaps the most important factor of evolution towards liberal arrangements. There are no reasons not to believe him when he said of himself and his group that 'we, having matured in a religious milieu, transcended Hayek and his school of thinking. From the very beginning religion has been shaping our understanding of the world, including thinking about society.'[16] This accounted for what he called his 'unorthodoxy' as a liberal, which was distinguished by the belief that 'the problems of poverty and social inequality are real dilemmas' and 'poor people must be helped'.[17] The influence of Catholic social teaching is also visible in his critical evaluation of contemporary Western civilization and in many other matters. Kazimierz Z. Sowa stated not without reason that Dzielski was close to formulating the 'thesis on the primacy of morality not only over politics but also over the economy'.[18]

---

[14] Revd J. Piwowarczyk, op. cit., p. 270.

[15] M. Dzielski, 'Kim są liberałowie?', in his *Duch nadchodzącego czasu* (Wrocław: Wektory, 1989), pp. 43–4.

[16] 'Credo. Z Mirosławem Dzielskim rozmawia Wiesław Walendziak', in *Widzieć mądrość w wolności. Księga pamięci Mirosława Dzielskiego*, ed. B. Chrabota (Kraków: KTP, 1991), p. 175.

[17] Ibid., p. 174.

[18] K. Sowa, 'Czy Dzielski był liberałem? Dwa spojrzenia na liberalizm', in his *Socjologia, społeczeństwo, polityka* (Kraków: KTP, 1991), pp. 11–12.

The problem, however, is that Dzielski was not only influenced by the religious tradition; he also made a *de facto* reinterpretation of this tradition whether under the influence of Hayek or other liberals. Dzielski highlighted individualistic motives and reduced the social teaching of the Church to 'moral theology', from which no 'recipes for political and economic life'[19] can be deduced. Finally, in his rehabilitation of capitalism he went even further than the encyclical *Centessimus Annus* published after his death.

One can say that Dzielski in Poland tackled the same problem that Michael Novak took up in the USA. He went even further, however, for Novak only attempted to reconcile Catholicism with capitalism and with 'liberal institutions' treated as something largely independent of liberalism as a doctrine. Dzielski, on the other hand, made an effort to reconcile Catholicism with *liberalism*, which required (and requires) overcoming an even larger number of misunderstandings and biases.

It is not for me to judge whether Dzielski's Catholicism remained pure or became 'Protestantized', so to speak. What is important is that his unquestioned liberalism acquired a special colouring; it combined with a strong aversion to 'rationalism without imperatives'[20] and the call for a moral revolution that would lead to both a religious renewal and to the restoration of capitalism. What is more, despite his aforementioned dislike for institutionalized (and state-sponsored) religion, Dzielski praised the Catholic Church as a teacher of political culture. In his opinion, the Catholic Church 'during the entire period of its mission under communism rejected radical democracy and supported the position of a liberal conception of political culture. . . . Outside the Church, the liberal conception of political culture was virtually non-existent.'[21]

There is no room here for a detailed analysis of Dzielski's views on the ties of liberalism with Christianity, even though the subject merits such an analysis on account of the originality of his conception. During the years when the views of the author of *Spirit of the Time to Come* were taking shape, liberalism not limited to economic problems was possible (for reasons given below), but it would have been a liberalism free from any thought of the complete laicization of social life, a liberalism strongly rooted in Christianity. This was a noteworthy ideological creation, for it was unabridged liberalism, that is, in attempting to retain all of the essential elements of the European liberal heritage. This Christian liberalism gave both Catholics and liberals a lot to think about; yet, despite the terms of praise lavished on Dzielski, this thinking bore few fruits in subsequent years.

[19] Ibid., pp. 13–14.
[20] See M. Dzielski, 'Powrót cywilizacji', *Duch nadchodzącego czasu*, op. cit., p. 258.
[21] M. Dzielski, 'Kultura polityczna a sytuacja polska', *Duch nadchodzącego czasu*, op. cit., pp. 294–5.

The second conception – chronologically somewhat later – of arranging relationships between liberalism and the religious tradition dominant in Poland was based on the assumption that liberalism can and should be radically limited, thanks to which the conflict between it and this tradition would be to no purpose. Reduced to a certain minimum, above all to a specific economic strategy, liberalism ceases to be an ideology claiming to have its own position on every area of social life and thereby becomes capable of peacefully coexisting with orientations that are more competent than it in non-economic matters and that are more deeply rooted in society than it. This, of course, required the further assumption that the liberal tradition is so heterogeneous or even incoherent that one can and even should have a definite choice within it, retaining or even strengthening some elements and rejecting others. As a critic of this position put it, the result of such an operation would consist in 'fusing a procapitalist economic programme with conservatism, which is understood as maintaining Christian values'.[22]

Perhaps this position was expressed most clearly by Lech Mażewski, who in his criticism of 'total liberalism' or liberal 'integrism' distinguished 'three liberalisms: economic, political and cultural', among which – as he cogently argued – 'there are no clear connections'.[23] In Mażewski's opinion, the 'first two forms of liberalism, if they are not regarded as absolute and are not subject to moral evaluation, can be . . . easily reconciled with the social teaching of the Church. . . . On the other hand, the third form, i.e., cultural liberalism, remains an important and difficult problem. By its nature this is an ideology unfriendly to religion, an ideology that absolutizes the individual and his liberty, and as a result one that can tear apart the tissue of social life.'[24]

If one accepts this point of view, 'one can be but doesn't have to be a liberal in one's outlook on life'.[25] In other words, a liberal option that is not an ideological option in the most common meaning of 'ideology' is not a matched sale: there is no objection to accepting economic liberalism without reservations, supplementing it in one way or another with political liberalism, while totally rejecting cultural liberalism and replacing it with *conservatism*. Such a solution was proposed by Mażewski, following the example

[22] Janusz Lewandowski, 'Czy i jaka centroprawica?', *Przegląd Polityczny* 1992, no. 3 (16), p. 9.

[23] Lech Mażewski, 'Thatcheryzm po polsku', *Przegląd Polski* 1992, no. 3 (16), p. 10. See also his 'Liberalizm i chrześcijaństwo', *Życie Warszawy*, 5 September 1991; his 'KLD: ruch w prawo', *Biuletyn Informacyjny KLD*, January 1992, no. 1 (9), pp. 6–7; and his 'Opcja konserwatywno-liberalna', *Filozofia liberalizmu*, ed. Józef Tarnowski (Warsaw: Oficyna Liberałów, 1993), pp. 90–9.

[24] L. Mażewski, 'Thatcheryzm po polsku', op. cit., p. 10.

[25] Statement of L. Mażewski, quoted in the report 'Obserwator Codzienny' from the Third KLD Conference on 26 February 1992.

of the combining of ideas of freedom and order by the 'new right', to which Roger Scruton ascribes a dual origin: from the theory of the free market and social conservatism.[26]

Mażewski was the moving force of the conservative-liberal group in the Liberal-Democratic Congress and often simply referred to himself as a conservative. In time, he switched to the newly formed Conservative Party. Logically, one can imagine that the same reasoning would lead someone in an entirely different direction. In fact, there are cases of combining cultural liberalism with an extremely non-liberal position in economic matters. It seems, however, that such a disintegration of liberalism is most useful for someone who wants to convince himself and others that liberalism does not necessarily mean disloyalty to religion and to dispel any suspicions that as a liberal deep in his heart he harbours views that disqualify him as a devout person and a member of the right. The supporters of cultural liberalism do not have troubles of this kind – unless they are confirmed socialists and thus want to openly demonstrate their hostility to economic liberalism.

I see no point in dwelling longer on Mażewski's classification of three liberalisms. It is very useful as a tool of historical analysis, and for this reason has been used by historians for a long time.[27] I myself used it in this book (see Chapter III). When used to construct a liberal programme, however, it has purgative effects. In compensation for this, the proponents of this approach claim that it will attract more supporters to this programme and make new alliances possible. This means a return to the old situation on the Polish political scene in which larger or smaller doses of liberalism were added to entirely different ideologies. Mażewski's proposal is not very convincing to the declared opponents of liberalism. They are generally hostile to economic liberalism, which, in fact, is hard to square with the social teaching of the Church, despite noticeable changes in the latter in recent years. Janusz Zabłocki called this entire operation 'rather artificial' and the thesis on the lack of a 'clear link' between various forms of liberalism 'somewhat arbitrary', adding that even if the proposed division were accepted, this would not alter the fact that 'there are also significant differences between economic and political liberalism and the social teaching of the Church, not even smaller perhaps than in the case of cultural liberalism.'[28]

M. Dzielski's conception seems much more immune to criticism from this

---

[26] See Roger Scruton, 'The New Right in Central Europe I: Czechoslovakia', *Political Studies* 1988, XXXVI, pp. 449–62.

[27] See Michael Mandelbaum, 'The Long Life of Liberalism', in *The Relevance of Liberalism*, eds Zbigniew Brzeziński, Seweryn Bialer, Sophia Slusar and Robert Nurick (Boulder CO: Westview Press, 1978), pp. 201–33.

[28] Janusz Zabłocki, 'Spór a nie sojusz', *Życie Warszawy*, 27 September 1991.

angle. Whether successfully or not, he undertook the more difficult task of reinterpreting the entire liberal doctrine to adapt it to the Christian context (which he also reinterpreted to some extent). Mażewski, on the other hand, simply made a crosswise cut through this doctrine, leaving essentially unchanged what he wanted to retain in it and giving up all the rest without discussion and regret. Dzielski was not indifferent to the 'rest' that had been lopped off by Mażewski, as evidenced by the former's attempts to create a theory of civilization and an ethical conception which would not merely be a replica of traditional religious ethics but which would admit the 'spirit of capitalism'.

In short, Mażewski's conception is basically a conception of two truths, each of which has a different scope of application, whereas Dzielski's conception – justifiably or not – assumes that it is possible to create a uniform and harmonious world-view drawing from both the liberal and the Christian tradition. It is not my intention here to deny that there were important similarities between these two conceptions. Both of them were interested in pushing liberalism to the right and reconciling it with the dominant religious tradition. In my opinion, however, these are two different conceptions of placing economic liberalism within the context of a particular world-view. Both of them seem very characteristic of the anti-communist 'liberal revolution', in which, naturally, the theme of *restoration* had to be present as well as sometimes exaggerated restraint in questioning what had been combated by the communists.

The third way of going beyond 'pure' economic liberalism, meanwhile, was much more hazy, but it deserves careful attention. It meant a return to the mainstream of liberal thought – intentionally limited in its postulates on account of containing no extremes and allowing for an extended sphere of privateness. None the less, it aspired to form itself in a *sweeping* programme for arranging society in a fundamentally non-traditional manner. To put it in a nutshell, this way recognized that in the long run it was impossible to practise economic liberalism without undertaking the task of modernizing the entire culture, and without in one area or another locking horns with tradition and orientations keen on keeping this tradition unchanged. In speaking of the existence of such a way, I have in mind especially the influential group of KLD activists as well as the Faction of the Social Democratic Union, who for some time now (but not from the very beginning) have been giving an ever more negative answer to the earlier quoted question whether in Poland it is possible to carry out 'a reinterpretation of Christianity in the style of Michael Novak',[29] that is, whether real agreement between liberals and the dominant religious tradition is possible.

[29] See note 13.

It is worth emphasizing that the turn in this direction by some Polish liberals was not doctrinally motivated. On the contrary, everything indicates that they were as far removed as possible from anti-traditionalism as a supposedly binding dogma of liberalism. They declared that they were 'pragmatists' and that philosophy was not their primary interest. In April 1991 Janusz Lewandowski wrote: 'It is not by chance that we have not joined the Liberal International . . . We have different attitudes towards tradition; some of them are more anti-clerical. We esteem stabilizing, Christian values. Our intention is to introduce every political change with somewhat conservative methods.'[30]

Many other Polish liberals from various circles and parties expressed themselves in a similar vein at this time. Yet, in their utterances it would be hard to find any manifestations of liberalism as a 'world-view', any 'total', 'integral' or 'radical' liberalism. Only later could a noticeable but rather small change be observed in this respect. This change unquestionably was a response to the political offensive of the Church. It was also due to growing awareness that the emerging liberal electorate would feel better 'in its own liberal skin',[31] that is, in a situation enabling it to clearly define its political identity. Initially, a rather widespread diagnostic error came into play here. From the indisputable fact that the vast majority of Polish society are Catholics the wrong conclusion was drawn that most of the members of this society think and behave as Catholics should and that, consequently, a politician's chances of getting support depend directly on the extent to which he or she is in agreement with the Church. This accounts for the oddity of political life in the first few years after 1989, an oddity which, as Lewandowski observed, consists in the 'fondness for donning Christian Democratic attire, declaring Christian values, and courting the Church'.[32]

I am unable to fully explain the change which was manifested both in the behaviour of liberal deputies in voting in the Diet on the anti-abortion law and on the requirement to respect Christian values on radio and television. Furthermore, liberal journalists and leaders ever more often expressed doubts – still toned down but unequivocal – about the advisability of 'baptizing' liberalism and 'washing away' the liberal identity. One of these liberals wrote: 'We fully understand the value of continuity and tradition, we appreciate the importance of Christian values as anchors in our life . . . But it isn't a matter of repeating such things so as to join the multi-coloured procession of supporters of Christian values.'[33] This issue became the

[30] 'Liberalizm praktyczny', an interview with Janusz Lewandowski, *Gazeta Wyborcza*, 13 April 1991.

[31] J. Lewandowski, 'Jaki liberalizm jest Polsce potrzebny?', op. cit., p. 12.

[32] Ibid., p. 13.

[33] Ibid.

subject of an interparty debate in connection with the LDC Programme Conference in 1992, which ended with the defeat of the supporters of 'baptizing' liberalism.[34]

Without going into the details of this dispute, which really concerned no essential philosophical questions that could have been raised in this context and which remained a political debate, it is worth mentioning the general line taken by journalists. It was argued ever more often that liberals should not confine their attention to a sweeping reconstruction of the economy, but should also strive to create a *new civilization*, which is an indispensable supplement to and consequence of this reconstruction.

This matter too was most clearly expressed by Janusz Lewandowski, who is unquestionably the most outstanding representative of liberalism in Poland today, even though as a 'pragmatist' he often lays himself open to criticism by orthodox neoliberals. He questioned Mażewski's conception in its entirety by arguing that capitalism

is a complete civilizational model and not building blocks that can be arranged in any way at all. The program of democratic capitalism will only acquire full meaning and content when the need is recognized for modernization of life in Poland on a wide scale. Capitalism has many shades . . ., but in each successful manifestation it required overcoming attitudes and habits inimical to market mechanisms and enterprise. Always, only part of the national heritage could enter into the new capitalist synthesis. The more sudden the changes of structures, the faster the progress of the market, the more dynamic the adjustment processes have to be and the less room there is for conservatism.[35]

Underpinning this reasoning was the belief that there are Christian values which 'harmonize with the vision of democratic capitalism' (Lewandowski in this context refers to the names of Irving Kristol, Wilhelm Roepke and Michael Novak), but they constitute 'a different set than the one encoded in Polish tradition and reinforced by the parish priest'.[36] Thus, it is necessary to 're-evaluate' the national heritage, while those liberals who want to

[34] See Andrzej Zarębski, 'Spory w Kongresie', *Nowa Europa*, 23–25 October 1992; Piotr Skwieciński, 'Dylematy liberałów', *Życie Warszawy*, reprinted in *Biuletyn Informacyjny KLD*, March–April 1992, no. 3 (11).

[35] Janusz Lewandowski, 'Czy i jaka centroprawica?', op. cit., p. 9. See the same author's 'Elementarz', *Wprost*, 19 July 1992, pp. 55–6.

[36] J. Lewandowski, 'Czy i jaka centroprawica?', op. cit., p. 9. See the same author's 'Kościół a wolny rynek', *Res Publica Nowa* 1993, no. 10 (61), pp. 13–14. Another liberal economist put this even more emphatically: 'Catholicism once again in history has turned out to be a factor impeding procapitalist changes' (Jan Winiecki, 'Przyczyny społeczne i polityczne', *Rzeczpospolita*, 9–10 October 1993).

present their views 'in a conservative-Christian wrapping' are encouraging people – Lewandowski says – to bury their heads in the sand. Even if a successful synthesis of neoliberalism and conservatism is possible in the West (in the form of Thatcherism, for instance), such a feat is impossible in Poland, where conservatism is too weighed down by a pre-capitalist mentality that in certain respects was made even stronger by communism. Liberals are thus faced with 'the task of an overall reform', not just reform of the economy carried out under the patronage of tradition. Just as one cannot lean too far towards conservatism, neither can one afford too much neoliberalism, which in Polish conditions is too revolutionary.

The discussion was conducted on a rather abstract level, or at most referred to some issues of day-to-day politics; therefore, it is difficult to draw up a detailed list of disputable points and modernization postulates. There is no question, however, that the discussion took up the problem of separation of Church and state and assigned to the private sphere a wider range of activities than wished for by traditionalists, who with their all-encompassing conception of the good know how a person should behave as an individual and as a member of a group. It is also obvious that the postulate of 're-evaluating' tradition also had to address such questions as Poland's opening up to the world, the 'return to Europe', overcoming xenophobia, changing the attitude towards time and money, etc. It does not take a genius to see that fanning nationalism, the cult of native ways, or xenophobia are direct threats to the budding capitalist economy through their repercussions in such areas as privatization policy, the tariff system, international relations, etc.

It is not entirely clear whether the aforementioned aloofness to traditional Catholicism was necessarily premised on such a broad understanding of liberal values. In any case, the reason is not always clearly spelled out. We may suppose that sometimes this criticism of the parish priest is restricted to the fact that he has not fully digested the contemporary stance of the Church on economic issues and not to the fact that he cannot divest himself of his hostility to liberalism as a world-view. In this sense, the dividing line between different liberal attitudes towards Christianity is not as clear as it might appear.

There is no room here for a detailed analysis of this complicated subject. The point is that the problem was raised of the *cultural* conditions for the expansion of the 'spirit of capitalism' in countries weighed down not only by the legacy of real socialism but also by the legacy of pre-capitalist traditionalism, which could be an invaluable support for resistance against communism but not necessarily for modernization of the country after the fall of communism. Even if such an opinion is somewhat biased, what is at issue is a problem that liberals (or at least some of them) could not help taking up if they wanted to be true to the 'liberal canon', to liberalism in its classic, more or less integral, form. Otherwise, not only would they have been banished to shamefaced regions of silence, but the mission of defending many liberal values would have been taken up by the rallying left. By ceding economic liberalism to conservatives and cultural liberalism to the left, liberals might easily disappear completely from the scene as an independent political force. Liberals appeared on the scene because they were the first to put forward a programme for building capitalism, but today this programme no longer guarantees their identity, even though they are the first to be blamed for its failures.

Still another attitude associated with liberalism may be distinguished, though this time not with economic liberalism. This is so-called *leftist liberalism*, which is rooted in the tradition of cultural and political liberalism but lacks strong ties with the tradition of economic liberalism[37] and is *sometimes even hostile to it*. Traditionalist critics of liberalism probably have this variety in mind when they say that liberalism acquired far-flung influence among the Polish intelligentsia, and they associate it directly with the so-called secular left and with the democratic opposition of the 1970s and 1980s.[38] The habit of associating all liberalism with the economic liberalism that constituted itself in Poland in the last decade makes it hard to perceive the possibility that such a liberalism can also exist. It should be remembered, however, that in many countries the word 'liberalism' is primarily associated with the former. It is characteristic that one of the experts on Polish affairs argues that after 1989 a 'crisis of liberalism' has been taking place in Poland and that in the pre-communist past the socialist left was the main carrier of liberal values.[39] So one can say that a liberalism whose conflict with traditionalism is not so much due to concern over the future of the 'spirit of capitalism' as to the conviction that basic liberal values in themselves are worth propagating exists at least potentially in Poland.

[37] See Wojciech Sadurski, 'Etos lewicy, etos liberalny', *Po prostu*, 28 June 1990.

[38] See Jarosław Marek Rymkiewicz, 'Dlaczego jestem taki wściekły?', *Życie Warszawy*, 1993, no. 113. There we read: 'This is now the most important Polish question: will the Poles permit themselves to be reshaped into some other nation, or will they live as they want to live? As they always lived here?'

[39] See David Ost, 'Introduction to Adam Michnik's Church – Left – Dialogue' (manuscript, subsequently published by University of Chicago Press); 'The Crisis of Liberalism in Poland', *Telos* 1991, no. 89, p. 85.

3. *The situational and doctrinal context*

Once again it should be reiterated that the criticism of tradition on the part of some Polish liberals was far from radical or militant. On the contrary, on the Polish political scene these critics in the main (apart from Janusz Korwin-Mikke and his Union of Realistic Politics, which emphasizes its conservatism) were paragons of reason and moderation, objectivity and tact. The reason they are attacked so vehemently is partly due to semantic misunderstandings, in which the word 'liberalism' is taken to mean a lack of principles and social discipline; partly to the attempt by many political groupings to make liberals the 'scapegoat' for the excessively high costs of building a capitalist economy on the post-communist base; and partly to the fact that they are 'different from everyone else', with their own style, which is an open challenge to many national habits and customs and which for this reason may gall both the right and the left.

In any case, just as noteworthy and surprising is that the conflict between liberalism and the dominant religious tradition did not appear earlier and more sharply. A serious effort was made to stave off this conflict by searching for a formula of Christian liberalism or by attempting to redefine Polish liberalism. At one time, Dzielski was even a member of the Primate's Council, and openly liberal publications appeared in the Catholic press.[40] This circumstance is worth examining more closely, because it may shed light both on the nature of liberalism and on the situation in Poland after the recent birth of liberalism there.

Attention should be called to a few matters which in one way or another paved the way for the rather unimpeded circulation of liberal ideas, notwithstanding the fact that these ideas lacked solid support in the historical tradition and were associated with the conflict of their advocates with the defenders of religion, if not with religion as such.

The enormous influence of Catholicism and the Church in Poland unquestionably was also of paramount importance. This influence stemmed from the high percentage of Catholics in the population and from the fact that for a very long time Catholicism and the Church had played a major role in preserving the identity of a nation which lacked its own state. There are good reasons for stating that 'liberals are pragmatics; and if they live in a

---

[40] Bohdan Cywiński later said: 'It is a paradox, but over the last decade the Catholic Church in Poland as well as the entire Polish Catholic society seem to have been unusually well-disposed to liberal capitalism.' This author sees the reason for this 'romance with liberalism' is 'unfamiliarity with the teachings of the Polish Pope', and predicts that when these teachings become known Polish Catholics will turn their backs on liberalism. ('Krajobraz po bitwie', an interview with Bohdan Cywiński in *Przegląd Polityczny* 1993, no. 19/20, p. 71.)

country in which Catholics make up 90 percent of the population, they take account of this fact and behave accordingly, despite the essentially secular nature of the liberal doctrine'.[41]

Although it certainly applies to some liberals, this formula is not very convincing to me. First, in certain cases (for example, Dzielski) this was not 'pragmatism' but a genuine bond with the religious tradition. Second, liberals – Christian or lay – never showed a tendency to conform to the majority; on the contrary, they were always ready to defend the view of the minority, something which seems to lie at the heart of their doctrine. It might have been expected that in conditions of the dominance of one religion, liberals would represent the opposite orientation – the more so as in the past many of them had good reasons to do so. Third, the thesis that 90 percent of Poles are Catholics is nonsense. A very high percentage of people who were brought up as Catholics are not Catholics in their views or their behaviour. In any case, in Polish society there are (and over the past two centuries always have been) sizeable groups of people who are real or potential clients of secular or religious ideologies far removed from Catholic orthodoxy. In this Catholic country the Christian Democratic Party was never a real political force; and in the absence of a National Democratic Party closely affiliated with the Church, neither is it a major political force today. In short, one cannot argue that the lack of ostentatious secularity on the part of Polish liberals is simply a statistical and tactical necessity. It is quite another matter that most conducive to the development of liberalism is the existence of a multitude of so-called non-orthodox churches and religious sects – not one great dominant Church claiming the right to speak for the entire society.[42]

Colin Barker noted the 'seeming paradox' consisting in the fact that 'the social values that the Catholic Church claims to defend in contemporary Poland are, essentially, those associated with liberalism in the West: personal authenticity, individual rights, civil society's claims against the State. This seems odd, for in the period when these liberal ideas were being forged in the West . . . one of liberalism's key enemies was the hierarchical and feudal Catholic Church.'[43] In passing, it is worth mentioning that for many people of the West this 'seeming paradox' was perhaps the biggest obstacle to understanding what was happening in Poland. In their experience, even if the fight for liberal values does not necessarily take place against the Church, no support for this fight may be expected from the Church.

[41] Barbara Szczepuła, 'Spisek liberałów', *Tygodnik Gdański*, 27 January 1991.
[42] R. Dahrendorf, *Society and Democracy in Germany* (Anchor Books, 1969), p. 135.
[43] Colin Barker, *Festival of the Oppressed: Solidarity, Reform and Revolution in Poland 1980–81* (London: Bookmarks, 1989), p. 57.

This was a misunderstanding in a double sense. It resulted, first, from sticking fast to a stereotype which in certain respects had long since lost touch with reality on account of the changes that had taken place in Catholicism in the last decades; and, second, from failure to appreciate the influence of the historical and situational context on how the very same doctrines function in society. The evolution of Catholicism is a separate and vast subject, and as such lies outside the framework of this book. It suffices to say that the idea of human and civil rights has changed over the last hundred or more years from an object of absolute condemnation to an essential part of Christianity, which does not mean that the Church simply approved the ideological legacy of modern revolutions.[44] The same thing happened with many other liberal ideas, starting from the idea of liberty itself. This was a completely natural process, which did not spare any institution of long standing – irrespective of its nature and mission.

More important in our case is the *context*. Most generally speaking, on the one hand the rule of communists had made even people and groups that in other circumstances would have been hostile to liberal ideas interested in the development of liberties; on the other in Poland the Catholic Church remained the only institution with a large degree of independence and capable of successfully resisting attempts to subordinate all social life to control of the party-state, thereby setting an example for all the 'unsubmissive' to follow. In a certain sense, the Church became the first institution of nascent civil society. It is not surprising, therefore, that people of different orientations saw the Church as an invaluable model, even those who did not belong to it and had little sympathy for its real mission.

Indeed, one could believe that 'the symbiosis of the Church and the opposition, most of whose members by various paths had reached some form of liberalism, would be a lasting process of mutual enrichment'.[45] A document of fundamental importance from this point of view is Adam Michnik's celebrated book *Kościół – lewica – dialog* (The Church – the Left – Dialogue). The 'secular left' of which Michnik wrote is nothing but what other people in other circumstances simply called liberals or cultural liberals. A testimony of another kind are the biographies of persons who during the period of real socialism discovered religion as an important dimension of spiritual life.[46]

This is another subject too vast to discuss in detail here. In a nutshell, for many people the idea of emancipation in those days unexpectedly became

[44] On the Catholic interpretation of human rights see Mieczysław Albert Krąpiec, *O ludzką politykę* (Katowice: Tolek, 1993), chapter 4.

[45] J. Gowin, 'Chrześcijaństwo – liberalizm: zapełnianie pustki', op. cit.

[46] Jacek Kuroń, *Wiara i wina. Do i od komunizmy* (London: Aneks, 1989), especially the last chapter.

inseparably linked with the idea of religion and the Church, criticism of which was readily associated with the official ideology and as such was virtually excluded.

In times when communism donned the cloak of an heir of the Enlightenment tradition, a liberal-freethinker and anti-cleric had to revise his or her views in order to avoid being taken for an ally of communism – even an unwilling one. This is unquestionably an oversimplification. The new attitude towards religion and the Church was not entirely free of doubts and reservations; nor did traditional freethinking imply political support for communism. In any case, a major rearrangement of ideological positions took place. The Church became the harbour for many of the 'unsubmissive', whom it took in not only as reformed sinners. In the existing conditions, these persons were its allies for they opposed forces hostile to the Church and were in favour of freedom, which the Church also needed.

In many respects, this was a different Church from the one that had been the object of attacks by freethinkers in the pre-communist era. In any case, there were good reasons to regard it as different; and, consequently, criticism of the Church became morally suspect. No one who was on the side of the opponents of communism was eager to criticize the Church – irrespective of whether he or she was a Catholic and of how strongly he or she was attached to the values which the Church still lacked. The tendency to see in the Church only what was best and to exaggerate the otherwise very important changes which had taken place in the Church during the time of persecutions and restrictions gained the upper hand in anti-communist circles.

From the very outset, this 'religious revival' contained the makings of a great misunderstanding. It is obvious that the Church was primarily interested in expanding the ranks of faithful and non-opportunistic supporters and strengthening its own position. On the other hand, these political allies and catechumens were not necessarily fully aware of the nature of the institution whose value they had discovered; they often were content to point out superficial similarities between views which attracted them to the Church and the views professed by the Church. When opposed to communism, these views might seem almost identical; when placed side by side in the absence of a common enemy, these views had to reveal their incommensurability and even incompatibility – and not only in details.

Someone who opposed communism in the name of values that did not necessarily fit into the Catholic tradition inevitably had to run into 'trouble',[47] someone who – as A. Michnik wrote – was unable or unwilling

---

[47] I refer here to Adam Michnik's essay entitled 'Kłopot' in the volume *Obecność. Leszkowi Kołakowskiemu w 60 rocznicę urodzin* (London: Aneks, 1987), pp. 197–219.

to give up 'his or her subject nature and identity for the sake of identification with Catholic doctrine and the Church hierarchy'.[48]

Here I will not go into how many people in Poland experienced such 'trouble', which Michnik himself described as the trouble of Polish intellectuals. No matter how elitist this trouble was, it unquestionably affected a considerable part of the protoliberal and liberal circles described in this book. It is these groups which came out with ideas lacking deep roots in the tradition of the Polish Church, ideas which enjoyed only a modicum of popularity in the few Catholic circles vitally interested in the renewal of the Church.

In speaking of those who might have had this 'trouble', I have in mind not only the democratic opposition with its conception of the individual and civil society but also the economic liberals, who – coming out strongly in favour of capitalism – had to be aware that they were proposing a real 'cultural revolution'. To be sure, this revolution was supposed to be directed against real socialism, but for many liberals it was also apparent that it would require profound changes in the traditional mentality and would also cause such changes. It was also obvious that the social teaching of the Church – despite the positive attitude towards private ownership – was very far from unreserved praise of the 'spirit of capitalism'[49] that economic liberals were attempting to awaken. Dzielski tried to resolve the problems resulting therefrom, but the matter remained controversial.[50] Even more controversial were all questions connected with reaching a *modus vivendi* between the Church and political and cultural liberalism.

To put it briefly, the two kinds of 'trouble' about which Adam Michnik wrote came into play here. They correspond roughly to the two lines of development of liberal ideas that I attempted to distinguish here: political and economic liberalism. In the first case, the difficulty consisted in reconciling the liberal ideal of an open pluralistic society based on the coexistence of many different conceptions of truth and good with the ideal of a society organized around one conception regarded as absolute truth. In the second case, the difficulty consisted in squaring the liberal ideal of a free market with the ideal of an economy subordinated to moral principles. Progress of

[48] Ibid., p. 198.

[49] The best elucidation of this matter is given by Michael Novak in *The Catholic Ethic and the Spirit of Capitalism* (New York: The Free Press, 1993). Novak is an exceptionally good witness not only because of his knowledge of the subject, but also because he makes every effort to tone down the opposition and show that the teaching of the present pope contains a certain rehabilitation of capitalism. See Michael Novak, *Catholic Social Thought and Liberal Institutions: Freedom with Justice* (New Brunswick NJ: Transaction Publishers, 1989).

[50] See the exchange of views between Revd Krzysztof Paczos MIG and Maciej Zięba OP in *Tygodnik Powszechny*, nos 49, 50/1993, and no. 6/1994.

liberal thought cannot be imagined without facing these two difficulties. For the reasons presented above, these difficulties were not recognized immediately. As long as real socialism existed, they were at most theoretical difficulties. What mattered in practice was that the Church was vitally interested both in the establishment of pluralism and in the restoration of an economic system in which private ownership would play a major role. In this sense, the dispute between the Church and liberalism was inopportune and seemingly belonged to the past.

After 1989, the situation changed fundamentally. In the new situational context, recent alliances were dissolved, and old disputes came to life again. The mounting criticism of 'liberalism', of which we have spoken earlier, was a clear sign that Catholic thought in many instances was returning to pre-communist ways of thinking, to the stereotype of Poland as standing aloof from the 'moral corruption of the West', ways of thinking that seemingly had been forgotten, or cast aside for good.

For people who had been accustomed to see the Church as the avantgarde of civil society in the Western style, this was a real shock. They now discovered that the most ardent supporters of the Church professed views glaringly in contradiction with their expectations.[51] These Catholics not only were unwilling to enter into a dialogue with people who thought differently, a dialogue that liberals believed would be common practice in a society liberated from communism, but they also professed the seemingly discredited view that the good can be decreed and put into practice using the machinery of government. This shock was all the greater for veterans of the fight against communism, who now had no place in the triumphant Church. They were attacked sharply and often treated as though they were, if not 'reds' at least 'pinks', and had done nothing to overthrow communism. Sometimes it appeared as if the democratic opposition had been nothing but a game of appearances, from which nothing should remain that did not fit into the traditional Polish ways whose mainstay is the Church. Implacable enemies of communism about whom no one had ever heard before suddenly came out of the woodwork and now were lauded as conquerors of 'liberalism' and 'demo-liberalism'.

An analysis of these views and frames of mind does not belong to our subject; neither does trying to identify those responsible for fanning them to such an intensity. Nor do I wish to dwell on the seriousness of various misunderstandings, which – as someone remarked – resulted primarily from getting lost in the 'labyrinth of freedom' and looking for a way out by

---

[51] See the characteristic article from this point of view of Czesław Miłosz, 'Państwo wyznaniowe', *Gazeta Wyborcza*, 11 May 1991 (reprinted in *Kultura* 1991, no. 7/527, pp. 3–11). See also Adam Michnik, 'Kościół, prawica, monolog albo ludzie podwójnego wyzwania', *Gazeta Wyborcza*, 27–28 March 1993.

ramming new ways of thinking into old patterns. Whatever these misunderstandings were like, it cannot be denied that through them the real problems
were laid bare which before 1989 had been masked by threats to the very
existence of the nation, not just to some ideology or other. In normal conditions these problems had to be expressed, though not necessarily in the way
this happened in Poland.

This initiated the debate on what liberalism really is and how far it should
go. As long as real socialism existed, circumstances did not require a real
intellectual effort on the part of its opponents. Everything that was against
the status quo was acceptable to them. It was to this way of thinking that
liberalism owed its career in Poland. Liberalism could be perceived as
communism *à rebours* and deserving of sympathy and support on this
account alone. As soon as real socialism fell, it became apparent that
nothing is self-evident or, what amounts to the same thing, something is
self-evident only within the boundaries of one world-view or one party.
Liberalism was forced to define itself in respect to orientations other than
communism. Now the separateness or even antagonism of these orientations
became glaringly apparent, and they in turn had to define themselves in
respect to liberalism. This did not happen overnight, of course. This is a
process that has just begun, and its final outcome is not yet clear. Already
today, however, one can see what the dispute is about and where Polish
liberalism[52] encounters barriers which are difficult to surmount.

4. *The line of division*

These barriers are not as high for all varieties of liberalism. Economic liberalism seems to have the most secure future. To be sure, this does not mean
that it is absolutely clear just what economic liberalism is in the post-
communist world; nor does it mean that there are no threats to economic
liberalism. Quite the contrary, there are many reasons to believe that various
opinions are held about economic liberalism, some of them quite outlandish.
What are commonly regarded as the practical failures of economic liberalism swell the ranks of its opponents, who tend to believe that the economy
can be reformed in some other, entirely non-liberal, way. My point is that
the general programme of moving to capitalism has been largely accepted
and, in fact, has ceased to be a uniquely liberal programme.

The question of the identity of economic liberalism shifted either to

[52] Here, as in this entire chapter, I am speaking about *Polish* liberalism on account of
the unusual situation of liberalism in a Catholic country. It seems, however, that a fundamental problem appears not only in this context. Also involved here are views on social
life which Catholicism shares with many other non-liberal ideologies.

specific economic discussions on what sort of capitalism this was to be or to a public debate on its consequences. In other words, the situation in the post-communist countries became similar in some respects to the one in Western countries. In the latter, economic liberalism, however defined, is a constantly present orientation. There it not only posits the necessity of a market economy, but understands this economy in a certain way. The economy is a subject of constant debate, in which liberals do not always have the upper hand, but are never completely defeated. Every practical triumph of their opponents makes the future of liberals brighter. After years of the predominance of anti-liberal economic policy, the scales finally seem to be shifting in their favour.

In this sense, economic liberalism has established a place for itself in the post-communist world. In one way or another, in one form or another, economic liberalism will make itself felt. It is quite another matter what this liberalism will be like. It is highly probable that it will be ever less dogmatic and that the revolutionary pathos which permeated it right after the fall of real communism will constantly wane.

Let us not toy with predictions. In any case, liberals are faced with the Herculean task of reconciling their principles with the exigencies of local conditions. This notwithstanding, it is hard to imagine that these principles have become completely unattractive. No matter what follies are committed by liberals, their opponents will do their utmost to thwart them by sinning on the side of interventionism, thereby once again opening up the field for liberals. Moreover, the chance for economic liberalism lies in the fact that in normal conditions the majority of its opponents are not so much against its principles as against going beyond acceptable limits in their application. Whatever orthodox liberals think of this, outside the confines of real socialism the dispute is largely over the *degree* to which their principles are recognized as correct and practical, not over whether they should be accepted or rejected in entirety.

One can argue that it is the same in the case of political liberalism. In the world today, as a rule the so-called liberal minimum is not rejected *in toto*, despite examples showing that its postulates are not respected in practice either on account of alleged special circumstances or contradictions between these postulates and some fundamentalist ideology or another. Like the market economy, liberal democracy is rarely questioned today; at most, reasons are sought to restrict it in some way. The more widespread the acceptance of the liberal minimum, the less it may be regarded as accep-tance of liberalism as such, whose political identity depends mainly on whether it goes beyond this minimum. Similarly, proclaiming oneself in favour of a market economy does not yet make someone an economic liberal; and neither is recognition of certain civil liberties, even though postulated by liberals in the past, by itself political liberalism today.

If liberalism is still a very special ideology and distinct from others, the reason is that it postulates *something more* and also holds some assumptions which the supporters of other positions decidedly reject.

Without repeating what was said in Chapter II, some additional remarks are necessary to fit earlier statements into the context of this chapter so as to answer the most important question posed here, namely, why was a conflict of liberalism with the traditional view of the world officially represented by the Catholic Church in Poland sooner or later unavoidable? Furthermore, why in this case was the issue not a difference of *degree* in recognition of liberal principles but an uncrossable *dividing line* between liberal and non-liberal principles?

This dividing line can be defined in various ways. The best approach to describing it, however, will be to recall that in principle the freedom defended by liberals is *negative* freedom. In other words, the aim of the advocates of this freedom is to remove the obstacles that rise up on the way to realization of the innate rights of the individual, not to decide what the individual should do to be good, wise and happy.[53] Only liberals seem to hold a concept of liberty restricted in such a way. All other conceptions of liberty speak about *positive* freedom, answering the question *for what* man should be free, and combining the idea of liberty with a certain idea of the good, whose attainment is the calling of the individual and the collectivity. Perhaps the latter view appears in its purest form in Catholic social thought, which fuses the concept of liberty with a concept of absolute truth and questions the liberal idea of liberty as empty and dangerous because it leads to subjectivity, licence and the dissolution of society.[54]

The *minimalism* of the liberal conception of political society is closely bound up with the understanding of liberty as negative freedom. The liberal position was most clearly expressed by John Rawls, but it is also characteristic of many representatives of political liberalism and seems fully consistent with the old liberal tradition. This minimalism consists in setting aside the question on absolute truth as a necessary foundation for cooperation in society. By ascribing inalienable rights to individuals and postulating the

[53] A classic exposition of the concept of negative freedom may be found in Isaiah Berlin, 'Two Concepts of Liberty', in *Four Essays on Liberty* (New York: Oxford University Press, 1982).

[54] See Maciej Zięba OP, 'Kościół wobec liberalnej demokracji', in Michael Novak, Anton Rauscher SJ, Maciej Zięba OP, *Chrześcijaństwo, demokracja, kapitalizm* (Poznań, 1993), p. 129. See also Józef Tischner, 'Wolność – łaska wszystkich łask', *Nieszczęsny dar wolności* (Kraków: Znak, 1993). I intentionally refer to these two authors, because their example shows that even sympathy for many aspects of the liberal tradition (both even speak of 'Christian liberalism') does not permit Catholics to become reconciled with political liberalism on this pivotal point for it.

abolition of all restrictions on these rights whenever this does not threaten the liberty of other individuals, liberals thereby consent to a chronic and unavoidable state of differences and conflicts. Since this must be so, they agree that – as Richard Wollheim wrote – 'the identity and continuity of society resides not in the common possession of a single morality but in the mutual toleration of different moralities'.[55]

Liberalism does not say which of these different moralities is better than others. It is neutral on this question and regards its neutrality as a virtue. Liberalism as a political doctrine assumes that – as Joseph Raz wrote – 'there are many worthwhile and valuable relationships, commitments and plans of life which are mutually incompatible'.[56] It recognizes that – as John Rawls put it – 'a modern democratic society is characterized not simply by a pluralism of comprehensive religious, philosophical and moral doctrines but by a pluralism of incompatible yet reasonable comprehensive doctrines'.[57] What is more, for a liberal this is not only a fact to take note of; he or she is ready to acknowledge that 'now this variety of conceptions of the good is itself a good thing, that is, it is rational for members of a well-ordered society to want their plans to be different'.[58]

Thus, the task of politics cannot and should not be to resolve the dispute among different conceptions of life. This is completely unattainable or is attainable only by a totalitarian enslavement of society in the name of some one conception. This being the case, according to Dworkin, 'political decisions must be as far as possible independent of conceptions of the good life, or what gives value to life. Since citizens of a society differ in these conceptions, the government does not treat them as equals if it prefers one conception to another.'[59]

Thus, the basic question is: 'How is it possible that there may exist over time a stable and just society of free and equal citizens profoundly divided by reasonable though incompatible religious, philosophical, and moral doctrines? Put another way: How is it possible that deeply opposed though reasonable comprehensive doctrines may live together and all affirm the political conception of a constitutional regime.'[60]

[55] Quoted after Raymond Plant, *Modern Political Thought* (Oxford: Blackwell, 1991), p. 76.
[56] Quoted after R. Plant, ibid.
[57] John Rawls, *Political Liberalism* (New York: Columbia University Press, 1993), p. xvi.
[58] John Rawls, 'A Theory of Justice', in *Liberalism and its Critics*, ed. Michael J. Sandel (New York: University Press, 1984), p. 50.
[59] Ronald Dworkin, *A Matter of Principle* (Cambridge MA: Harvard University Press, 1985), p. 191. See Peter Jones, 'The Ideal of the Neutral State', *Liberal Neutrality*, ed. Robert E. Goodwin and Andrew Reewe (London: Routledge, 1989), p. 9.
[60] J. Rawls, *Political Liberalism*, op. cit., p. xviii.

This is a fundamentally different way of putting the question than the approach we find in virtually all of political thought, whose main effort has been to ensure society as much consensus as possible in many fields. Political liberalism, especially in its contemporary form, so-called *modus vivendi* liberalism, seems to have totally abandoned this claim. It is content to establish the principles of peaceful coexistence within a state of contending people and groups, all of which have an equal right to have their views recognized as rational. 'Liberal democracy is government by conflict', stated Ralf Dahrendorf, not without reason, and he argued that such conflict is irremovable.[61]

It is hardly surprising that for a long time this 'neutrality' of liberalism has been strongly criticized. It has been censured by traditional conceptions, such as Catholicism, which profess ideas of absolute truth and the common good, and by entirely new conceptions (such as communitarianism). Advocates of these new orientations do not necessarily repeat all of the traditional arguments, but they do reproach liberalism with similar flaws. Just as traditionalists, they try to expand the sphere of social consensus and find a way to eliminate conflicts which liberalism regards as irremovable. Both groups of critics seem to assume that if liberalism were taken to its final logical consequences, this would result in the elimination of morality from politics, the destruction of social bonds, and anomie and disorganization.[62]

It is not my intention to show that criticisms of liberalism from start to finish were and are wide of the mark and unjust. There are many liberals who willingly admit that their political project is 'cold' and does not give members of society the 'feeling of belonging and identity' which traditional societies gave them.[63] In this sense, liberals admit that their antagonists are partially right. It cannot be denied that humanity has paid a high price for liberal negative liberty in the form of rootlessness and anomie, which Durkheim described as the lack of uniform social norms capable of controlling the behaviours of individuals and forming them into a community. The results of such a position have been catastrophic for liberty. 'Demokratie und Anomie sind unglückliche Bettgenossen.'[64]

On the other hand, one should be aware that the discussion with liberalism on some of its real weaknesses usually also abounds in misunderstandings. As a consequence, liberalism time and again is represented in grotesque form and becomes unrecognizable to its supporters and to all

---

[61] R. Dahrendorf, *Society and Democracy in Germany*, op. cit., p. 141.

[62] See Stephen Holmes, *The Anatomy of Liberalism* (Cambridge MA: Harvard University Press, 1993).

[63] R. Dahrendorf, 'Freiheit und soziale Bindungen' in *Die liberale Gesellschaft: Castelgandolfo-Gespräche 1992*, ed. Krzysztof Michalski (Stuttgart: Klett-Cotta, 1993), p. 11.

[64] Ibid.

those who have authoritative knowledge of it. The less knowledge of liberal theory and practice there is in society, the more such misunderstandings there are.

The critics of liberalism often seem to ignore the fact that liberalism simply asks different questions than ones to which they would like answers. For this reason, they interpret liberalism as though its main intention was to negate everything which they hold dear. By refusing to take a position on the common good, liberalism by no means tries to invalidate moral problems. Liberalism only states that in modern society these problems are resolved in many different ways and whatever one thinks about individual solutions, it cannot be otherwise.

In any case, the state is not called upon to resolve these problems. In order to be fair to all its citizens, the state must refrain from deciding on which of them are right in their choice of world-views. The task of the state, therefore, is to arrange dealings between citizens in such a way as to reduce the damage from the irremovable conflicts between them to a minimum. In this sense, Paul Ricoeur is right when he says that lying at the foundation of the liberal state is the principle of abstracting from truth.[65]

As Stephen Holmes observed, 'the real starting point for liberal morality was not the subjectivity of values, but the historical intractability of moral conflict'.[66] Thus, it is going too far to charge liberals with 'aversion to fixed moral values'.[67] Liberals are only against establishing these values by political measures; they are not opposed to holding such values or to defending them resolutely by other means and in a forum other than state institutions.[68]

Liberalism is not identical with moral relativism and does not call upon its followers to accord equal value to all conceptions. There are not and cannot be any liberals who would be neutral in this sense. Their doctrine only requires them to recognize that our opponent has the same right as we do to regard his or her conception as the best and to live in accordance with it within the same state.

In short, the dispute is not over whether morality is necessary in public life but over whether the government may be a party in conflicts over

---

[65] Paul Ricoeur, 'Wolność religijna – podstawy filozoficzne', *Res Publica Nowa* 1993, no. 10 (61), p. 9.

[66] Stephen Holmes, 'The Permanent Structure of Antiliberal Thought', *Liberalism and the Moral Life*, ed. Nancy L. Rosenblum (Cambridge MA: Harvard University Press, 1991), p. 243.

[67] See Emmet John Hughes, *The Church and Liberal Society* (Princeton NJ: Princeton University Press, 1944), pp. ix–x.

[68] See Leszek Kołakowski, 'Wo sind die Kinder in der Liberalen Philosophie? Eine Anmerkung zur Definition des Liberalismus', in *Die Liberale Gesellschaft: Castelgandolfo Gespräche 1992*, ed. Krzysztof Michalski (Stuttgart: Klett-Cotta, 1993).

morality and whether such conflicts will ever be resolved once and for all. Liberalism gives negative answers to both questions. For this reason, anti-religious crusaders trying to establish the domination of secular morality and a secular world-view were very bad liberals. Unfortunately, they are often wrongly taken to be typical representatives of the entire species.[69]

It goes without saying that the above reservations by no means eliminate the problem of opposition between liberalism and Catholicism or between liberalism and numerous other conceptions which hold forth the promise of creating a political society founded on a broad moral consensus of all, or at least most, of its members.

These reservations only suggest that the ongoing debate should be redefined. It is not a dispute over the need for morality but over the *possibility and limits of politics*. In this dispute, liberals take a clearly *minimalistic* position based on the conviction that no perfect community can be rebuilt today on a national scale (if such a community ever existed). This being so, one has to accept diversity and plurality, discovering as many of their good sides as possible and improving principles of behaviour which preserve social peace and equilibrium in the existing conditions without resorting to methods of government that threaten the liberty of the individual.

5. Is dialogue possible?

Political liberalism does not claim to have a solution for all difficult problems of contemporary society; it does not offer any universal key, any new 'religion'.[70] It only gives a rather general blueprint for setting up political society, without assuming that this design will encompass all social life, whose perhaps most important part will lie outside its ambit. 'Liberalism is not a programme covering all 24 hours of a person's life', Janusz Lewandowski observed.[71] Liberalism does not provide an idea on how to create an ideal society. Rather, it tries to answer a clearly limited number of questions resulting from the existence of real society, one in which individuals were granted rights which they did not have in more perfect societies.

In taking a minimalistic approach to politics, liberalism unquestionably leaves many 'empty spaces', which will be filled in without its participation

---

[69] See Juan Miguel Garrigues, 'Kościół, państwo liberalne i wolne społeczeństwo', *Znak* 1993, no. 461 (10), p. 32.

[70] Such an interpretation of political liberalism is given by Maciej Zięba OP, following which he argues that it is impossible to build a society on the basis of liberal 'religious pluralism' (see Zięba, 'Kościół wobec liberalnej demokracji', op. cit., p. 128).

[71] *Biuletyn Informacyjny KLD*, March–April 1992, no. 3 (11), p. 13.

and even at its cost. On this is based the possibility – admitted so far by only a few authors – of overcoming the old antagonism between liberalism and Catholicism, which Michael Novak calls a tragedy for both sides, because, as he argued, 'liberalism needed the Catholic feeling of community, transcendence, realism, irony, sense of the tragic, and evil. Catholicism, on the other hand, needed liberal institutions in order to actualize its own vision of the dignity of the human person in society; it needed irrevocable free associations and a state with limited authority which would respect liberty of conscience.'[72]

The matter is much more complicated, of course, and requires a long and substantive discussion. The first part of this discussion might consist in clearing up misunderstandings that have accumulated over two centuries, especially treating liberalism and Catholicism as two competing ideological systems giving answers to basically the same questions and claiming to be infallible in all their parts, thus excluding the possibility of genuine dialogue. There is no need to recall that this was so. It suffices to look closely at some contemporary polemics to get an idea of the scale of these misunderstandings and the difficulties on the way to overcoming them. In the light of historical experiences, it is no surprise that Catholics are so prone to mistake liberalism for militant atheism and anti-clericism; and for liberals on their part to detect in Catholicism a fundamentalist commendation of closed society. A tremendous effort will be required by both sides to turn the discussion towards the future and to replace the desire to discredit one's supposed opponent at all cost with the search for the most important points of disagreement and confronting them with new arguments.

Already today there are many signs of changes going in the right direction. Unfortunately, one cannot say that in Poland they have gone very far. It might have seemed that the joint opposition to communism and the presence of Christian inspiration in Polish liberalism coming back to life after so many years would have favoured the softening of historical antagonisms. It is not my business to pronounce an opinion on what these changes look like from the Catholic side, though I do note with satisfaction attempts to rethink the problem by writers in *Znak* and *Tygodnik Powszechny*[73] and by individual Catholics who in recent years have been committed to the promotion of not only economic liberal ideas.

---

[72] M. Novak, *Liberalizm – sprzymierzeniec czy wróg Kościoła*, (Poznań: 'W drodze', 1993), p. 70.

[73] The most serious attempt of this kind thus far is the earlier cited treatise of Maciej Zięba OP, 'Kościół wobec liberalnej demokracji'.

6. The weakness of political liberalism

On the side of liberalism progress is really not great. On the one hand, we see the avoidance of all discussion by closing oneself up within the confines of purely economic postulates. The liberal nature of these postulates is no obstacle to refusing to take liberalism seriously in any other area or even to combating liberalism. On the other hand, we can observe self-defence reactions against the offensive of anti-liberal forces – a self-defence which rarely goes beyond generalities about tolerance, civil society or a secular state and that are, what is even worse, often just carbon copies of polemics in a very old style. There are few publications which show that their authors have assimilated the legacy of contemporary liberal political thought.[74]

To all appearances, political liberalism has aroused incomparably less interest than economic liberalism and has incomparably fewer dyed-in-the-wool supporters. In Poland today the word 'liberalism', without a qualifying adjective, is typically associated mainly with economic and not political liberalism. Traces of the latter are visible here and there, but it has not coalesced into a political movement with a coherent vision of the state and a wide intellectual base. David Ost, not without reason, recently wrote of the crisis of liberalism in Poland.[75]

'Crisis' is not the most appropriate word, however, for it suggests that something bad is happening to something that was recently hale and hearty. Ost can use this word because he sees the culmination of Polish political liberalism in the democratic opposition, in which I see at most the still unfulfilled harbinger of political liberalism. In other words, I contend that political liberalism has yet to be born in our country and that the fear of it disseminated by the right is highly exaggerated. At most one can discern certain elements of political liberalism scattered along the spectrum of the Polish political scene. Adam Michnik (or someone of a similar orientation) could become the theoretician of political liberalism, but it would be a great exaggeration to say that he has become its theoretician.[76] An even greater exaggeration would be to state that the liberal

---

[74] An example of such a publication is the earlier cited book of Wojciech Sadurski, *Racje liberała: Eseje o państwie liberalno-demokratycznym* (Warsaw: Presspublica, 1992), and some publications of Marcin Król, Jacek Kurczewski, Paweł Śpiewak and others.

[75] See note 39.

[76] See Michnik's article, 'The Presence of Liberal Values', *East European Reporter* 1991, vol. 4, no. 4, pp. 70–2. I was unable to determine where and when this article was printed in the Polish press.

political philosophy is being articulated by leaders of Polish political parties with liberal labels. Thus, the question of why a serious dialogue was not struck up between liberals and Catholics is largely rhetorical. If one partner was unprepared for such a dialogue, the other partner simply refrained from entering into it.

It is worth pondering on the reasons for this poverty of political liberalism (greater in Poland, it seems, than in the Czech Republic or in Hungary). The remarks below will be an updated version of the problem posed earlier (see Chapter III).

A reason not worth dwelling on because it is so obvious is the overall poverty of political thought in the post-communist world. All political parties seem equally deficient in this area, even though it might have been expected that the Great Transformation would unleash a flood of ideas comparable to what happened after 1789. Nothing of the kind took place, however. Perhaps the reason for this is that 1789 hugely complicated the political world, whereas 1989 simplified it by swallowing the argument of its most good-hearted and naive interpreters that communism was an aberration, after which everything would return to normal.

Another obvious reason for the backwardness of liberal thought in the countries of Eastern Europe is the lack of a tradition on which liberals could base themselves. It is only they who in Poland do not have their Cardinal Wyszyński, their Piłsudski, their Dmowski, their Witos, their PPS, etc. They alone must start from the very beginning if even historians are able to find some information about forgotten predecessors.

Less obvious are three other reasons. The first is historical. For two centuries, with brief interruptions, Poles were a 'nation without a state'. This compelled them to pay special heed to moral unity. Their existence as a nation depended on whether they could establish a community of values outside and in opposition to the existing political institutions. Thus, divisions and conflicts within society were treated as threats to the most vital national interests, not as something normal that one had to get used to and to which political solutions had to be adapted. In other words, until very recent times there was little place in Polish thought for the kinds of problems which political liberalism addresses. The special role of Catholicism in our country was also an important factor. In Poland, Catholicism is not just another religious denomination but an important medium of searching for a national consensus.[77] In this context, the opposition of many politicians today to liberal arguments has two motivations:

---

[77] See Mieczysław A. Krąpiec, 'O podstawach tożsamości narodu polskiego', *O ludzka politykę*, (Katowice: Tolek, 1993), pp. 263–78.

attachment to the idea of the common good as the foundation of political society and the belief that the nation-state above all should express the moral unity of the nation.

The second reason for the weakness of Polish liberalism is sociological, namely, the considerable homogeneity of the population of the contemporary Polish state. Political liberalism in the West was a response to the great diversity of society – first religious, then political, class, moral, and in some countries even ethnic. Confronted with such diversity, political liberalism searched for a state model which would ensure domestic order without imposing a moral order on anyone with different beliefs and without infringing on the right to be oneself (it is quite another matter whether such a model has ever been put into practice). In a country in which divisions are less clearly drawn or in which one group strongly dominates over others, liberalism loses some of its *raison d'être*: it has to appeal not so much to the necessity of finding a *modus vivendi* between different systems of values as to the goodwill of the advocates of the dominant system to show tolerance towards difference for one reason or another. Instead of mutual tolerance as a principle of political life, at best tolerance is shown towards someone whom the members of the dominant group regard as morally inferior.

The third – political – reason for the weakness of political liberalism seems to be the tendency in Poland to understand democracy archaically (etymologically). It is assumed that the political majority should have special rights in all areas of life and that the restriction of these rights depends on the benevolence of the majority. Liberals, in contrast, appeal to the inalienable rights of individuals and on this basis argue that minorities have rights too. Many supporters of archaic democracy believe that majority rule should not be restricted in any way and that someone who has the majority behind him can shape things after his own fashion.

The more the spheres of social life are controlled by the state, the more dangerous this way of thinking is for political liberalism as a programme. Civil society, in which the minority would have its own institutions enabling it to preserve its identity and to speak up for its rights, is restricted or destroyed. It is obvious that the liberal programme assumes the existence of an extensive sphere of social relationships which no majority can abolish and with which it has to reckon. There is no liberalism without this separation of political and civil society, combined with the belief that the most important processes take place in the latter. In the post-communist world, this extra-state sphere is poorly developed and is highly dependent on political decisions. As a result, as George Schöpflin correctly noted, the countries emancipating themselves from communism immediately started to imitate the forms of Western liberal democracies, but in practice the post-communist countries are leaning towards less liberal forms, in which the emphasis is put on 'the nation as the key group, not on the rights of individuals articulated through civil society'.[78]

Given all of these factors, political liberalism is not very fashionable. It has not really formed itself into an independent orientation or, even less so, developed a theoretical position. It remains a strange Western doctrine, which has some attraction for some people, but clearly loses out in the competition with doctrines more strongly rooted in the traditions and present day of Eastern Europe. Political liberalism has turned out to be less attractive on a mass scale than economic liberalism and has a much less certain future than the latter.

[78] George Schöpflin, *Politics in Western Europe* (Oxford: Blackwell, 1993), p. 257. See John Gray, 'From Post-communism to Civil Society: The Reemergence of History and the Decline of the Western Model', *Social Philosophy and Policy*, vol. 10, no. 2, 1993.

VII Epilogue

This book cannot have a summary because it concerns history in the making, and all conclusions very quickly become outdated or at least need to be greatly modified soon after they are stated. I already experienced this problem during the writing of this book, which I started at the crest of the liberal wave in Eastern Europe and finished soon after the defeat of Polish liberals at the polls – when in many circles the word 'liberal' was used as an insult or in any case as an epithet to discredit an opponent.[1] By a strange twist of fate, the heirs of communism and proponents of the most extreme right-wing ideologies participated equally in the anti-liberal crusade.

Hence, the 'triumph of liberalism' proclaimed by many authors (not only liberal ones) after 1989 was short-lived. It was by no means a *return* of Eastern Europe *to nature*, which for the entire Western world meant liberal democracy historically shaped on the pillars of the free market. Liberalism was only one of many projects for overcoming the legacy of real socialism. Perhaps liberalism was the most drastic and effective remedy for the after-effects of socialism, but its programme is not very well suited to the realities of the backward countries commonly referred to as Eastern Europe or the post-communist world. The scepticism which I voiced in writing the first article on liberalism in Eastern Europe[2] turned out to be more prophetic than I had expected.

It can be argued, however, that the very appearance of liberals on the political scenes of Eastern Europe bordered on a miracle, for everything

---

[1] I leave aside the fact that after a few years some of the names of political parties mentioned now and then in this book have become historical names (for example, the disappearance of the Liberal-Democratic Congress, which did so much to promote liberal ideas, from the Polish political scene).

[2] Jerzy Szacki, 'A Revival of Liberalism in Poland', *Social Research* 1990, vol. 57, no. 2, pp. 463–92.

seemed to be against them: no liberal tradition; the legacy of real socialism both in the organization of social institutions and in people's minds; the kinds of expectations societies had when they entered this new period of their history. The only thing in favour of liberalism was the naive faith that the fall of communism signalled the 'end of history'.

Three things apparently were out of kilter with this optimistic vision, which simultaneously was spread all over the world by numerous friends of the young East European democracies and by the ideologists of these democracies with their slogans of the 'return to Europe'.

First, the post-communist countries were hardly on the verge of the *return* to Western liberal democracy, from which they were hopelessly far removed not only under the rule of communism but also earlier. Communism may be accused of depriving these countries of the hypothetical chance of catching up with the West after the Second World War and of becoming a part of it, but not of tearing these countries away from the West. Communism unquestionably destroyed many of the former ways of life of these societies, but at the same time it petrified and consolidated many others. In speaking of the absence of a liberal tradition in the countries of Eastern Europe, I have in mind not only the destruction wreaked by communism but also the former condition of the countries that came under communist rule.[3] This does not mean that there were no liberal ideas in these countries, but the reception of these ideas was limited and selective; and what is more important, these ideas were absorbed more in ideology than in practice. Why it happened this way is less important here. What is important is the result, namely, that no civil society in the full sense emerged in Eastern Europe.[4]

Second, during the decades of its rule communism not only did its utmost to extirpate liberal ideas from society, but it also tried to destroy all enclaves of citizens' independence from state authority to which potential adherents of these ideas could appeal. The cardinal role here was played by the almost total nationalization of the economy, which transformed the mass of citizens

---

[3] See George Schöpflin, *Politics in Eastern Europe* (Oxford: Blackwell, 1993), pp. 5–37.

[4] I accept the idea of civil society presented recently by John Gray: 'In dialectical contrast with Marxian totalitarianism or Islamic (or other) fundamentalism, civil societies have three defining features. First, their political institutions are not those of a Weltanschauung-state, embodying a totalistic world-view, but instead permit a diversity of perspectives and values to coexist in peace. Second, by contrast with traditional despotism, civil societies are governed by the rule of law . . . . Third, in all civil societies, the bulk of economic life is conducted in autonomous institutions, themselves defined and protected by law – in voluntary associations, intermediary institutions, and markets operating under institutions of private property and contractual liberty' (John Gray, 'From Post-communism to Civil Society: The Reemergence of History and the Decline of the Western Model', *Social Philosophy and Policy* 1993, no. 2.).

into hired workers, who, into the bargain, lacked the possibility of organizing themselves to defend their group interests. Much less success was achieved in taking control of people's minds, though communism did block many channels of social communication and abolished the market-place of ideas which to a certain extent existed even in non-democratic countries. Many people experienced this general *étatism* as a serious burden, but it was risky, even hopeless, to protest; but on the other hand, dependency on the state had its pluses, since it relieved the citizen of responsibility and provided social security on at least a minimum level. In any case, this system was deadly for the institutional infrastructure conducive to liberal democracy as well as for ways of thinking required for its existence.

Third, only on the surface did the resistance against this system swelling in time in some countries have anything in common with the Western liberal tradition. To be sure, a vital role was played by the liberal defence of civil rights and the idea of civil society as a form of assembling individuals in a manner enabling them to express their individual and group needs independent of the state. What is more, for the democratic opposition against communism, Western liberal democracy was a positive model. It must be stated, however, that at the same time this democratic opposition was far removed from liberalism in all of its numerous meanings except the etymological. The unquestioned individualism of this opposition, manifesting itself in support for the autonomy of the individual, was directed against the communist state, but it did not require non-conformist behaviour towards the society. Quite the contrary, it called for a reaffirmation of the social bonds that *étatism*, as people correctly believed, had destroyed. The severe criticism of *étatism* left the economy almost untouched; as a rule it did not go beyond postulating worker–manager cooperation in state enterprises. Finally, the bulk of specific postulates (such as those of Polish Solidarity) not only were addressed to the state, but also called upon the state to make good the promises of the socialist ideology to which it had appealed. In addition, where this protest was on a mass scale, ideas belonging to the pre-communist heritage of the collectivity came to the fore – especially religious and national ideas. In some countries the latter almost completely overshadowed the flashes of liberalism.

Thus, conditions for expansion of the liberal ideology in Eastern Europe were not favourable. Liberalism had only two advantages. The first was the widely held belief that liberalism had been 'tested' in the entire 'normal' world and consequently also was the most obvious solution for the problems of the post-communist countries. The second was that liberal ideas suggested themselves spontaneously as an alternative to communism. Since the greatest evil had been the swallowing up of society by the state, for a remedy people looked to the soil on which liberal ideologies grew. With either no or only superficial knowledge of these ideologies, liberalism was discovered as a sort of communism *à rebours* by deducing opposite features to the existing system, especially its *étatism*.

In short, liberalism appeared in Eastern Europe above all as a *utopia* – as a vision of the good society resulting from protest against existing social arrangements and having hardly any historical roots. The main problem for East European liberalism was that it had to create its base of support, and this accounts for its relative originality. For the first time in its history liberalism had to be *constructivist*, though the dislike of constructivism is indigenous to its nature.

The entire history of liberalism in the post-communist countries is nothing else but a number of attempts to transplant solutions that supposedly had been 'tested' elsewhere to local soil. Sometimes these efforts bore fruit. At other times, liberals had to operate in a vacuum by attempting to create capitalism in the absence of capitalists and capital, a civil society in the absence of a middle class, entrepreneurship without people ready to act independently, liberal institutions without the custom of living in liberty. As Zygmunt Bauman put it: 'The cover was taken off and the pot turned out to be empty. It did not contain a society ready to spread its wings and live differently. There was no class or group ready to embrace the new type of social relationships without reservation and to feel at home in them.'[5]

Liberals like Stefan Kisielewski could take consolation in the fact that 'politicians now and again formulated their programmes in a "classless vacuum", after which these programmes sometimes unexpectedly took on social content'.[6] For now, however, this 'vacuum' meant that liberals would either have to abandon some parts of their original design or introduce it by force with the assistance of the state and with no heed to growing resistance on the part of society. This observation applies especially to economic liberalism, since no other kind of liberalism had emerged full blown. Other varieties of liberalism had been pushed to the margin by doctrines closer to local tradition and customs of citizens. From the very outset political liberalism found itself in an incomparably more difficult situation than economic liberalism, because the problems usually addressed by the former seemed much less important to people than achieving the economic efficiency promised by economic liberals. Political liberalism could not even count on

[5] 'Rewolucje pożerają ojców', Ewa Nowakowska and Jacek Poprzeczko interview Professor Zygmunt Bauman, sociologist, in *Polityka*, 17 April 1993, p. 21. See Z. Bauman, 'The Polish Predicament: A Model in Search of Class Interests', *Telos* 1992, pp. 113–30.

[6] S. Kisielewski, 'Wstęp do programu opozycji', *Bez cenzury* (Paris: Editions Spotkania, 1987), p. 261.

the support of economic liberals, many of whom had made entirely different political choices by adopting the strategy of building civil society from its economic foundations and not worrying about whether its 'superstructure' would be liberal.

Thus, the cleavage of liberalism into two separate trends was not overcome after 1989, and economic liberalism remained dominant.

Economic liberalism enjoyed a period of great successes. In the face of the total discreditation of the socialist economic system, the proposal of introducing a system based on diametrically opposite principles was accepted as almost self-evident. No small role here was played by ignorance of what this would mean in practice. It was widely believed that the realignment of the economy would bring all gains and no losses. People naively expected market reforms to bring immediate results.

These illusions were so great in Poland that the anti-communist trade union movement became the social base of economic liberalism (though not for long) and held its protective 'umbrella' over the reforms. In other post-communist countries as well, the support for pro-capitalist reforms was out of all proportion to the political power of liberals themselves.

These were pyrrhic victories, however. The dilemma for liberalism was whether it could move in its chosen direction without betraying the principles which until now seemed to constitute its very essence. In the post-communist countries, liberals only had an *ideological blueprint* which was openly at variance with the existing state of affairs.

When the first liberal ideas appeared before the breakthrough of 1989, this problem really did not exist. As long as power was held by the communists, liberals in Eastern Europe found themselves in a similar situation to the one faced by their predecessors in the West centuries ago, who simply tried to create enclaves of the new economic order in an unfavourable setting. In the pre-1989 situation, Polish liberals naturally banked on evolution and 'piecemeal engineering'. This path may have seemed longer and more bumpy than others, but it had been travelled successfully before. And in setting out on this path liberals, as always, could warn against the danger of sudden changes and 'reformatory romanticism'. They were free from the temptation of constructivism.

The revolution of 1989, to which economic liberals contributed little, radically changed this situation. Now, unexpectedly, there was a chance to institute a new economic order quickly, an order which promised a rosy future to the post-communist societies tired out with socialism. It was hard to pass up such an opportunity. A unique experiment got under way consisting in planning and rapidly building a capitalist order whose main feature elsewhere was that it was supposed to develop spontaneously and without any preconceived theoretical assumptions. In the post-communist world, capitalism had to be invented and then put into practice – in the reverse order to its entire previous history.

The purer the model of capitalism accepted, the greater the contrast between this model and post-communist reality. Guided by this model, liberals become convinced of the necessity of some great act of *creation*, which would bring into being nearly everything that does not exist and that seems vital for the new order to arise: a free market, real money, capital, private ownership, a middle class, etc. Right after the fall of communism, capitalism developed spontaneously at the bazaar level, but moved beyond these confines with difficulty; the economy as a whole displayed surprising lifelessness, reacting weakly to 'market signals' from the top. The state had to be enlisted to jump-start the march towards capitalism and to assume the main responsibility for the fate of the liberal reform. Willingly or unwillingly, the state had to lay the foundations of the new economic order.

'Practical' liberals are right, of course, when they contend that every 'pure' liberal policy would inexorably lead to catastrophe; but neither is it certain whether their 'pragmatism' provides any safeguards whatsoever against a set-back. In any event, the case of Poland leads one to have serious doubts about this.

The history of liberalism in the post-communist countries is the history of a partial success. Its unquestionably greatest achievement is that it came into being at all on alien and difficult soil for it and, moreover, that it was able to impose on at least some of these countries the general direction of economic changes. It must be admitted that the countries which decided not to adopt liberalism gained no measurable advantages thereby, while all modifications in this direction take (and must take) the conceptions of liberals as a frame of reference.

At the same time, however, the balance sheet of liberalism in the post-communist world is negative in more than one respect – not only because liberalism rather quickly lost its initial popularity and, rightly or wrongly, is blamed by many for the high social costs of the economic and political reforms. To some extent, liberals themselves are responsible for this turn of events. Firmly convinced of the rightness of their views, they showed little understanding for the realities of the post-communist world, especially for the mentality of people for whom capitalism is or until recently was a reality from another planet.

Yet, the mistakes of liberals do not seem to have been the decisive factor here – the more so as it was hard for liberals to commit them when they found themselves, against their wishes, in the situation of practitioners of utopian social engineering. There was no good way out of this situation. Liberals either had to remain absolutely true to their principles and ram them through in the teeth of mounting social resistance, thereby running the risk of being defeated and becoming a marginal social force; or they had to compromise on their principles to some degree – though this would still not guarantee a victory, which perhaps is not possible at all in the existing conditions.

I do not deny that this is so. One of the dogmas of economic liberalism is the thesis that there is no 'third road' between socialism and capitalism. In my opinion, this is absolutely true in the context of economic theory. This excludes the possibility of building models of a 'social market economy' or 'market socialism' with the same consistency and elegance as models of two pure forms. The point is, however, that pure forms can be conceived only in a social vacuum but not in a real society in which economists do not wield absolute power, while people who are not economists have the right to defend their 'fallacies'. Contrary to what economic theory says, in reality we have to do with an almost infinite variety of 'mixed' economies, and the practical disputes are primarily over *proportions*. Nowhere is it written on stone that in the post-communist countries these proportions must be in favour of the pure capitalism for which liberals pine. This is, perhaps, the sad lot of these countries, but not every misfortune can be turned around. The opinion that the classical liberal model cannot be adapted to the reality of the post-communist countries is being voiced ever more often.

Index of Names